Reading Error

Modern Poetry

Series editors:
David Ayers, David Herd & Jan Montefiore, University of Kent

Volume 1

PETER LANG
Oxford • Bern • Berlin • Bruxelles • Frankfurt am Main • New York • Wien

Nerys Williams

Reading Error

The Lyric and Contemporary Poetry

PETER LANG

Oxford · Bern · Berlin · Bruxelles · Frankfurt am Main · New York · Wien

Bibliographic information published by Die Deutsche Bibliothek
Die Deutsche Bibliothek lists this publication in the Deutsche
Nationalbibliografie; detailed bibliographic data is available on the
Internet at ‹http://dnb.ddb.de›.

British Library and Library of Congress Cataloguing-in-Publication Data:
A catalogue record for this book is available from *The British Library*,
Great Britain, and from *The Library of Congress*, USA

ISSN 1661-2744
ISBN 978-3-03911-025-4

© Peter Lang AG, International Academic Publishers, Bern 2007
Hochfeldstrasse 32, Postfach 746, CH-3000 Bern 9, Switzerland
info@peterlang.com, www.peterlang.com, www.peterlang.net

I
Una a John Williams

gorau arf, arf dysg

Contents

Acknowledgements

Grateful acknowledgement is made to the following sources for permission to reprint material copyrighted or controlled by them:

Charles Bernstein – 'A Defence of Poetry', *My Way: Speeches and Poems*, Harvard: Harvard U.P., 1999. 'Lives of the Toll Takers' *Dark City*, Los Angeles: Sun & Moon Press, 1994. 'Riddle of The Fat Faced Man' and 'The Kiwi Bird in the Kiwi Tree', *Rough Trades* Los Angeles: Sun & Moon Press, 1991. 'Matters of Policy', *Controlling Interests*, New York: Roof Books, 1980.

Michael Palmer – 'A Dream Called "The House of the Jews"' *Notes for Echo Lake*, San Francisco: North Point Press, 1981. 'The Baudelaire Series', *Sun*, San Francisco: North Point Press, 1988. 'Letter 5' from 'Letters to Zanzotto' *At Passages*, New York: New Directions, 1995. 'Autobiography 5', *The Promises of Glass,* New York: New Directions, 2000.

Lyn Hejinian – Excerpts from *The Guard* and *The Person* in *The Cold of Poetry*, Los Angeles: Sun & Moon Press, 1994. Excerpts from *The Cell*, Los Angeles: Sun & Moon Press, 1992. Excerpts from *Happily* Sausalito: Post Apollo Press, 2000.

My sincere thanks to Charles Bernstein, Lyn Hejinian and Michael Palmer for enabling publication from archived correspondence held at *The Mandeville Library* at UC San Diego.

Please note that every attempt has been made to contact the authors and publishers represented here for their permission to use their poems. Please contact the author if there have been any inadvertent omissions

I express immense gratitude to the Fulbright Commission in Ireland for a scholar's award spent on sabbatical leave at UC Berkeley. A major debt is also acknowledged to the guidance of Pete Nicholls at University of Sussex University, for the initial research that helped shape *Reading Error*. Thanks also to colleagues at the School of English and Drama, University College Dublin – in particular to the generosity of Michelle O'Connell, Ron Callan, J.C.C. Mays, Andrew Carpenter and Maria Stuart. For his patience thanks to Alan Mauro and also the staff at Peter Lang UK. Special thanks as always go to Sally Perry, Elsa Evans, Bethan Evans, Angharad Penrhyn, Gaynor Jones, Ifor Owen and Yoshie Suzuki. Friends Sarah MacLachlan, Sue Currell, Frances Barry, Ciara Hogan, Stephanie Newell and Clare Walker provided a lively and constructive forum throughout. My most happy and continuing thanks to Myles Dungan who lived with ms. malapropism and 'the room for error', viewing the enterprise as an adventure 'with a plan.' I dedicate the book to my parents who gave me books, humour and the mnemonics of poetry – *Cymraeg*.

Introduction
Language Writing and the Lyric

Although it is over twenty five years since the emergence of a body of poetry loosely configured under the rubric of 'Language Writing',[1] we are possibly only now in a position to evaluate the broader impact of this work upon contemporary American poetics. The proverbial coming of age of any so called movement presents notorious dangers of appropriation. Not least in this case is the temptation towards a retrospective levelling of the multiple claims of Language Writing to an aesthetic of composition. While the proliferation of published scholarship within this field indicates that there can be no immediate agreement on the taxonomy of the project, it suggests that an important mapping of the expanding trajectories of this work is already in progress.[2] Originally a small core group, Language Writing has developed to become an expansive and complex phenomenon. Broadly speaking, and perhaps at the danger of simplification, Language Writing can be characterised as a poetry which frequently works in terms of diminished reference, questioning the transparency of language, or

---

1   Here I am following Lyn Hejinian's sketch of the emergence of Language Writing in her collection of essays *The Language of Inquiry* (Berkeley: University of California Press, 2000). Hejinian suggests that as a 'specific social moment' it could be situated 'around 1976', p. 320.

2   Examples include: Christopher Beach, *Contemporary Poetry Between Community and Institution* (Evanston, Illinois: Northwestern U.P., 1999), Ann Vickery, *Leaving Lines of Gender: A Feminist Genealogy of Language Writing* (Hanover & London: Wesleyan U.P., 2000). A further range of reference and inclusiveness is suggested by the recent *The World in Time And Space: Towards a History of Innovative American Poetry in Our Time*, eds. Edward Foster and Joseph Donahue (New Jersey: Talisman, 2002), *Assembling Alternatives: Reading Postmodern Poetries Transnationally*, ed. Romana Huk (Middletown, Co: Wesleyan, 2003) and *Poetry and Pedagogy: The Challenge of the Contemporary*, eds. Joan Retallack and Juliana Spahr (New York: Palgrave, 2006).

language's unequivocal claim as a finite medium of representation. The disruption of syntax, narrative and the foregrounding of language's generative properties through its slippages, puns and word play serve to create a poetry of intense linguistic opacity. Furthermore, this writing is predicated on the belief that the divergence of poetic language from customary discourse does itself mark out the ground for political agency.

Yet there is an immediate problem in situating this diverse range of writing, not only restricted to the problem of naming. While the earlier confusion of whether we address the work as 'L=A=N=G=U=A=G=E Poetry', or 'language-centred poetry' has dissipated to a general preference for Language Writing, historicising this tendency in American poetry presents some pertinent problems. As Jeff Derksen asserts 'past the ambiguity and hesitation of naming the internal defining process of the Language writers is neither singular nor uncontested.'[3] In his literary account of the phenomenon Bob Perelman poses that one is immediately faced with the dilemma of whether to approach the writing as a historical literary 'movement', or as a 'set of generalisable concerns'[4] applicable to the writing of the present. Given that the majority of the key practitioners associated with this movement are still publishing new work there must be a certain element of mobility in this identification. As Perelman asserts, there is a definable literary history to be traced, through the initial and pivotal publications of *This* (1971), *Hills* (1973), and *L=A=N=G=U=A=G=E* (1978).[5] But Language Writing's notorious resistance to a pedagogical summation of its poetics is indicative not only of the multiplicity of its poetics, but of a strategic indeterminacy which is at the core of the writing. In surveying the compendium of early poetics

3   Jeff Derksen, 'Where have all the Equal Signs Gone? Inside/Outside The L=A=N=G=U=A=G=E Site' in *Assembling Alternatives*, pp. 41–65 (p. 43).
4   Bob Perelman, *The Marginalization of Poetry* (Princeton: Princeton U.P., 1996), pp. 15–16.
5   Edited respectively by Robert Grenier and Barrett Watten; Bob Perelman; Bruce Andrews and Charles Bernstein. For an extensive history of the many small magazines and presses see Ann Vickery's *Leaving Lines of Gender*.

in *The L=A=N=G=U=A=G=E Book* and *In The American Tree*,[6] Jed Rasula asserts that the only consensus that may be said to have been attained through the diverse writings is 'the restoration of the reader as coproducer of the text, and an emphasis on the materiality of the signifier.'[7] Yet even this abbreviated account, however alluring, needs some consideration.

Possibly the most evident characteristic of Language Writing is its openness to engage and examine a range of theoretical discussions from fields as diverse as continental philosophy, linguistics, language philosophy, aesthetics, phenomenology and psychology within its poetics.[8] Rather than seeing theory and poetry as distinct taxonomies, Language Writing attempts to enact the considerations of theory within the writing of poetry and poetics. This intervention of theoretical concerns, particularly in early Language Writing, are not discursive accounts of propositions themselves, but are attempts to motivate some of the tenets of these discussions into a certain textuality of writing.

Rasula's observation on Language Writing's overall focus upon the reader as a 'coproducer', appears to align the tenor of their poetics neatly with Roland Barthes's identification of the 'writerly text.'[9] Barthes suggests that the writerly text can be understood as 'ourselves writing' (5), and characterises its goal as a desire 'to make the reader no longer a consumer, but a producer of the text' (4). Although Language Writing by its detractors has been characterised as merely ventriloquising the investigations of post-structuralist theory,[10] the dy-

6   *The L=A=N=G=U=A=G=E Book*, eds. Bruce Andrews and Charles Bernstein (Carbondale: Southern Illinois University Press, 1984), *In the American Tree: Language, Realism, Poetry*, ed. Ron Silliman (Orno Maine: National Poetry Foundation, 1986).

7   Jed Rasula, *The American Poetry Wax Museum: Reality Effects 1940–1990* (Urbana: National Council of Teachers of English, 1996), p. 397.

8   Here I am using 'theory' in its broadest application, a consideration which will be discussed in conjunction with Hejinian's remarks later.

9   Roland Barthes, *S/Z*, trans. Richard Miller (Oxford: Blackwell, 2000).

10   See for example Tom Clark, 'Stalin as Linguist', *Partisan Review*, 37.3 (1989), 299–304. Clark characterises Language Writing as 'a pretentious intellectual *argot* that sounds a little like an assistant professor who took a wrong turn on his way to the Derrida Cookout and ended up at the poetry reading' (p. 301).

namic interaction between theoretical considerations and poetry is one which is performed with considerable sophistication. Indeed, what is worth initially noting in approaching the poetics is the transformative aspect of the imbrication of theory and poetry. Michael Greer astutely notes in examining Lyn Hejinian's pivotal essay 'The Rejection of Closure',[11] that the particular value of this writing is the way in which 'many of the familiar-sounding terms are transformed, rewritten in a largely post-structural mode and context'.[12] Greer adds importantly that 'at the same time, a common vocabulary, an already existing discourse for talking about poets and poetry, is reactivated and, quietly politicized' (350). Hejinian herself notes more recently that the distinctions between theory and poetry in her own work are indeed negligible:

> Theory asks what practice does and in asking, it sees the connections that practice makes. Poetic language, then, insofar as it is a language of linkage, is a practice. It is practical. But poetry insofar as it comments on itself ... is also theoretical.[13]

This transformative impulse while at once seeming liberating, also poses some pertinent problems to the reader of the work. Although the poetics often cite the context of the writing, the sheer range of reference calls for an idealised reader,[14] at the very least one who is aware of where the contextualisations of the work may be sourced. Equally it is fair to say that Language Writing's pronounced willingness to engage with theory, makes the work vulnerable to readings which occasionally traverse the field of the work. While perhaps 'co-production' may be an efficient shorthand for this tendency, I want to propose that a further way of understanding this process of reading could be

11 Hejinian, *The Language of Inquiry*, pp. 40–58. Originally published in 1985.
12 Michael Greer, 'Ideology and Theory in Recent Experimental Writing or, The Naming of "Language Poetry"' *Boundary 2* 16.2/3 (1989) 335–55 (p. 350).
13 Hejinian, *The Language of Inquiry*, p. 356.
14 As Ron Silliman admits the danger with this tendency that 'the idealized absent author of the New Critical Canon has been replaced by an equally idealized, absent reader.' 'Who Speaks,' in *Close Listening: Poetry and the Performed Word*, ed. Charles Bernstein (New York Oxford: Oxford U.P., 1998), pp. 360–78 (p 365).

14

formulated through a poetics of *erring*. Although the imbrication of error here might appear to gesture to a misreading, my focus throughout *Reading Error* is to illustrate how the engagement demanded by the writing could be approached as a form of wandering, or errancy by the reader within the interstices of the text. Cast in this light, a reading of erring becomes a provisional testing out of hypotheses and propositions both in accordance with, and occasionally against, the grain of the text.

Before examining how a methodology of error provides a way of engaging with this body of work, we need to situate Language Writing's problematic relationship to the lyric in contemporary American poetry. Historically the emergence of Language Writing has been read as a reaction to the predominance of the workshop lyric of the seventies and eighties. In this account the writing performs a general swipe in the face of what Charles Bernstein calls 'official verse culture'.[15] Although we can see how this narrative has a certain attraction, framing the poetics of Language Writing solely as an oppositional impulse, seems to offer us little more than a nostalgia for the re-emergence of an avant-garde. Indeed the danger in this sole accounting of the Language Writing is not only the reduction of its poetics to a position of self advocated marginality, but also to diminish its acknowledged debt to an important historical lineage of experimental writing in both American and European poetry. All three early Language Writers under focus: Charles Bernstein, Michael Palmer and Lyn Hejinian stress the influence of an earlier tradition of innovative poetry, which includes the work of Louis Zukofsky, Gertrude Stein and Robert Duncan.[16] As Bernstein puts it Language Writing would appear to be Janus-like, establishing a dialogic engagement with a past and an immediate future:

> I am sufficiently skeptical of the presumption of 'advance' in 'avant-garde' to equally distrust formulations that appear to pit 'the new' against tradition. What

15   Bernstein, 'The Academy in Peril: William Carlos Williams meets the MLA', in *Content's Dream: Essays 1978–1984* (Los Angeles: Sun & Moon Press, 1986), pp. 244–51 (p. 247).

16   This listing would be an extensive one and this question of 'influence' in Palmer's work is discussed extensively in Chapter Four.

is presented here exemplifies a continuing dialogue with the past(s)– surely not, though, just a narrow line of hallowed English verse!– and the future(s). Yet because it is a dialogue, it does not only involve repetition of old forms but also a response to them.[17]

Language Writing's polemical attacks of workshop poetry cannot be disputed. During the years synonyms for the workshop lyric have included Bernstein's 'official verse culture', Rasula's coining of '*PSI*– Poetry Systems Incorporated',[18] and the more general referencing of the poetry as a conveyor belt of personal experience in 'the commuter' or 'Mc Poem.' Here perhaps the trials of historicising a literary tendency which Perelman draws attention to becomes most evident. Retrospectively it is fair to assert that the historical emergence of Language Writing was a considered response to a cultural deficit in the writing of poetry. But before wading into the minefield of 'margins' and 'mainstreams' in American poetic culture, it is worth addressing what lies behind the rather ponderous category 'the workshop lyric', and begin to consider whether a critique of this form amounts to a total dismissal of lyricism. By now it appears, at least for the purposes of *Reading Error*, that the more urgent question is how the early critiques of workshop poetry have propelled a reconfiguration of a static model of lyricism.

Recent discussions of the workshop lyric relate its rise to prominence during the seventies and the eighties as the inevitable outcome of the proliferation of creative writing programmes in the academy. The increasing professionalisation of poetry has its roots in the post war years, and in the flourishing of New Criticism we can trace the basic premise of the workshop poem as a well crafted, self sufficient composition. Charles Altieri identifies the dominant model of the seventies as the 'scenic mode',[19] and suggests that this model of the lyric is firmly rooted in the extension of a romantic ideology. The impetus

17 Bernstein, 'Introduction: "Language Sampler"', in *Content's Dream*, pp. 239–43 (p. 242).
18 Rasula, 'Literary Effects in the Wad: Handling the Fiction, Nursing the Wounds', *Sulfur*, 24 (1989) 77–8.
19 Charles Altieri, *Self and Sensibility in Contemporary American Poetry* (Cambridge: Cambridge U.P., 1984), p. 10.

of the work is towards an expression of an inchoate interiority and the poem in his words:

> places a reticent, plain-speaking and self-reflective speaker within a narratively presented scene evoking a sense of loss. Then the poet tries to resolve the loss in a moment of emotional poignance or wry acceptance that renders the entire lyric event an evocative metaphor for some general sense of mystery about the human condition. (10)

This impetus towards description and expression is characterised by the poet Robert Pinsky as 'discursive writing.' Pinsky states that the discursive lyric presents 'the poet talking, predicating, moving directly and as systematically and unaffectedly as he would walk from one place to another.'[20] Broadly speaking it is fair to propose that both these models of an 'expressive lyric', posit the self as the primary organising principle of the work. Central to this tendency is the articulation of the subject's feelings and desires, and a strongly marked division between subjectivity and its articulation as expression. This focus on expression is frequently evoked with reference to the speaker's voice and a suggestion of a certain 'sincerity' and 'authenticity.' What is apparent in this dominant model of the lyric is the immanence of the self, its centrality within the composition as the subject of the writing, and the role of language as a transparent medium for communicating intense emotion.

I am aware that this descriptive accounting of the more mainstream writing of this period is guilty of generalisation. But following the configuration of Language Writing purely as an oppositional impulse to a dominant ideology, the lyric seems the inevitable casualty of the narrative. What becomes apparent in this model of the lyric as personal expression, is the problem facing the poet in attempting to move beyond the personal data of the quotidian, and the tendency towards a harnessing of the poem to a retrospective account of experience. Indeed, the inherent restrictions of this model are the general evocation of the everyday as immediately available material for the poetry, and the annexing of public address as mere rhetoric. At its

20 Robert Pinsky, *The Situation of Poetry* (Princeton: Princeton U.P., 1976), p. 133.

very worst the workshop lyric has been caricatured as little more than a serialisation of indistinguishable free verse diary entries. It must be affirmed that recent critical thinking is beginning to address the development and refiguration of the lyric form through provocative theoretical perspectives and an expanding range of poetic traditions.[21] As Daniel Barbiero emphasises American experimental poetics of the seventies and eighties 'did not entail a wholesale negation of the lyric tradition; rather it would seem instead that the lyric tradition was given a refigured reading.'[22]

At the core of Language Writing's early critiques of the workshop lyric, is not only a resistance towards an aesthetic of writing which inscribes subjectivity as a static point of reference, but a dissatisfaction with the commodification of this writing practice and both its circulation and consumption within the academy. Bernstein in explaining 'official verse culture' suggests that it is 'not mainstream, nor is it monolithic, nor uniformly bad or good.'[23] Instead he objects to the criterion of value which is placed on its circulation: 'What makes official verse culture official is that it denies the ideological nature of its practice while maintaining hegemony in terms of major media exposure and academic legitimation and funding' (248–9). As an early response to the marginalisation of their work, many of the poets associated with Language Writing established small presses to publish and promote their poetry. Within this action is a broad consensus to establish a sense of community on a practical level, and the general practices of collaborative writing and establishing open forums for discussing poetics are identifiable characteristics of this ten-

21   For some theoretical perspectives on the lyric see *New Definitions of the Lyric: Theory Technology and Culture*, ed. Mark Jeffrys (New York and London, Garland Publishing, 1998), *Theory into Poetry: New Approaches to the Lyric* eds. Eva Muller-Zettelmann and Margarete Rubik (Amsterdam: Rodopi, 2004). Marjorie Perloff's close reading of American poetry have been key to this development and also Norman Finkelstein's *Lyrical Interference: Essays on Poetics* (New York: Sputyen Duyvil, 2003). See my Bibliography for full details

22   Daniel Barbiero, 'Reflections on Lyric Before, During and After Language', in *The World in Time and Space*, pp. 355–66 (p. 361).

23   Bernstein, *Content's Dream*, p. 248.

dency.[24] Evidently the academic recognition of many of the writers associated with Language Writing problematises the peripheral status of the original movement, and we can no longer consider the writing as marginal. Yet I will suggest that the conceptualisation of community, even if now only at a theoretical level, informs the poetics of Language Writing.[25] Furthermore the elusive word 'community', has an important conceptual point of reference to the examination of lyricism in recent innovative poetry.

Initially this yoking of both 'lyric' and 'community' seems to present two irreconcilable impulses. But reconsidering both as a dialectic provides a useful site for an investigation. Theodor Adorno, writing specifically on the tradition of German Expressionism, warns against approaching the lyric as merely a form of solipsistic aestheticism. He suggests that the lyric's withdrawal into subjectivity cannot be separated from the social realm, since it is an action which implies critique or even opposition in itself:

> You experience lyric poetry as something opposed to society, something wholly individual. Your feelings insist that it remain so, feel strongly that lyric expression, having escaped from the weight of material existence, evoke the image of a life free from the coercion of reigning practices, of utility of the relentless pressures of self-preservation. This demand, however, the demand that the lyric word be virginal, is itself social in nature. It implies a protest against a social situation ... In its protest the poem expresses the dream of a world in which things would be different.[26]

Language Writing's initial preoccupation with the expressive workshop aesthetic as the dominant model of lyricism, would perhaps not read Adorno's reference to the lyric in the same light, or at least as not

---

24　The pivotal examples here are Michael Davidson, Lyn Hejinian, Ron Silliman and Barrett Watten's collaboration *Leningrad: American Writers in the Soviet Union* (San Francisco: Mercury House, 1991) and *Writing/Talks*, ed. Bob Perelman (Carbondale: Southern Illinois U.P., 1985).

25　For an extended study of the relationship between Language Writing, community and the academy see Christopher Beach's *Poetic Culture*.

26　Theodor Adorno, 'Lyric Poetry and Society,' in *Notes to Literature: Volume One*, trans. Shierry Weber Nicholsen (New York: Columbia U.P., 1991), pp. 37–54 (p. 39, 40).

having the same force of critique. Yet, it is useful to note that an early essay by Hejinian draws on the similar danger of reducing community, or what we have encountered in Adorno's case as the social realm, to a static entity. 'Community' in Hejinian's consideration is a mobile and transitional locus:

> The question of community and creativity is not one issue but a whole complex of interrelated public and private issues, and as one brings the pressures of one's attentions to bear on one of them, another of them rises up, requiring that one adjust one's emphasis. But this adjusting of emphasis is essential to keeping the relationship between oneself and the community viable and productive ... A community consists of any or all of those persons who have the capacity to acknowledge what others among them are doing.[27]

Hejinian's comments advocate an open-ended description of what a community may entail. What is of interest is how this 'acknowledgement of others' and its indication of responsibility, may be performed by the poetry and formulated within a configuration of lyricism. Interestingly, Roger Gilbert in surveying an extensive range of American poetry in the eighties, suggests that there are shared preoccupations linking what would appear as so-called antithetical encampments. In his view the poetry of this period may be characterised by its performance of 'the rival claims of pleasure and politics, the aesthetic and the social, private experience and public responsibility.'[28] While Gilbert recognises that these are of course not new preoccupations, he suggests that what distinguishes the poetry of the eighties is how the rift between the private and the public is mediated through 'exaggerated dislocations and shifts of reference' (242).

Somewhat inevitably this discussion of community, private and public experience and responsibility returns us to the problematic question of whether a static model of the lyric can sustain these investigations. Gilbert's general reference to a 'dislocation' in the writing can certainly be extended to Language Writing's disruption of syntactical and grammatical conventions. As Peter Middleton points

---

27 Hejinian, 'Who is Speaking', in *The Language of Inquiry*, pp. 30–9 (p. 34).
28 Roger Gilbert, 'Textured Information: Politics, Pleasure, and Poetry in the Eighties', *Contemporary Literature*, 33.2 (1992), 242–72 (p. 242).

out 'Language Writers had to oppose an earlier model of community based on authenticity and individuality, and this led to something of a paradigm shift in American avant-garde Poetry.'[29] What is important to emphasise is that for Language Writing this rupturing of the text and the divergence of poetic language from customary discourse, has both a political and ethical agency. By now Bernstein's familiar comment that language must be seen as 'not accompanying but constituting the world,'[30] has become axiomatic for understanding the original tenets of this writing. It is also of no surprise that Ludwig Wittgenstein's philosophy, with its examination of a 'shared grammar in use',[31] has had an extensive impact on the poetics of Language Writing. Evidently the traditional subject-object dichotomy of the lyric, and its clear demarcation between private expression and public address, are strategically problematised in the writing of these poets. But rather than approaching the writing as purely 'anti' lyrical, we can begin to approach this rupturing of the text as a necessary step in the attempt to disperse the infamous tyranny of the lyric 'I' and open the work to epistemological uncertainty. I will suggest that understanding Bernstein, Palmer and Hejinian's poetry through an aesthetic of error will allow us to examine the different methods they employ to rupture the lyric in an attempt to extend its address.

One might well ask how do we begin to make that leap from linguistic and epistemological indeterminacy to the claim for political efficacy or even community? Following the poetics, the role of the reader is fundamental to this equation, and the difficulty of this poetry requires as Michael Palmer neatly puts it '[that] the reader completes the circuit.'[32] While Bernstein, Palmer and Hejinian share a broad ambition to refigure the lyric from a model of emphatic interiority, their approach to how poetry may begin to orchestrate a communal address, and the ultimate efficacy of these claims are decidedly differ-

---

29 Peter Middleton, *Distant Reading: Performance, Readership, and Consumption in Contemporary Poetry* (Tuscaloosa: Alabama U.P, 2005), p. 134.
30 Bernstein, 'Thought's Measure', in *Content's Dream*, pp. 61–86 (p. 62).
31 The relationship between Bernstein's work and Wittgenstein's *Philosophical Investigations* is discussed in the second chapter
32 Palmer, 'A Conversation', *American Poetry*, 3.1 (1986), 72–88 (p. 74).

ent. Initially it may serve as a useful preliminary to their work to broach what a configuration of community suggests for the three poets.

Bernstein suggests that his poetry is harnessed to the possibilities for creating an alternative polis:

> Against the Romantic idea of poems as transport, I prefer to imagine poems as spatializations and interiorizations– blueprints of a world I live near to, but have yet to occupy fully. Building impossible spaces in which to roam, unhinged from the contingent necessities of durability, poems and the books they make eclipse stasis in their insatiable desire to dwell inside the pleats and folds of language.[33]

In this light the poem becomes an architectural or textual utopia, and this sketching of a public space is concomitant with Bernstein's demand that poetry and poetics have a public function. Indeed his poem 'Matters of Policy' suggests that 'love of the /public good is the only passion that really/ necessitates speaking to the public.'[34] While perhaps Bernstein's evocation of a senatorial address might suggest a grand authoritarian flourish, his poetics maintain an aversion against an authoritarian rhetoric. Palmer is more cautious in his conceptualisation of community. The policy making of Bernstein's public space, is replaced by a distinctly literary configuration. Palmer reflects on '[the] idea of imaginary community in which poets tend to dwell with others. Not to say that it's outside the real, but it's constructed through the imagination and sometimes in opposition to the principles of reality that are laid on us.'[35] Although this account of a community appears to be a hermetic one, Palmer seems to suggest that poetry has a role for both a political critique and the tentative formulation of an oppositional discourse. But Palmer's sketching of the relationship between poetry and a broader community appears highly speculative in comparison with Hejinian's ambitions:

---

33   Bernstein, 'The Book as Architecture', *My Way: Speeches and Poems* (Chicago: University of Chicago Press, 1999), pp. 56–7 (p. 57).
34   Bernstein, *Controlling Interests* (New York: Roof Books: 1980) p. 6
35   Palmer, 'Interview: Conducted by Peter Gizzi', *Exact Change Yearbook No. 1*, ed. Peter Gizzi (Boston: Exact Change, 1995), pp. 161–79 (p. 162).

> For a writer, it is language that carries thought, perception, and meaning. And it does so through a largely metonymic process, through the discovery and invention of associations and connections. Though it may seem merely technical, the notion of linkage– of forging connections– has in my mind, a concomitant political and social dimension. Communities of phrases spark the communities of ideas in which communities of persons live and work.[36]

Hejinian makes a link between interpretative practices and their translation to the social sphere. Indeed her poetics suggest that there can be a viable and productive relationship between aesthetics, and the establishing of sustainable social relationships. Later in the discussion, *Reading Error* examines these claims in considering the ethical performance of her poetry.

Given the conceptual differences between the work of these poets, I want to make it clear from the outset that the aim of this study is not to propose an entirely new or all encompassing theory of the lyric. In focusing on the poetry of Bernstein, Palmer and Hejinian this work attempts to delineate a range of innovative writing in American poetry over the past three decades. Arguably other poets could have been chosen, yet while I am reluctant to suggest that Bernstein, Palmer and Hejinian's work is somehow representative of a large body of American innovative poetry, there are certain important continuities which link the three. Bernstein and Hejinian are strongly identified with Language Writing's original core group. While Palmer has always expressed extreme scepticism in affiliating his work with a group of movement, his work has been published under the auspices of early Language Writing anthologies and journal publications.[37] All three have edited and contributed to collections of poetics. But most importantly, I will suggest that their poetry illustrates how an initial dissatisfaction with the workshop model, has evolved into compendium of complex strategies for refiguring the lyric within an experimental praxis.

---

36   Hejinian, 'Materials (for Dubravka Djuric)', *The Language of Inquiry*, pp. 161–76 (p. 166).
37   See Palmer's contribution in the *L=A=N=G=U=A=G=E Book* and *Writing/Talks* and *'Language' Poetries*, ed. Douglas Messerli (New York: New Directions, 1987).

23

The final chapter of *Reading Error* considers the legacy of Language Writing to the work of other American poets, focusing specifically on the poetry of Jennifer Moxley. Moxley somewhat playfully recognises that she has been identified as a lyric 'poster child'[38] for her generation, yet her initial impressions of contemporary American lyricism in the mid 1980s were far from auspicious:

> This was the mid eighties, a time when if you opened a mainstream literary magazine all of the so-called lyric poems were little stories from an individual's perspective broken into lines and ending in an epiphany usually with a sense of either moral or political superiority) directed toward an absent interlocutor.[39]

Moxley's poetry has been characterised too readily as part of a 'post' Language generation's renewed appreciation of the lyric. I argue that her poetry provides a way of contemplating the legacy of Language Writing for recent poetry and the reception of lyric forms in the 21st Century. Notoriously Moxley's preface to her first major volume *Imagination Verses*, champions the rights of the 'universal lyric I' the universal lyric "I."[40] As Steve Evans points out the gesture can be read as 'a dare to the doxological avant-gardist who learned in the 1970s to sneer at it as an "ideological construction" But that neither this facile rejection nor any equally facile return to some prior state of self transparency.'[41] Moxley's lyric is not a return to the scenic mode that Altieri characterises; moreover the issue of community remains an integral consideration in recent writing by a younger generation. Evans warns against a levelling of a recent generation's poetry to a shorthand of 'perceived rehabilitation of musical forms' and emphasises instead 'the actual multiplicity of new composition' (655). He proposes that a characteristic of this new work is a commitment to 'the articulation of suffering' and 'the democracy of perception' (655). While I may be guilty of revisiting the specter of lyricism upon Mox-

---

38   Jennifer Moxley 'Lyric Poetry and the Inassimilable Life', *The Poker*, 6 (Cambridge, MA: 2005), 49–58 (p. 49).

39   Moxley, 'Lyric Poetry and the Inassimilable Life', p. 55.

40   Moxley, *Imagination Verses* (New York: Tender Buttons, 1996), p. x

41   Steve Evans, 'The American Avant-Garde after 1989: Notes Toward a History', in *The World in Time and Space*, pp. 646–73 (p. 670).

ley's poetry (and her work certainly cannot be read as an unproblematic continuation of Language Writing), her poetry renegotiates central issues raised in Bernstein, Palmer and Hejinian's relationship to lyricism.

A methodology of 'error'

In the early critical accounts of Language Writing, the tendency has been to use the lyric as the 'straw man' in the discussion, equating lyricism with a generic model of workshop poetry. While the focus of *Reading Error* is not to redeem the workshop aesthetic, I want to address the tendency within critical discussions to project the lyric as the generic other of innovative writing. The key difficulty faced is how to formulate a strategy for approaching the lyrical inflection in the work of these poets, without forcing the poetry into yet a further didactic model. Central to this problem is the general consideration of what reading of lyricism can we formulate, once the self is displaced from centre stage and an 'experience' of language takes its place.

One way of beginning to address this problem is offered in a reading of Michael Davidson's study *Ghostlier Demarcations*.[42] Davidson lineates the modern poet's foregrounding of the materiality of language, and examines how the poetic text can be read as a site for phantasmagorical writings and the layering of previous inscriptions. In describing the multiple strata of writing, Davidson draws on the inflection of palimpsest which becomes in his own coining 'palimtext'. The palimtext in his account is an attempt at describing:

> Modern writing's intertextual and material character, its graphic rendering of multiple layers of signification. The term also suggests the need for a historicist perspective in which textual layers refer not only to previous texts but to the discursive frame of the present in which they are seen. (9)

42   Michael Davidson, *Ghostlier Demarcations: Modern Poetry and the Material Word* (Berkeley: University of California Press, 1997).

Approaching the lyrical inflection in the work of Bernstein, Palmer and Hejinian less as a model imposed upon the poetry, but as a series of palimtextual traces encrypted within the strata of the poetic text, allows us to formulate a more problematic account of the lyric impulse. This initial consideration of traces and encryptions in the text lends itself to a reading of the poetry through a configuration of error. Understanding 'configuration' as a 'mode of arrangement,' my examination will provide different interpretative strategies for understanding the varying ways error may surface (for example humour, mistakes, malapropisms, polyphony), in the work of recent poets. Already I have suggested how the strategic indeterminacy of these texts demands a certain form of engagement by the reader, one that could be broached as an *erring* or errancy within the text. Broaching the work of the three poets through a configuration of error allows for a consideration of the more localised difficulties of approaching the poetry, while negotiating the relationship of this body of work to a tradition of modernist mastery. Read through an aesthetic of error, we can begin to approach the work of these three poets as a response to what Perelman draws attention to as modernism's 'ideology of accuracy.'[43] This erring impulse can be interpreted as both a reaction to Ezra Pound's exhortation for linguistic precision in poetic language, and the grand scale ambition of a pedagogical instruction which could be organised around the rhetoric of the 'ego scriptor.' Bernstein, Palmer and Hejinian share a mistrust of poetry as a mastery of form, and the linguistic indeterminacy of their poetry could be read as a strategy safeguarding against the dangers of an authoritarian rhetoric.

Initially error is broached through Bernstein's work as a reading of typographical mistakes and solecisms as his recent poem, 'A Defence of Poetry',[44] demonstrates. This preliminary reading of error as a series of intentional mistakes, appears throughout his poetics and is linked with political agency. Bernstein's poetics suggest that the deformation of 'prescribed rules of grammar & spelling',[45] opens the

43   Perelman, *The Marginalization of Poetry*, p. 88.
44   Bernstein, *My Way*, pp. 1–2.
45   Bernstein, 'Three or four things I know about him', in *Content's Dream*, pp. 13–33 (p. 26).

text to affirmation of language as a shared commonality. Indeed Bernstein proposes polemically that, '"bad grammar" can speak more truthfully than correct grammar, that learning & expertise don't really impart knowledge, that private fantasies don't coincide with public property' (29). The poet indicates throughout his essays that these linguistic 'pratfalls' attempt to deflate the authority of the speaker through humour. Central to this conceptual mapping of error as a means of opening up the social sphere of the lyric, are the poet's own references to the reading of Wittgenstein's dismissal of the concept of private language and the philosopher Stanley Cavell's scrutiny of the social contract.

Yet the recourse to humour as a strategy for navigating a way from an authoritarian rhetoric does present us with some pertinent problems. Although Bernstein insists that his polyphonic texts opens the univocal lyric to a multiplicity of what he terms 'ideolects', this tactic could also justifiably be read as series of ventriloquised speech acts. Does Bernstein's insistence on humour navigate a way from the dangers of ironic commentary which he is keen to avoid? In attempting to read these breaches or aberrations in the poet's work, a considered response will be given to the claims of the poetics and how error may be read a series of trace marks within the work. In this context Nicholas Abraham and Maria Torok's psychoanalytic analysis of encryptions or provides a useful strategy for reading the poetry. Following through this mapping of an erring poetics, the work of the language philosopher Donald Davidson allows us to link a consideration of the malapropisms of Bernstein's poetry with the broader configuration of what knowing a language might entail. I will suggest that this line of enquiry is vindicated by Bernstein's own questioning when he poses 'Is it possible, for example, to allow typographical errors, mistypings, to remain integral?'[46]

The key descriptors of the workshop lyric 'authenticity' and 'sincerity', are given a surprising reconfiguration in approaching Palmer's poetry. Typically Palmer's work has been read as a citational response to a tradition of American and European lyricism. While this approach is certainly validated by the frequently seamless inclusion of textual

46   Bernstein, 'Straw Dogs and Straw Men', in *Content's Dream*, pp. 40–9 (p. 48).

references in the poetry, there remains the problematic consideration of how this intertextual impulse may be read. The justifiable temptation with Palmer's poetry is to pursue the sources, itself a form of bibliographic or scholarly errancy, without recontextualising their impact upon the work. Palmer's pivotal volume *Sun* (1988), demonstrates an acute anxiety of how its text may relate to borrowed sources and whether a process of constellation shifts the citation from its original context. The volume as a whole hints at a process of inclusion, citation and even plagiarism. But far from suggesting a poetics of play or a paradigm of postmodern pastiche, the poet indicates that there is a serious intention at work. In a telling remark Palmer suggests that:

> It's an interesting time to rearticulate an idea of authenticity. Not in a mystifying way, but in some urgent relationship to work, beyond the post-modern queries which drove so many people into endless ironization, endless play, endless 'screen' so to speak which became a sort of protection against that deconstructive critique. Well then, what, after that, can one possibly reassert about an ethics of representation? [47]

Unsurprisingly, Palmer like Bernstein, attempts to distance himself from a fetishisation of the text as a combative measure against ventriloquising poststructuralist theory. But problematically, Palmer could equally be charged with hiding behind his own literal screen of palimpsestual layerings through borrowed citations.

An entry in Palmer's *The Danish Notebook*, helps the reader to somewhat retrospectively broach the ethical problem between concealment and representation which these comments gesture towards. In this work the poet asserts that 'Now I know that I would rather embrace the flaws.'[48] A further conceptual reading of error as a series of aberrations, halts and plateaux in the text, may help us to provide a more acute understanding of the intertextual density of Palmer's work and its relationship to the reconfiguration of the lyric. Prompted by

47   Palmer, 'Interview: Conducted by Peter Gizzi', p. 163.
48   Palmer, *The Danish Notebook* (Penngrove: Avec Books, 1999), p. 43.

Palmer's own reference to Michael Riffaterre's *Semiotics of Poetry*,[49] the discussion considers whether Riffaterre's conceptualisation of intertextuality as a series of 'ungrammaticalities' in the poetic text may help to problematise an understanding of citation as more than the locating of the sources. Although I will illustrate the diverse sources which Palmer's work draws from, it is more provocative to suggest what the poem's referencing of an European lyric tradition, ranging from Rainer Maria Rilke, Charles Baudelaire and Andrea Zanzotto, may begin to tell us about the poet's own project.

Reading Palmer's poetry against Bernstein's work through a conceptual configuration of error highlights some surprising allegiances between their poetry. In writing on the presentation of memory in poetry, Palmer suggests that the syntactical indeterminacies and aberrations in the text may paradoxically perform with a certain 'integrity.' Palmer suggests that 'what is taken as a sign of openness– conventional narrative order– may stand for concealment, and what is understood generally as signs of withholding or evasion– ellipsis, periphrasis, etc.– may from another point of view stand for disclosure.'[50] It may seem tenuous at first to link a conceptualisation of error with a work that performs with integrity or even ethical consideration, yet it is evident that for Bernstein error is strongly linked to a political gesture, providing the refutation of an authoritarian rhetoric through humour. Similarly Palmer refutes the lyric as merely a space for an unproblematic anecdotal recounting. Although his comments are more speculative, Palmer indicates that his work in examining the epistemology of the lyric has a certain political critique; 'I'm very conscious of the role that poetry can play as resistant to and as a critique of the discourse of power by undermining assumptions about meaning and univocality.'[51]

---

49   See 'From the Notebooks', *19 New American Poets of the Golden Gate*, ed. Philip Dow (New York: Harcourt Brace Jovanovich, 1984), pp. 341–50 (p. 347).

50   Palmer, 'Autobiography, Memory and Mechanisms of Concealment' in *Writing/Talks*, pp. 207–29 (p. 227).

51   Palmer, 'Interview: Conducted by Keith Tuma', *Contemporary Literature*, 30.1 (Spring 1989), 1–12 (p. 6).

What starkly distinguishes a reading of error in Palmer's work is the poet's concerted anxiety over the rupturing of the lyric. While framing Palmer's work as an agonistic response to the lyric may be overstating his project, his work certainly dramatises a personal responsibility towards an extensive lineage of lyrical investigation. Citing Riffaterre, Palmer clearly makes a link between error or 'ungrammaticalities' and the problematising of the subject-object dichotomy of the traditional lyric:

> Riffaterre observes that 'the arbitrariness of language conventions seems to diminish as the text becomes more deviant and ungrammatical, rather than the other way around.' Poetry seems often a talking to self as well as other as well as self as other, a simultaneity that recognizes the elusive multiplicity of what is called identity.[52]

Frequently the subject in Palmer's poetry is evoked through an aphasic stuttering. Prompted by the poet's remarks and journal excerpts, broaching the poetry through accounts of schizophrenic language guides us in an understanding of the violent rupturing of the single speaking voice in Palmer's work. I will also suggest that a reading of the intertextual impulse within a conceptualisation of error allows us to consider the complex evocation of memory in Palmer's poetry. Harnessing a reading of the intertextual to Julia Kristeva's discussion of 'transposition' in poetic language and its relationship to the subject in process, enables an assessment of Palmer's scrutiny of the speaking subject. The poet cannot provide us with an alternative lyric model, and ultimately the poetry indicates that this is an untenable aim, the figurative and elusive backdrop of the European lyric in his work suggests that Palmer is battling quite seriously with a scrutiny of the responsibilities of the lyric voice.

In an interview Palmer draws attention to error as a form of wandering or errancy in the text, and suggests that there is a valuable relation between erring as a compositional strategy and the syntactical indeterminacy of his work:

---

52   Palmer, 'Autobiography, Memory and Mechanisms of Concealment', p. 227.

Robert Duncan and I talked a good deal about this– a trust to a kind of errancy, which is also an erring, making errors, and wandering, at the same time, through the passages– this dark wood which the poem is. Finding one's way through that without a map beforehand, to see what specific information would rise from the words themselves.[53]

The temptation with Palmer's remarks is to assert that his focus on the 'words themselves', draws us conveniently to the axiomatic attention of Language Writing to the materiality of the signifier. Throughout the study a conceptualisation of error will help to refine an understanding of the aesthetics of opacity associated with this broad range of writing. But it will also be useful to consider whether we can also read this erring impulse in conjunction with a poetics of transition. In this light an 'erring' poetics that is wandering, roaming irregularly, and without a predetermined itinerary, provides a strategy for bypassing the problems of rhetorical performance these three poets are keen to avoid.

The consideration of an erring poetics comes to the fore in approaching Hejinian's poetry. Already we have noted that Hejinian's poetics challenge the distinction between theory and the practice of poetry. 'Theory' in her configuration is neither pedagogical nor predetermined. Instead, she suggests that theory is a synonym for 'thought that is rigorously speculative, ongoing, and by virtue of looking out toward the world as well as self-critically inward, it resists adherence to first principles, immutable truths, authoritarian formulations. Theory as I understand it, is always everywhere mutable.'[54] Hejinian makes a connection in her writing not only between theory and thought, but also with the configuration of a speculative or provisional poetics. Key philosophical terms and critical idioms are often adapted and re-deployed in Hejinian's discussion, and this presents the primary difficulty in executing an examination of the poet's work. As readers we are required to translate Hejinian's adaptation of philosophical terms and how these amended concepts perform within the poetry. Understanding this transformative impulse as a speculative erring not only

53   Palmer, 'Interview' in Thomas Gardner's *Regions of Unlikeness: Explaining Contemporary Poetry* (Lincoln: University of Nebraska Press, 1999), pp. 272–91 (p. 272).
54   Hejinian, 'Reason', *The Language of Inquiry*, pp. 337–54 (p. 338).

31

performed by the writer, but also by the reader, grants us the opportunity to evaluate the engagement demanded by Hejinian's open text.

My configuration of an erring poetics draws from Hejinian's own remarks, and is an attempt to understand the provisionality which her poetics appear to endorse. Beginning with Hejinian's early poetics, erring is initially evoked as a figurative wandering in the text, and indeed her poem *The Guard* opens by evoking Dante's journey in *The Divine Comedy*. This intertextual reference serves as a vehicle for an extended meditation on what the essay 'Language and Paradise,' draws attention to as the 'lyric dilemma.'[55] In this essay the impossibility of harnessing experience through language is seen less as inadequacy than a celebration of a desire located within language. What is most alluring in Hejinian's account of this 'dilemma', is the suggestion that language generates a persistent 'restlessness'. The erring trajectory of Hejinian's poetry is an attempt to sustain the temporal mobility and phenomenological enquiry of her work. Understanding this initial dilemma or 'aporia' as an irresolvable 'overspill' in the text, allows us to reflect upon the tensions performed strategically in the poetry. Frequently the momentum of Hejinian's poetry is halted by a general aphoristic display which appears to run against the speculative criterion examined in her essays. But this aphoristic impulse is complex, since often the aphorism's rhetorical flourish is sabotaged by the poet's substitution of a word or phrase which renders the epithet ludic, if not slightly ridiculous. This slippage in the aphorism could initially be read in conjunction with Bernstein's poetics of error and its relationship to humour. Yet Hejinian's intention is markedly different since the aphoristic tendency not only staggers the poem's impulse towards phenomenological description and undercuts a pedagogical rhetoric, but also strikes a reminder of the lyric form that Hejinian is working within.

A reading of erring is useful in approaching the inconsistencies and tensions set up intentionally in Hejinian's poetry. The complexities of this erring impulse are developed in examining Hejinian's later work. Her essays suggest that the epistemological uncertainty the

---

55   Hejinian, 'Language and Paradise', *The Language of Inquiry*, pp. 59–82.

poetics delineates is strongly allied to an understanding of ethics.[56] In an attempt to understand what Hejinian repeatedly refers to as 'altruism in poetry',[57] *Reading Error* will scrutinise how an ethical engagement may be performed by the poetry. Furthermore Hejinian indicates that a responsible aesthetics can read as a 'poetics of encounter.' This configuration of encounter points us towards an understanding of the lyric as inscribing a sense of responsibility and acknowledgement of alterity. Hejinian like Palmer is anxious to re-evaluate what understanding of sincerity poetry can propose beyond a model of the lyric as self-expression. It becomes clear that Hejinian relates the opacity or difficulty of recent poetry, with a configuration of sincerity as an ethical engagement or responsibility:

> The difficulty of the work, then, does not constitute an intransigence; on the contrary, it is the material manifestation of the work's mutability, its openness, not just a form, but, more importantly, a forming, a manifestation of what the Objectivists would have termed its 'sincerity', the ethical principle by which a poet tests words against the actuality of the world, the articulation of our status as presences in common (and only in common) with other presences on the world.[58]

Overall this study will consider whether this gesture of altruism in Hejinian's poetry is entirely self-sacrificing, or if it also betrays the irresolvable complexities created by the attempt to move beyond the lyric 'I'. A configuration of erring as both a figurative wandering performed by Hejinian's poetry, and as a speculative interpretation executed by the reader tests the poet's use of key critical idioms against a range of theoretical and philosophical discussions. While the erring impulse in Hejinian's poetics does not give us an entirely interpretative free rein, the philosophical density of her work does on occasion

---

56 Interestingly, in her account of the emergence of Language Writing, Hejinian proposes that the 'intersecting of aesthetic concerns with ethical concerns is one of the basic characteristics of Language Writing.' 'Barbarism' in *The Language of Inquiry*, pp. 318–36 (p. 322).

57 Hejinian, *The Person* in *The Cold of Poetry* (Los Angeles: Sun and Moon Press, 1994), p. 146.

58 Hejinian, 'Barbarism', p. 331.

warrant brief readings of philosophical concepts outside those gestured to in the poet's own discussion.

The final chapter speculates upon an erring poetics as a way of negotiating recent literacy experimentation and a lyric tradition. I argue that Moxley's fascination with narrative digression, inconsistency and errancy in the poetic text has its precedent in 19th Century lyric practice. Moreover Moxley's stress upon lyric artifice as integral to her understanding of poetry, moves the discussion to ideas of linguistic transgression which Alexander Pope infamously addressed as 'bathos' in his mock and parodic treatise *Peri Bathous, or The Art of Sinking in Poetry*. I propose that her poetry draws attention to a transatlantic passage and transcription of a poetic tradition, as well to acts of deliberate misreading and an errant narrative momentum. Seth Lerner's reading of error as embracing 'both the erring and the errant– the latin word *"errare"* means of course "to wander,"' provides a way of reading the contemporary lyric's need for responsiveness to the world and a past tradition.[59] Moxley's lyric indicates that the recent lyric need not jettison tradition but that its journeying and momentum can be empathetic to a world beyond self-reflexivity.

Throughout *Reading Error* a consideration of an erring poetics will be a way of expanding the scope of the lyric, while retaining the important conceptual differences between the poets. Although my primary aim is to establish how an aesthetic of error enables us to approach the reconfiguration of the lyric in recent innovative poetry, I will evaluate whether the political and ethical claims of these three poets can be sustained by their aesthetics. In approaching the poetry as a plurality of constructive responses to the problematics of situating subjectivity and public address in poetry, the discussion will avoid reducing Bernstein, Palmer and Hejinian's poetry to a general aesthetic. In this overall ambition, I am forewarned by Hejinian's comments that the historicisation of Language Writing threatens to 'do violence to what were its large-scale intentions, those that hoped to exceed the boundaries of mere aesthetics.'[60] The parallels established with Mox-

59   Seth Lerner, *Error and the Academic Self: The Scholarly Imagination, Medieval to Modern* (New York: Columbia U.P., 2002) p. 3.
60   Hejinian, 'Barbarism', p. 321.

ley's poetry in at the close of *Reading Error* indicate a productive consideration of the preoccupations of a preceding generation. As Moxley puts it in her negotiation of literary and political history: 'Will a loss-strewn personal history/ swallow or create our relevance?'[61]

While the trials of historicising Language Writing is not the focus of *Reading Error*, I will suggest that error offers us a possibility of countering literary history's tendency to define the contemporary lyric as a static model of personal expression. In beginning to understand the recent history of the lyric as a transitional locus, we may eventually find some correspondence between our own enquiry, and Martin Heidegger's alluring proposal that 'error is the space where history unfolds ... Without errancy there would be no history.'[62]

61   Moxley, 'The Occasion' *The Sense Record* (Cambridge: Salt, 2003), p. 89.
62   Cited in Peter Baker, *Obdurate Brilliance: Exteriority and the Modern Long Poem* (Gainesville: University of Florida Press, 1991), p. 45.

Chapter One
Error, Malapropisms, 'Ideolects' and 'Knowing' a Language in Charles Bernstein's *Dark City* and *Rough Trades*

The lyric and the 'show me' business

It may seem surprising that Charles Bernstein draws attention to the lyric tradition as informing his poetics. Given Bernstein's role as a key polemicist of Language Writing, his acknowledgement of the lyric might seem incongruous with Language Writing's early attacks on the workshop aesthetic.[1] But looking attentively at his comments, it is clear that the lyric Bernstein has in mind is not the anecdotal expressive model associated with creative writing programmes:

> The lyric tradition, with its emphasis on the enunciative, on sound, and on subjectivity remains extremely valuable to my poetic concerns. But lyric poetry needs to be viewed in its specific historical contexts and read for its specific rhetorical forms; that is away from the Romantic ideology that makes the lyric a generalized, even universal, expression of human sentiment.[2]

In direct contrast, Michael Scharf's comments in a survey of the lyric for an edition of *Poets & Writers*, perpetuates the well-worn analogy of Language Writing as the antagonistic 'other' of the lyric impulse:

> Language poetry often seems ambivalent about, and even hostile to, the lyric imagination, with its reputation for straightening things up and pointing them toward the sublime of small epiphanies. The challenge for poets today is to find

---

1   The Introduction situates Language Writing's general dissatisfaction with the workshop model.
2   Charles Bernstein, 'The Revenge of the Poet-Critic, or The Parts are Greater than the Whole', in *My Way: Speeches and Poems* (Harvard: Harvard U.P., 1999), pp. 3–17 (p. 10).

ways of writing from the lyric imagination without getting stuck in its history, or in the uses to which it is most often put.[3]

Clearly Bernstein unlike Scharf, points to the importance of situating the lyric's rhetorical impulse within its historical context. Furthermore his comments indicate the necessity of reformulating an approach to the lyric away from its more recent dispersal as a generalised address, or expression of emphatic interiority. Reading Bernstein's approach to the lyric not as a dismissal of subjectivity itself but as a critique of the expressive lyric's configuration of subjectivity, allows us to examine his poetry from a more productive perspective. Examining Bernstein's poetry through a configuration of error allows us to link the rupturing of the lyric form in his work, to his ambitious claims for the public function for both poetry and poetics.

Provocatively, Bernstein's celebrated essay in verse 'Artifice of Absorption',[4] draws attention to what he calls 'official verse culture' and its privileging of authenticity and sincerity:

official verse culture
of the last 25 years has engaged in militant
(that is to say ungenerously uniformitarian)
campaigns to 'restrict the subversive,
'independent-of-things' nature of the language'
in the name of the common voice, clarity, sincerity,
or directness of the poem (46)

Bernstein associates the workshop lyric with a certain directness or 'transparency', which can be understood as the conceptualisation of language as an unproblematic vehicle for communicating thought and perception. By now it has become somewhat axiomatic to attend to the contrasting 'opacity'[5] of poetry associated with Language Writing,

3   Michael Scharf, 'Imagination vs.', *Poets & Writers*, 27.2 (April 1999), p. 59.
4   Bernstein, 'Artifice of Absorption', in *A Poetics* (Harvard: Harvard U.P., 1991), pp. 9–89 (p. 46).
5   Bob Perelman argues that the disjunction and fracturing of reference in some recent poetry is not particularly innovative. He comments upon the danger of using such strategies as 'fashion tips', adding that, 'disjunction and opacity are getting a little too long in the tooth; try connectedness'. From Perelman's 'Polemic Greetings to the Inhabitants of Utopia', in *Assembling Alternatives*:

understanding this 'density' in the text as the foregrounding of the generative properties of language itself. What is most compelling about this essay is how the key terms 'artifice' and 'absorption', are given provisional interpretations, both terms shift notably during the course of the discussion. While one would intuitively associate the 'transparency' of the workshop aesthetic with a certain 'absorption', and the 'opacity' of more innovative poetry with a certain 'artifice', Bernstein problematises these categories by suggesting that a poetry of 'impermeability' can also be 'absorbing'.

One way of exacerbating this seemingly paradoxical configuration in Bernstein's essay is to turn to the poet's conceptualisation of language in his poetics. Intrinsic to his refutation of language as a vehicle of direct mediation is Bernstein's suspicion of the language of public discourse. Indeed his poetics stress that there is a troubling relationship between the hierarchies of language's ruled-governed conventions and authority. The relationship between convention and a rhetorical address he suggests can be located as an attempt to master language. This link between rhetoric, rule-governed conventions and public discourse has for Bernstein an explicitly political dimension; since he stresses that once 'we consider the conventions of writing, we are entering into the politics of language ... Convention is a central means by which authority is made credible.'[6] Before equating Bernstein's poetics with the refutation of all ruled-governed principles in language, it is clear that the poet considers not all conventions and authorities as 'corrupt' (222). Instead he proposes that:

> It is essential to trace how some uses of convention and authority can hide the fact that both are historical constructions rather than sovereign principles. For convention and authority can, and ought, serve at the will of the polis. (222–3)

Bernstein's comments indicate that a critique of convention is a legitimate method for revealing an authority which perhaps does not serve,

Reading Postmodern Poetries Transnationally, ed. Romana Huk (Hanover, NH: Wesleyan U.P.), pp. 375–88 (p. 375, 6).

6   Bernstein, 'Comedy and the Poetics of Political Form', in *A Poetics*, pp. 218–28 (p. 218, 220).

what he gestures to as the 'love of the public good.'[7] But can we begin to link this ambition to the writing of poetry? In an early essay, the poet suggests that the disruption of established rules of grammar and syntax is linked with a political agency in effect opening the text to an affirmation of language as a shared commonality:

> Prescribed rules of grammar & spelling make language seem outside of our control. & a language, even only seemingly, wrested from our control is a world taken from us– a world in which language becomes a tool for the description of the world, words mere instrumentalities for representing this world.[8]

His poetics indicate a mistrust of poetry as a mastery of form, and acts of linguistic indeterminacy become strategies safeguarding against the dangers of an authoritarian rhetoric. Returning to our initial dilemma over the terms 'artifice' and absorption', it is apparent that Bernstein associates the foregrounding of language's generative properties with an engagement from his reader. This is apparent when he gestures to a 'writing that incorporates the issue of interpretation and interaction.'[9] Approached from this perspective of readerly engagement, it is not surprising that Bernstein suggests that the term absorption could be read as 'engrossing, engulfing completely, engaging ... enthralling: belief, conviction.'[10] Indeed, Bernstein links the 'artifice' of poetry, or what he calls, 'writing centered on its wordness',[11] with an ambitious political and social claim:

> Language is commonness in being, through which we see & make sense of & value. Its exploration is the exploration of the human common ground. The move from a purely descriptive, outward directive, writing toward writing centered on its wordness, its physicality, its haecceity (thisness) is, in its impulse, an investigation of human self-sameness, of the place of our connection: in the world, in the word, in ourselves. (32)

---

7   Bernstein, 'Matters of Policy', in *Controlling Interests* (New York: Roof Books: 1980), p. 6.
8   Bernstein, 'Three or four things I know about him', in *Content's Dream* (Los Angeles: Sun & Moon Press, 1986), pp. 13–33 (p. 26).
9   Bernstein, 'Writing and Method', in *Content's Dream*, pp. 217–36 (p. 233).
10 Bernstein, 'Artifice of Absorption', p. 29.
11 Bernstein, 'Three or four things I know about him', p. 32.

Bernstein's dissatisfaction with the workshop lyric stems not only from a refutation of a certain aesthetic, but is also linked with his own approach to poetics as necessarily social in its address and political in its intention. He addresses the domestication of the recent lyric in no uncertain terms, suggesting that for the 'subjectivized, gutted lyric', imagination and subjectivity 'have become house pets of the personal lifestyle industry, cousins to a creativity that seems to apply more to earrings than to hearing.'[12] But as is frequently the case with Bernstein's poetics this wit belies a serious intention. Within this discussion of 'official verse culture' Bernstein, echoing Theodor Adorno, stakes an important claim:

> No artist can remain entirely free from collaboration with the society in which she or he works– history is too consuming for that– but relative degrees of resistance are possible. Art can provide a means by which to read culture, cognitive maps if you will. New forms provide new methods of critique. (20)

Bernstein's criticism of the workshop lyric as a solipsistic aesthetic is evident, but we need to consider what strategies the poet offers us for opening up the address of the lyric, to situate it within a social and political nexus. Reading Bernstein's poetry through a configuration of error allows us to simultaneously consider Bernstein's aesthetic of 'artifice' in conjunction with his political aims. Understanding error initially as intentional typographical mistakes, misspellings and the disruption of syntax, we can examine the relationship between error and Bernstein's conceptualisation of language. Usefully an explicit aesthetic of typographical error features most prominently in Bernstein's recent poetry especially proclamations in his 'A Defence of Poetry'[13] where the surface of language is defaced so violently as to be practically unreadable:

> We
> have preshaps a blurrig of sense, whih
> means not relying on convnetionally

12 Bernstein, 'Poetics of the Americas', *Modernism/ Modernity*, 3.3 (1996), 1–23 (p. 19, 20).
13 Bernstein, 'A Defence of Poetry', in *My Way*, pp. 1–2. Originally published in 1991.

methods for *conveying* sense but whih may
aloow for dar greater sense-smakinh than
specisi9usforms of doinat disoucrse that
makes no sense at all by irute of thier
hyperconventionality (Bush's speeches
calssically). (1–2)

Bernstein's 'Defence' has elicited a sceptical response. Remarkably amidst this disruption of the 'prescribed rules of grammar & spelling', the loaded word 'hyperconventionality' remains intact. Bernstein's orthographic disruption of the lyric with its implications of an ironic commentary presents some pertinent problems in reading his refutation of an authoritarian discourse.

The surfacing of an explicit aesthetic of typographical error in Bernstein's 'The Lives of the Toll Takers' in *Dark City* (1994) can be sourced to his earlier volume *Rough Trades* (1987). Bernstein's early poetry offers the reader a more persuasive linking of error and the configuration of an alternative polis, than the explicit aesthetic of error mediated through the typographical mistakes. The temptation is to view his poetry solely through his poetics, since their close correlation makes it difficult to distinguish between proposition and praxis. Alternative or supplementary approaches help develop the initial reading of error as a series of typographical mistakes. Approaching the intentional syntactical and grammatical solecisms of Bernstein's work through a psychoanalytic reading, grants a further perspective on the poet's aesthetic of artifice. Most importantly, this enquiry will attempt to relate Bernstein's mediation of error as a strategy for challenging authoritarian conventions, with the broader problematic of what indeed knowing a language may entail. The insistent malapropisms in Bernstein's poetry demand attention, and we need to consider whether these deliberate slippages in the text can be aligned to the poet's proposition of poetry as a composition of 'ideolects'.[14] American language philosopher Donald Davidson, offers an interesting twist on how to begin reading these garbled phrases or malapropisms within a broader context of linguistic competence and communication.

---

14   Bernstein's coining of an 'ideolectical' approach to poetic language is introduced in his essay, 'Poetics of the Americas'.

Persuaded by Bernstein's invocation of poetics as errant enquiry, this chapter examines how the engagement demanded by the writing can be approached as a form of wandering, or errancy performed by the reader within the interstices of the text. Approaching error in this light provides a reading of Bernstein's poetry as a provisional testing out of hypotheses and propositions, both in accordance with, and against his poetics. A consideration of error in Bernstein's poetry enables a reading of the lyric not merely as a poetry of intense personal expression, or what the poet calls the 'show me business' but as a sustained attempt to configure a public address in poetry.

Configuring Error: Humour, Irony and Encryption in 'A Defence of Poetry' and *Dark City*

Following Bernstein's gestures to error as the disruption of rule-governed conventions; an essay in *A Poetics* extends the poet's meditations on error as a methodology for rupturing the lyric and configuring a public address:

> One of the main things I want to suggest is that poetics must necessarily involve error. Error in the sense of wandering, errantry, but also error in the sense of mistake, misperception, incorrectness, contradiction. Error as projection (expression of desire unmediated by rationalized explanation): as slips, slides ... Then again the issue of error is transformed for me into a question of humor. I am interested, insofar as possible, to try to put into talks like this, essays, certain kinds of pratfalls, the equivalent of slipping on a banana, or throwing a pie in my own face. So that error is made explicit as part of the process.
>
> And then the humor itself begins to make dialectical or trilectical or quadralectical some of the dynamics I am talking about.
>
> It can be like juggling four or five or six different things.
>
> But alas I can only juggle one thing at a time, so as I am juggling all these different things hopefully three or four of them will fall to the ground.
>
> Hopefully some of them will be rotten tomatoes.

And you'll say what happened to that one.
And you'll begin to get it.[15]

In Bernstein's formulation error is a contingent practice closely allied to humour. The space created for error is presented as a vaudeville act or a ludic performance; this configuration of a relationship between error and humour is important. Bernstein is wary of aligning his poetics with an ambition of mastery, and error through its association with humour is linked with an ambition to establish a public address that does not rely on authoritarian rhetoric. In this light error provides a way of dislodging the workshop poem's focus on the lyric as an expression of sincerity, since Bernstein stresses that 'anything that departs from the sincere or serious enters into the comic.'[16] Yet as readers we should remain wary of this immediate configuration of humour, error and the refutation of a rhetorical address. In Bernstein's configuration error also serves an important pedagogical role. Error is promoted as a context of instruction or even education. Radical poetics in eschewing rule-governed conventions, appears to promote its own regulations for reading, hence the joke is one that we shall begin to 'get', only if we pay attention. I am sceptical of Bernstein's easy dismissal of rationality within his configuration of error, since the error this passage illustrates seems to indicate strategy rather than randomness. Rather than dramatising a poststructuralist paradigm of play, Bernstein's conceptualisation of an errant humour is informed by a serious intention. Humour as a strategy for deflating a rhetorical impulse, may also err paradoxically, on the ironic commentary the poet is keen to avoid.

One way of unthreading the broader propositions posed by Bernstein's erring poetics is to consider whether a relationship can be traced between error, rationality and aesthetic practice. Alan Singer challenges 'perfection' as the ultimate criterion for aesthetic value and judgement.[17] He proposes that the dangers in this equating of perfec-

---

15   Bernstein, 'Optimism and Critical Excess', in *A Poetics*, pp. 150–78 (p. 153, 154).
16   Bernstein, 'Comedy and the Poetics of Political Form', in *A Poetics*, p. 227.
17   Alan Singer, 'Beautiful Errors: Aesthetics and the Art of Contextualization', *Boundary 2*, 25. 2 (1998), 7–34.

tion and aesthetic value is the allure of configuring the artwork within the rhetoric of genius and the sublime, in effect isolating it from a social or historical context. Cast in this context of aesthetic perfection, the artwork is presented as a timeless unity, separate from the process of its becoming; or as Nietzsche reminds us 'when something is perfect we tend to neglect to ask about its evolution.'[18] Singer asserts that error can be aligned productively to reconfiguring a model of aesthetic judgement premised on perfection, but insists that rationality is intrinsic to this process:

> Error has been the touchstone of political critiques that discount the aesthetic as a hopelessly unworldly preoccupation ... In this context, I want to allege that error might be a salutary link between the aesthetic and rational cognition, one that might suspend the mutual exclusions otherwise predicated between them. (9)

Singer develops the concept of error as an opposition of right and wrong, or rule and contingent practice, and indicates that any approach to error demands a context of aesthetic judgement. Error thus becomes a 'phenomenon of contextuality and not as a mutually exclusive wrong versus a right' (10). This highlighting of the evaluative process integral to formulating and understanding error is crucial to in Bernstein's poetry and its relation to humour and irony. There is in effect a threshold which error has to cross to be understood and interpreted, and in Bernstein's case this threshold is the passage from error to humour. Singer suggests that this boundary has an informing potential:

> There emerges in the cognizance of error, a threshold of negotiation between the wrongs of irrationality and right reason that might mitigate the morally precarious abstraction of both. It is particularly important to stipulate that these negotiations unfold in narrative order as a learning process. Errors can come to light only within an emergent context of judgement. The emergent context reveals prior conceptions to be inadequate to the intentionality instantiated through their deployment. (10)

18   Friedrich Nietzsche, *Human all too Human*, trans. Marion Faber with Stephen Lehmann (Lincoln: University of Nebraska Press, 1996), p. 131.

Error can to a great extent requires that one questions the rationality of rule-based values as themselves contingent practices. Singer's gesture to the questioning of convention makes a strong connection with Bernstein's configuration of error as the challenging of rule-governed hierarchies. Yet, it is worth bearing in mind that Singer places a focus on the evaluative judgement that an understanding of error demands. In Bernstein's case how free we are to make these interpretative and evaluative choices? A consideration of the rhetorical strategy of irony in Bernstein's poetry is integral to this assessment.

Bernstein disputes that the errant humour in his work could be read as ironic. Indeed, the following extract from a writers' symposium indicates that the configuration of humour in his poetics works as a strategy for countering the authoritarian dangers of an ironic commentary:

> I don't actually see my work as ironic in the way that irony tends to be conceptualized ... I think we share this conception of the humour of it, but I've been thinking just over the past few days of the term 'self-cancelling irony'. With irony, you're left with some sense of authoritative distance from whatever's being mocked or ironized, especially in the modernist form. I'm interested in coming back around, so that you're actually where you were if it weren't ironic. You've gone through the humorous turn, but it's self-cancelling in the sense that you're not remaining at a distance from it, nor are you ridiculing it. On the contrary, you've gone through a kind of comic spin cycle. It all depends on what people's attitude to humor is, as if humor were at odds with all kinds of things that it's not at odds with, as if humor were somehow always associated with mocking and therefore with belittling.[19]

The reference to a modernist tradition is not merely coincidental; high modernism's preoccupation with linguistic accuracy and mastery of technique could be read as antithetical to Bernstein's conceptualisation of an erring poetics. Reading irony as a rhetorical device it is evident that Bernstein's mistrust stems from the hierarchical distance that irony establishes between the poem and the public audience it is attempting to address. Furthermore the provisionality of Bernstein's configuration of error and its focus upon linguistic play as a gesture of

19   Bernstein, 'Poetry Community, Movement: A Conversation', *Diacritics*, 26.3 (1994), 196–210 (p. 206).

opposition, is presented as a strategy for deflating irony's rhetorical command. For Bernstein to admit to an ironical reading of his work would reintroduce the compelling authorial presence associated with a hectoring rhetoric, he is keen to avoid.

My correlation of irony with authority here, is taking irony at its simplest form as a rhetorical device. Bernstein's insistent focus on humour in his poetics is focused towards generating meaning through linguistic play, yet the examples of error in his poetry as intentional mistakes gesture towards an ironical reading. Candace Lang proposes that irony can be extended beyond its familiar role as a rhetorical strategy, and her attention to the alternating modes of ironic and humorous writing within texts stresses that neither are exclusive forms of writing.[20] Lang's conceptualisation of how an ironic text may be read sheds light upon the complex relationship between error, irony and humour in Bernstein's poetics.

For the sophist irony is the difference between phenomena and essence, in this philosophy Lang notes that 'man is condemned to struggle incessantly and vainly to obtain an abstract truth forever hidden or distorted by the veil of appearance' (2). This 'veil' could be extended to the use of language as a phenomenal screen which correlates with the romantic's longing for truth in the guise of sincerity and self expression. The ironist to a degree is guilty of mystification and the arrogance of assuming understanding through general indications of how a work should be read. While Bernstein's entire poetic oeuvre cannot be read as an ironist's quest for truth, there is a troubling reduction in his approach to error as mere play and its unproblematic transition to humour. Lang suggests that a humorous text differentiates itself from an ironic text through its conceptualisation of language. For the 'humorist', language is an essential determinant of thought, and meaning does not pre-exist in language in a symbolic order. While for the ironist meaning is reliant upon authorial intention, the humorist delights in textual surfaces and the multiple possibilities of language generating its own meaning. For the ironist Lang notes:

---

20   Candace Lang, *Irony/ Humour Critical Paradigms* (Baltimore & London: Johns Hopkins U.P., 1988).

> The multivalent text is unthinkable: discrepancies or incoherencies can only be interpreted as errors, as attempts to communicate anxiety over life's contradictions as despairing demonstrations of the inadequacies of language as a vehicle for self-expression ... a true meaning is elsewhere. (45)

This alluring sense of nostalgia for a rhetorical command proves most useful, and also most problematic in assessing the role of error in Bernstein's configuration of lyricism. There are several contradictory impulses in his poetics; he wants to critique culture to an extent out of culture, and promote meaning through linguistic play without abandoning an intentional command. This paralysis between an open-ended dynamic and authorial intention is replicated by the respective play between humour and irony within the poetry. Roland Barthes offers us a surprising way into considering the rather confusing realm of intentionality in the Bernstein's poetry. Barthes identifies a 'baroque' irony that is a form of irony which 'expands language rather than constricts it' and he indicates we should ask of an author not to 'make me believe in what you say, but rather make me believe in your decision to say it'.[21] This formulation of irony is useful in understanding the complications that an explicit aesthetic of error as typographical mistakes, creates as a strategy in Bernstein's poetics.

Bernstein's 'A Defence of Poetry' illustrates the problems the reader faces in approaching the more explicit aesthetic of error in his work:

> (I thin youy misinterpret the natuer of
> some of the poltical claims go; not
> themaic
> interpretatiomn of evey
> evey detail in every peim
> but an oeitnetation towatd a kind of
> texutal practice
> that you prefer to call 'nknsense' but
> for *poltical* purpses I prepfer to call
> ideological!
> , say Hupty Dumpty) (1)

---

21   Roland Barthes, cited by Lang, *Irony/Humour*, p. 57.

The retreat to error here is censorial to the reader of the poem since typographical errors do not actually further the content. We are required to translate by substitution, and one wonders how effective this challenging of rule-governed conventions of grammar, spelling and syntax may actually be. Indeed, the poem elicits a rather sceptical response from Bob Perelman who points out in that once the process of grammatical rewriting is completed, we are left with a sketchy poem:

> Bernstein recommends an omnivorous, non-judgmental process that would read without evaluating. But the surface of the poem flirts with the judgmental category of error. Doesn't '*poltical*' especially italicized, act out a kind of slapstick? Can the '*poltical* is the political' be taken as an unironic lesson? ... Bernstein is insisting on anti-mastery in a self-contaminating way. He is not bending orthography to criticize wrongful power outside the poem or to signal his own elect status; rather he is destroying the image of power within in his own writing, abjuring the conventional tasks of the poet and rewards for the reader. The line breaks seem deliberately non-significant; and if we make the orthographic corrections, we get prose, casually disguised as verse.[22]

Perelman suggests that Bernstein's 'Defence' extols the cause of 'non mastery and error,' and the poem's blurring of the dichotomies between sense and nonsense serve only to ridicule the process of evaluative judgement. As Perelman reminds us, we should bear in mind that it was Humpty Dumpty who proposed that 'the question is who is to be master that is all.'[23] Although Bernstein is not configuring his own private language in the poem, there is more than a tentative connection with this reading of mastery that Perelman draws attention to and Bernstein's poetics. Consider for example, the poet's exhortation in 'The Revenge of the Poet-Critic':

22 Bob Perelman, 'Write the Power: Orthography and Community', in *The Marginalization of Poetry: Language Writing and Literary History* (Princeton: Princeton U.P., 1996), pp. 79–95 (p. 88, 89).

23 Bernstein in an early interview suggests that the central ambition of innovative poetry is 'to take control over language, to take it within our hands and make it mean what we want it to mean, like Humpty Dumpty says in *Alice in Wonderland*.' See Bernstein, 'Socialist Realism or Real Socialism', in *Content's Dream*, pp. 411–27 (p. 426).

The men on the hill, they say, 'learn the rules, *then* break them.' I like to 'think the reverse' whenever possible and even if not: break 'em enough times you won't have to learn 'em, or the rules will have changed, or you will change them, or make up your own rules and don't follow those either; anyway whose rules are they?[24]

In jumping through the hoops Bernstein has set for his reader 'A Defence of Poetry' establishes an evident hierarchy. In spite of the poem's typographical disruption, there is paradoxically no possibility of reading it beyond the author's initial intention. Considering this interpretative stranglehold in conjunction with Lang's discussion one cannot but state that the text is ironic.

A readerly frustration with Bernstein's superficial disruption of poetic language and its claim for a political efficacy is examined by Margaret Soltan's article 'Hoax Poetry in America.'[25] Understanding 'hoax' as falsity, obsessive self-referential awareness and an aesthetic which shields a rather mundane or overworked content, Soltan's remarks on Bernstein's poetry link us directly to the explicit aesthetic of error in 'A Defence of Poetry'. Soltan's response to Bernstein's poem 'Thinking I think I think' is scathing:

> The meaning of Bernstein's poetry is blushingly plain; it is a puerile diatribe against what the poet thinks of as a repressive arts establishment ... while the pace and impudence of 'Thinking I think I think' suggests a sort of verve, its shabby language games and bootless cynicism betray an immobility rooted in the conviction of cultural constructionism. (54)

Soltan links her configuration of 'hoax' poetry to a general waning of evaluative judgement, and alarmingly suggests that this aspect of self-referentiality in the poetry is the poet's attempt to placate his audience's expectations.[26] Her discussion poses that an explicit aesthetic of error in 'A Defence of Poetry' has a tendency to immobilise the

---

24 Bernstein, 'The Revenge of the Poet-Critic', p. 3.
25 Margaret Soltan, 'Hoax Poetry in America', *Angelaki: Journal of the Theoretical Humanities*, 5.1 (2000), 43–62.
26 Soltan comments 'This poem tries hard to make itself appealing to college students, and some of their professors, to whom the manifest desire of this writer to be a poet, and of his writing to be revolutionary, is immediately recognizable as their own desire, too', p. 55.

50

poem in its foregrounding of artifice. Coincidentally Bernstein's re-working of Shelley's treatise diligently performs an exercise noted in Ezra Pound's *ABC of Reading*, where Pound suggests that the student of poetry may 'parody some poem he finds ridiculous ... or for any other reason that strikes his risible faculties, his sense of irony.[27] While parody may not be Bernstein's explicit intention in 'A Defence of Poetry', there is gamble to be staked in this exercise of rewriting. Pound states that the completed poem reveals 'whether the joke is on the parodied or the parodist' (69). Similarly in 'A Defence of Poetry' we are left wondering uncomfortably whether the last laugh is at the reader or indeed the author's expense.

An explicit aesthetic of error as a series intentional mistakes is tempered in Bernstein's long poem 'The Lives of the Toll Takers' from *Dark City*.[28] 'The Lives of the Toll Takers' delineates the wandering passage or errancy Bernstein promotes in his essay 'Optimism and Critical Excess'. The poem's found materials and conflicting speech acts enacts a libretto with constant digression and replication. There are traces of a chorus, but morphemic shifts destabilise phrases and refrains in the text. The fracturing of the single speaking lyric voice and the competing registers in the text enact a Bakhtinian polyphony. Although Mikhail Bakhtin notoriously privileges the novel's 'dialogism' over what he terms the 'monologic' discourse of poetry, there is an immediate correspondence with his observations on the heteroglossic texture of the novel and Bernstein's poem. Bakhtin illustrates how conflicting speech acts in the novel inform the author's voice: 'For the prose writer, the object is a focal point for heteroglot voices among which his own voice must sound; these voices create the background necessary for his own voice, outside of which his artistic prose nuances cannot be perceived, and without which they "do not sound."'[29]

27   Ezra Pound, 'Further Tests', in *ABC of Reading* (New York: New Directions, 1987), pp. 68–70 (p. 68).
28   Bernstein, *Dark City* (Los Angeles: Sun & Moon Press, 1994).
29   Mikhail Bakhtin, *The Dialogic Imagination*, ed. Michael Hoquist and trans. Caryl Emerson (Texas: University of Texas Press, 1981), p. 278.

A study of polyphony in Bernstein's poetry yields interesting results,[30] but I want to concentrate on how to read the inclusion and disruption of cliches and aphorisms in 'The Lives of the Toll Takers.' In this poem sayings become skewed intentionally, and while meaning may shift within an aphorism or a quotation, the cadence of the original remains as a trace mark within the text. Take for example the disrupted proverb in 'a picture/ [fixture]/ is worth more than a thousand words' (10), which disappears almost completely to a demarcation of syllables '[*a tincture gives birth to a gravely verve*]' (10). It then becomes a command for form above rhetoric, '[*a mixture is worth a thousand one-line serves*]' (11) and ludically collapses into a linguistic economy '(A picture is worth 44.95 but no price can be/ put on words)' (15). A further ghosted reference behind all these examples is the pertinent adage, 'Actions speak louder than words'. A psychoanalytic approach to these palimpsestual layerings and tracings enables a further conceptualisation of error as a series of determined encryptions hidden in Bernstein's text.

'The Lives of the Toll Takers' reads as an a mini biopic, one cannot fail to see resonances with Bernstein's career path as poetics professor:

> I had decided to go back
> to school after fifteen years in
> community poetry because I felt
> I did not know enough to navigate
> though the rocky waters that
> lie ahead for all of us in this field. (24–5)

But before one gets too comfortable with an autobiographical reading, this is also a poem that contains an intrusive visual trajectory of what could be a programming code:

---

30   For a 'polyphonic' reading of Bernstein's poetry see John Shoptaw, 'Measure and Polyphony in Ashbery and Bernstein', in *The Tribe of John: Ashbery and Contemporary Poetry*, ed. Susan M. Schultz (Tuscaloosa and London: University of Alabama Press, 1995), pp. 211–58.

```
=]ovwhiu2g97hgbcf67q6dvqujx67sf2197b.c.9327b97b987b87j 7
7td7tq98gdukbhq   g9tq9798   icxqyj2f108ytscxags62jc .<Mz[
   –\ io (27)
```

This is the ultimate in encoding or encryption, but how to read it? The reader is informed midway in the poem that there is a 'Fatal Error F27: Disk directory full' (15). This is an interpretative overload and since Bernstein plays with the conventions of nonsense rhyme throughout the poem, the problem could be that rather than lack of meaning, his poem inscribes too much, short-circuiting the whole operation. The mismatching of codas and refrains throughout the poem recalls the title of an earlier poem by Bernstein 'Dysraphism', a medical term which he takes much delight in footnoting. The note itself functions as a lexical insert and a tracing of etymology:

> Dysraphism is a word used by specialists in a congenital disease to mean a dysfunctional fusion of embryonic parts– a birth defect ... Raph literally means 'seam' so dysraphism is mis-seaming– a prosodic device! But it has the punch of being the same root as rhapsody (rhaph)– or in Skeat's–'one who strings (lit. stitches) songs together, a reciter of epic poetry, cf 'ode' etc. In any case, to be simple, Dorland's does define 'dysraphia' (if not dysraphism) as 'incomplete closure of the primary neural tube, status dysraphicus': this is just below 'dysprosody' [sic]: 'disturbance of stress, pitch, and rhythm of speech.'[31]

Bernstein relishes the wordplay in 'mis-seaming' and with due cause, since his poetry extols the instabilities of a defective or erring language and the skewing of aphoristic sayings. Yet the temptation with Bernstein's poetry is to characterize this pulverisation of language as word play. Reading these instances of error in 'The Lives of the Toll Takers' as a series of intentional encryptions in the text extends our reading of error from the literal challenging of grammatical rule-governed conventions.

---

31   Bernstein, 'Dysraphism', in *The Sophist* (Los Angeles: Sun & Moon Press, 1987), p. 44.

Nicholas Abraham and Maria Torok's psychoanalytic work *The Wolfman's Magic Word: A Cryptonymy*,[32] with its formulation of 'crypt words' understands intentional errors not as obstructions to interpretation, but as initiatory acts which prompt a sequence of further questions. Nicholas Rand identifies cryptonymy as 'a verbal procedure leading to the creation of a text whose sole purpose is to hide words that are hypothesized as having to remain beyond reach' (lviii). In the case of the Wolf Man, Abraham and Torok's analysis of Freud's casenotes reveal not only the command of the analyst's authorial judgement, but an interior debate of the patient as author. The case notes become a life poem of puns and verbal contortions. Rand emphasises that it is 'not a situation comprising words that becomes repressed; the words are not dragged into repression by a situation. Rather the words themselves expressing desire are deemed to be generators of a situation that must be avoided and voided retroactively' (lix). The crypt word moreover 'inhibits the process of definition or meaning by concealing a segment of the associative path that normally allows one to move freely from one element to another in a verbal chain' (lix).

In 'The Lives of the Toll Takers' crypt words gesture towards a threshold of error without conferring an evaluative judgement, since Bernstein commits himself only to the indeterminacies of signifieds:

> The things I
> write are
> not about me
> though they
> become me.

You look so bec
       oming, she said, attending the flower pots.
          I'm a very
                        becom

ing guy
(tell it to
)
. That is, better

32   Nicholas Abraham and Maria Torok, *The Wolfman's Magic Word: A Cryptonymy* (Minneapolis: University of Minneapolis Press, 1986).

                to
become than
                (gestalt f[r]iction)
                                {traction?}
                                {flirtation?}
                to
be: ac
   tuality
   is just around
the corner (just a spark
                in the dark); self actualization a glance in
a tank of concave [concatenating] mirrors. Not
                                angles, just
tangles. From which
a direction emerges, p
                                urges. Hope
gives way
                to tire tracks. On the
way without stipulating
   the destination,
                        the better
to get there (somewhere
                other
).
                THE MAGIC PHONEME FOR TODAY IS 'KTH'.
Funny, you don't look
                gluish. Poetry: the show-
me business.
                You've just said the magic phoneme!
'Don't give me
any of your
show-me business'
She wore blue velvet but I was colour blind and insensible.
                Heavy tolls, few
advances. Are you cl
os
   e
                        to your m
        other? (15–18)

    Some of the crypt words make their presence known violently as
a splicing over linebreaks or within the perimeters of brackets, for ex-

ample: 'f[r]iction', 'p/urges' and 'm/other'. But what is provocative to our context of the lyric is the delineation of subjectivity, or the evolving 'be-coming' in the text and how this process is disrupted by the appearance of the magic phoneme. The speaker in writing herself into the poem is in a state of constant emergence; 'That is better to become than ... to be' as the poem aphoristically announces. Hence the rejection of Gestalt psychology as a possible 'fiction'. Furthermore the mirror-stage is presented as a disorientating chain of replications 'a tank of concave [concatenating] mirrors'. But the subject seems to resist this recognition or 'self-actualization' until the halt into an uppercase instruction 'THE MAGIC PHONEME FOR TODAY IS "KTH."'

Using Abraham and Torok's cryptonymic reading of the Wolf Man's case history in this final section yields some interesting results. Fortuitously to our context of a psychoanalytic reading, the repeated phrase 'the better to get there', resonates as a hijacking of the Wolf's refrain to Little Red Riding Hood. But how to apply a cryptonymic reading to 'kth'? Homophonic translations gesture to 'kith', not totally useless if one thinks of kin and also 'cuss'. In approaching 'KTH' as an acronym the results are more productive, suggesting criteria which 'mesh' with Bernstein's focus on an emergent subjectivity in this extract. Bearing in mind that the poem introduces an unstable and disruptive computer midway in 'The Lives of the Toll Takers', my associational chain ran to the acronym HAL in Stanley Kubrick's film *2001*. According to Kubrick this acronym was an intentional one-letter, alphabetical downshift from the giant IBM. So by shifting Bernstein's own acronym, one could muster J (e) U and I. Maybe not altogether implausible since the shift from I to you, and back to I, indicates more self-awareness than the solipsistic and constant 'becoming' in the opening of this extract. Once the 'you' and 'me become associated with a tacky poetry of revelation or, 'the show me business', a quizmaster/ instructor intervenes. Is there an evaluative judgement to the cry, 'You've just said the magic phoneme'? A threshold has been crossed, but whether it is an affirmation of voice or a trespass into encrypted silence, Bernstein does not grant his reader the co-ordinates.

Commenting on 'The Lives of the Toll Takers' Bernstein stresses that the work must be seen in the context of poetic language and its relationship to a public domain. He proposes that the poem could be read as:

> A social dimension to my preoccupation with the radical morphogenerativeness of language and its related instability and ambiguity, its unsettling and poly-dictory logics, which constitute, rather than impede, our mutual grounding in language as a grounding in each other that forms the basis not of nations or ethnicities or races but of polis.[33]

Yet, how successful is a reliance upon textual instability and indeterminacy in and of itself for establishing a public forum in poetry? Donald Davidson's focus on the malapropism extends a reading of error in Bernstein's earlier volume *Rough Trades* and its relationship to what 'knowing' a language entails.

Error, Malapropisms, 'Ideolects' and 'Knowing' a Language in *Rough Trades*

A cryptonymic reading of 'The Lives of the Toll Takers' applies a psychoanalytic approach to the misspellings and skewing of familiar aphorisms in Bernstein's poetry. While a psychoanalytic approach stresses the process of interpretation as an act of initiation, we need to consider what process of interpretation occurs when error is perceived as a form of miscommunication, or as an impediment between writer and reader. Error in this light complicates the process of reading, but has a further consequence to the broader question of what indeed it is to 'know' a language. Bernstein's poetics stress the applicability of context in his overall conceptualisation of language, but his initial configuration of error as a deviation from rule-governed conventions requires more scrutiny. What exactly do such forms of linguistic error

33 Bernstein, 'From an Ongoing Interview with Tom Beckett', in *My Way*, pp. 186–90 (p. 189).

generate in terms of the larger picture of linguistic competence? If language is a means of communication between parties, and the level of competence of knowing a language relies upon the efficacy of the communication between speaker and addressee, what happens in the case of misused aphorisms and phrases? In Bernstein's case this examination is further problematised by the intentional malapropisms in his poetry.

The work of language philosopher Donald Davidson forms a broader picture of how error in Bernstein's poetry may be aligned to a conceptualisation of language. Davidson's 'A Nice Derangement of Epitaphs'[34] concentrates on the role and use of malapropisms in language as a consideration of what a communicating language rests upon. Concentrating solely on malapropisms extends the discussion by linking some of Davidson's assumptions with the 'ideolectical' approach to poetry Bernstein designates in 'Poetics of the Americas'. Although Davidson takes spoken speech as his exemplar for the malapropism and does not explicitly discuss the written word, his examination introduces intentionality to our discussion of error in Bernstein's poetry.

Davidson's investigation draws some remarkable statements if solipsistic ones, which would appear to conflict with Bernstein's idea of what a socious language may be. Rather than seeing the role of error as a liberatory, Davidson's discussion presents the interpretation of a malapropism as the fleeting convergence of two languages in an agreed understanding or what he calls a 'passing theory'. In his consideration of humour Davidson's remarks in the opening of his paper conflict with the democratic intention Bernstein assigns to his poetry: 'A malapropism does not have to be amusing or surprising. It does not have to be based on cliche, and of course it does not have to be intentional. There need be no play on words, no hint of deliberate pun... the humour is adventitious' (433). What is most surprising about this paper is Davidson's final summation, which is both a dramatic and polemical statement:

---

34   Donald Davidson, 'A Nice Derangement of Epitaphs', in *Truth and Interpretation: Perspectives on the Philosophy of Donald Davidson*, ed. Ernest Le Pore (Oxford: Blackwell, 1986), pp. 433–46.

There is no such thing as a language, not if a language is anything like what many philosophers and linguists have supposed. There is therefore no such thing to be learned, mastered or born with. We must therefore give up the idea of a clearly defined shared structure which language users acquire and then apply to all cases. And we should try again to say how convention in any important sense is involved in language; or, as I think, we should give up any attempt to illuminate how we communicate by appeal to convention. (446)

Davidson argues the case that much of our communication rests upon the fleeting convergence of understanding misused clauses and phrases. Yet, he does not want to approach this convergence as an erring deviation from a rule-governed language. While he lineates contextual patterns for communication he wants to distinguish between convention and to some extent, performance.

Here the parallels with Bernstein's programme seem most apparent, since the poet attempts through the performance of misquoted cliches and citations to undermine convention and speech patterns. This challenge to linguistic rules is linked in Bernstein's poetics to an opening up of the lyric and ultimately is informed by a political aim. In moving beyond set patterns of a grammar Davidson argues for a more problematic idea of what constitutes not only learning a language, but knowing a language. If as the philosopher suggests malapropisms feature as a natural process of communicating, what exactly is happens then when Mrs. Malaprop declares a 'Nice Derangement of Epitaphs' which the reader interprets as a 'Nice arrangement of epithets'?

Davidson designates three possible stages to the understanding of an utterance, a procedure which he identifies are 'first meaning in language'. The three principles he identifies are: firstly systematic based on semantic properties, secondly shared meanings or properties of language as a method for communication, and finally meaning generated by conventions or regularities. He indicates that although a malapropism may gesture to the first two principles, it is not reliant upon convention. Davidson proposes that malapropisms offer more than an aberration from these principles for communication. The philosopher wants to abolish convention from the matrix of the equation, in his view a malapropism offers more than a deviation from a rule-governed practice of normative language:

59

Malapropisms introduce expressions not covered by prior learning or familiar expressions which cannot be interpreted by any of the abilities so far discussed. Malapropisms fall into a different category, one that may include such things as our ability to perceive a well-formed sentence when the actual utterance was incomplete or grammatically garbled, our ability to interpret words we have never heard before, to correct slips of the tongue, or to cope with new idiolects. These phenomena threaten standard descriptions of linguistic competence. (437)

If we rest briefly on the word 'idiolects' in the excerpt, one may get a clearer understanding of the parallels with Bernstein's poetry. The 'passing theory' which Davidson explains as the fleeting convergence of the speaker's and addressee's beliefs, creates in a sense a new and different language at each instance of translating garbled phrases. In response to Davidson's paper Ian Hacking argues that much of what Davidson would characterise as 'radical interpretation' relies heavily on homophonic resonance in the phrasing of an utterance.[35] To test Hacking's proposition we could take a further example from Mrs. Malaprop 'Illiterate him quite from your memory'. Although the phrase would make some sense if translated literally as a form of memory renegotiated through dismissal, we are led to the aural resonance of 'obliterate.' Could this be the new idiolect Davidson gestures towards?

The word 'idiolect', resurfaces in Bernstein's essay, 'The Poetics of the Americas', where it is transmuted to 'ideolect'. Bernstein argues for an 'ideolectical' approach to an American poetry reliant less on a multiplicity of identities than a plurality of different languages. Taken at its broadest sense, Bernstein's 'ideolects' draws a vast perimeter around an experimental poetics and the conceptualisation of a socious language. As opposed to dialect in poetry, Bernstein argues that an 'ideolectical' approach creates a 'virtual' poetics of the Americas, allowing in effect for a range of different idioms. Above all, Bernstein stresses that an 'ideolectical' poetics is provisional, and unlike dialect in poetry which is still 'informed', if not regulated, by its difference to 'standard' language practices:

---

35   Ian Hacking, 'The Parody of Conversation', in *Truth and Interpretation*, pp. 447–58.

By linking dialect and ideolect I wish to emphasize the common ground of linguistic exploration, the invention of new syntaxes as akin to the invention of new Americas, or of new possibilities for America ... nonstandard writing practices share a technical commonality that overrides the necessary differences of interpretation and motivation, and this commonality may be the vortical prosodic force that gives us footing with one another ... dialect understood as nation language, has a centripetal force, regrouping often denigrated and dispirited language practices around a common center; ideolect in contrast, suggests a centrifugal force moving away from normative practices without necessarily replacing them with a new center of gravity, at least defined by self or group.[36]

Bernstein is proposing languages of differentiation, not merely the placing words in unusual grammatical orders. Initially, this development in the poet's conceptualisation of poetic language, appears to promote a solipsistic enquiry advocating multiple forms of 'private' language. Yet Bernstein in an early essay categorically states that 'the idea of a private language is illusory because language itself is a communality, a public domain. Its forms and contents are in no sense private– they are the very essence of the social.'[37] On reflection, what is shared in this enterprise of an 'ideolectical' approach to poetry is the creation of a common social space for these linguistic endeavours, and an attempt to decentralise the informing role of rule-governed practices in poetic language:

The use of dialectical or ideolectical language in a poem marks a refusal of standard English as the common ground of communication. For poets wishing to obliterate or overcome such marks of difference, the choice of the conventional literary language whether understood as mask or not, reflects a willingness to abide by the linguistic norms of a culture and to negotiate within these norms. Nonstandard language practice suggests an element of cultural resistance that has as its lower limit dialogic self-questioning and as its upper limit secession and autonomy. (11)

The poet's reliance upon multiplicity may only promote an increasingly atomised resistance to the conventions Bernstein wants to challenge. Paradoxically he argues that the problematising of identity

36   Bernstein, 'Poetics of the Americas', p. 7.
37   Bernstein, 'Thought's Measure', in *Content's Dream*, p. 81.

that an 'ideolectical' approach provides may in effect 'forge new collective identities' (19). How do we begin to connect Bernstein's configuration of 'ideolects' in poetic language and Davidson's investigation of malapropisms in spoken speech? The connective thread linking both these papers rests upon their crucial dismissal of convention. While Davidson's claim is evidently the dismissal of standardisation, his approach is to focus on the process of interpretation by foregrounding intention. Most useful is his delineation of 'a passing theory' in the interpretation of an unfamiliar idiolect, a procedure which in the case of Mrs. Malaprop he designates as 'getting away with it'. Davidson looks at the case of Mrs. Malaprop in general:

> There is no word or construction that cannot be converted to a new use by an ingenious or ignorant speaker. And such conversion, while easier to explain because it involves mere substitution, is not the only kind. Sheer invention is equally possible, and we can be as good as interpreting it (say in Joyce or Lewis Carroll) as we are at interpreting the errors or twists of substitution. From the point of view of an ultimate explanation of how new concepts are acquired, learning to interpret a word that expresses a concept we do not already have is a far deeper and more interesting phenomenon than explaining the ability to use a word new to us for an old concept. But both require a change in one's way of interpreting the speech of another, or in speaking to someone who has the use of that word. (441)

Bernstein's 'Riddle of the Fat Faced Man' from *Rough Trades*[38] places these parallel conceptual and interpretative claims for malapropisms and ideolects into practice:

> None guards the moor where stands
> Receipt of scorn, doting on doddered
> Mill as fool compose compare, come
> Fair padre to your pleated score
> Mind the ducks but not the door
> Autumnal blooms have made us snore (14)

Bernstein evidently plays with received rules and grammar, the reader is left questioning initially whether the 'moor' of the first line is a subject or object. In approaching the poem 'ideolectically', interpret-

38   Bernstein, *Rough Trades* (Los Angeles: Sun & Moon Press, 1991).

ation is oriented by intertextual or literary allusions. There are words here which gesture to a broader context of canonical literature; the 'moor' could point the reader initially towards Othello, or a heath; 'fool', the act of deception or possibly a jester, 'padre' a father, figurehead or religious instructor. In this contextualisation the overall 'thematic' becomes a synopsis of Shakespeare's *King Lear*. Correspondingly if we move from an overtly literary context to a tentative philosophical one, the 'Mill' of Bernstein's poem since it is capitalised, could be a reference to the philosopher and social reformer John Stuart Mill whose examination of liberty as a social institution connects with Bernstein's own linguistic project. Inevitably these ambiguities in the text problematise our reading of the malapropism through Davidson's 'passing theory', since his discussion does not account for the multiple interpretations which 'Riddle of the Fat Faced Man' is reliant upon. As Hacking remarks the problem faced in reading the poem through Davidson's interpretation of malapropism is that the theorising is reliant upon a model of 'a duettist' (458). The intentional command in Bernstein's poem is strategically unclear, and Davidson's gesture to 'getting away with it' could equally be ascribed to the reader, as the writer of this poem. But reconsidering Bernstein's 'ideolectical' approach we could tentatively concur that this is a new 'provisional' language to be read, even if make recourse to paradigms of literary plots to make sense of it.

How does the reading malapropisms in Bernstein's poetry fit in a broader context of error? Certainly error is aligned in this poem with a strategic, interpretative indeterminacy. In 'Riddle of the Fat Faced Man' words lose their clear semantic intention, becoming simultaneously noun and verb for example: 'Mill', 'Mind', Receipt' and 'ducks'. This verse enacts the conditions of a misplaced vocabulary, and also redesignates conventions of grammar and syntax. Yet while this process may have some parallels with Davidson's desire to refute convention from the matrix of interpretation, the reading of the work is informed by homophonic translation. A single phonemic shift within the poem recontextualizes the whole strategy of interpretation. If we take 'moor' for a slip on 'moon', the verse translates as a pastoral if comic version of seasonal change, almost a sham lyric since the lunar landscape could be read as a breve on the 'pleated score', a harvest moon, or even a mock Keatsian praise of hibernation. Bernstein's 'Poetics of Americas' proposes that it is precisely this provisionality of meaning which validates the political efficacy of his project. The model of reading that the poem promotes is a shift from received ideas or meanings in language, to a form of radical interpretation. This process is neatly characterised by the poet Lyn Hejinian as the tactic of 'where once one sought a vocabulary for ideas, now one seeks ideas for vocabularies.'[39]

Can Bernstein's 'ideolectical' approach to poetic language effectively opens up the lyric to a social address? One of the key problems in approaching Bernstein's work lies in how to read the author's intention. Explicit typographical errors suggest that one may read the text as ironic, yet frequent malapropisms pull the reader towards a humorous reading. This raises further concerns in considering the overall tenability of Bernstein's project. While malapropisms in Bernstein's work question the idea of a monolithic language, the provisional configuration of multiple 'ideolects' in the poetry threaten to atomise the political efficacy of his claims.

Bernstein wants to open up the social address of the lyric and although it may be tempting to examine the humorous texture of his poetry solely through a poststructuralist reading, the poet's comments problematise this approach. He states that 'it is a mistake ... to posit the self as the primary organizing feature of the writing' but also asserts that:

> I do not feel that it makes sense to carry these views over to the extreme of cancelling authorship as a factor completely, making the text exclusively the product of a discourse or a period, since in crucial ways a poem is much a resistance as a product, and for the moment at least the individual is the most salient concept with which to describe the site of this resistance.[40]

39   Lyn Hejinian, 'If Written is Writing', in *The L=A=N=G=U=A=G=E Book*, eds. Bruce Andrews and Charles Bernstein (Carbondale: Southern Illinois U. P., 1984), pp. 29–30 (p. 29).
40   Bernstein, 'An Interview with Tom Beckett', in *Content's Dream*, pp. 385–410 (p. 408, 9).

This tension between a nostalgia for a rhetorical address and humorous word play in Bernstein's poetry can be read as the inevitable consequence of reconfiguring the lyric within a political and social nexus. Lang asserts in her discussion of humour and irony that neither are exclusive forms of writing, rather than seeing these tensions as irreconcilable impulses in his work, they remind the reader of the difficulty in rupturing the lyric form. 'The Kiwi Bird in the Kiwi Tree' from *Rough Trades*[41] grants a focus on the tension between rhetorical flourish and linguistic indeterminacy navigated in Bernstein's poetry. Moreover the poem enables some observations on the nonsensical texture of Bernstein's work in the light of malapropisms and error.

'The Kiwi Bird in the Kiwi Tree' is a surprisingly lyric declaration of aims and ambitions, and can be read as a metaphrastic imitation of Wallace Stevens's 'Of Mere Being.' Bernstein's rather dumpy Kiwi Bird could be a ludic reworking of the modernist's poet's of weighted proposition and image. Yet the revisionary aspect of 'The Kiwi Bird in the Kiwi Tree' moves the poem away from the simply polyvocal or brash pastiche. If anything, the slightly 'skewed' sonnet enacts what George Oppen referred to as 'a lyric reaction to the world'[42] beginning with an emphatic interiority and moving outside or beyond to a social realm, a realm made possible Bernstein would argue by an ideolectical poetics:

> I want no paradise only to be
> drenched in the downpour of words, fecund
> with tropicality. Fundament be
> yond relation, less 'real' than made, as arms
> surround a baby's gurgling: encir
> cling mesh pronounces its promise (not bars
> that pinion, notes that ply). The tailor tells
> of other tolls, the seam that binds, the trim,
> the waste. & having spelled these names, move on
> to toys or talcums, skates & scores. Only
> the imaginary is real– not trumps
> beclouding the mind's acrobatic vers

41   Bernstein, *Rough Trades* (Los Angeles: Sun & Moon Press, 1991), p. 11
42   Interview with George Oppen', *Contemporary Literature*, 10.2 (1969), 159–77 (p. 172).

ions. The first fact is the social body,
one from another, nor needs no other.

The poem performs as a loose sonnet, overrunning 'spliced' words from one line break to another. Even in their splicing syllables retain remnants of sense and become either individual words in their own right, 'be', 'cling', 'vers' and 'ions', or phonic connotations of others 'yond'– yonder, 'encir', possibly to 'incur.' What these line breaks in effect demonstrate are two simultaneously operating language systems generating multiple meanings, which in turn could be a broad definition of nonsense verse.[43] A nonsensical' texture is evidently apparent in Bernstein's 'Riddle of the Fat Faced Man.' Northrop Frye makes a distinction between riddle and nonsense suggesting that 'riddles are part of the process of reducing language to a visible form', whereas 'nonsense is part of the inverse process, reducing visible forms, both dreams and reality to language.'[44] In 'The Kiwi Bird in the Kiwi Tree' the 'nonsensical' texture of this poem enacts more convincingly a possible social space for the lyric than the insistent artifice and wit of 'Riddle of the Fat Faced Man.'

Read from an ideolectical perspective the poem strategically works on establishing relations in the text, and there is a sense that the poem builds its own vocabulary. Bernstein would argue that this interactive process of interpretation presents a possibility of configuring tangible social relationships beyond the terrain of the poem. The opening of the poem is a surreal visualisation of an earth bound paradise, it begins with an expressive speaker and an array of syntactical inversions; an adverb becomes a verb 'fecund with tropicality', 'fundament' is initially associated with the ethereal, but modified to frame a concept 'less "real" than made'. In its probing of relations between the everyday and the utopic, the social and the imaginary, the poem opts firstly for a familial tie. Yet, there is only a demarcation of proximity here; the baby may at first seem comforted but we realise that the contact is an embrace of sound 'arms surround a baby's

---

43 For a full study of the relationship between nonsense and contemporary poetry see Marnie Parsons, *Touchmonkeys: Nonsense Strategies in Contemporary Poetry* (Toronto: University of Toronto Press, 1994).

44 Northrop Frye, cited in *Touchmonkeys*, p. 36.

gurgling'. Any physical contact is certainly encrypted and needs some decoding 'encir/cling mesh pronounces its promise', the mesh here could be substituted by 'flesh', but this 'inscribed' image of cradling requires some lexical excavation.

We have already considered this procedure of rewriting in Bernstein's poetry as the interpretation of a series of determined encryptions beneath the text. John Ashbery's poetry most notoriously operates at this level of self-reflective encryption. In an interview Ashbery characterises this process; '[t]he original word literally had a marginal existence and isn't spoken, is perhaps what you might call a crypt word.'[45] Certainly these are not tactics restricted to the work of Ashbery and Bernstein, and as John Shoptaw notes in his comparative study of both: 'All poets, not only resolute experimenters, compose with crypt words. Reading for similar sounds, rather than simply for associated meanings is indispensable in reconstructing poetic meaning.'[46] Combining our reading of cryptonymy with Bernstein's 'ideolectical' approach to poetic language provides a productive methodology for understanding the poet's intention in rupturing the lyric form of this sonnet.

To return to the mesh/ flesh encryption, could there be more going on here than simply a sonorous inversion? Certainly mesh has a manufactured feel and a restrictive one if one is to read the splicing of encircling as 'cling'. Furthermore it has sinister resonance too, although there may be a 'promise' set within this action, the following 'bars that pinion, notes that ply', reinforce an impression of restraint. What conventionally marks domestic bliss, the gurgling child, is presented as a relation of enforcement. Moving on to the tailor, we are presented with craft once more, but craft at a cost. The crypt word 'tolls' gestures towards toil. Rather than the finished product there is a detailing of its making and most importantly the wastage involved.[47]

45   John Ashbery, 'The Imminence of a Revelation', in *Acts of Mind: Conversations with Contemporary Poets*, Richard Jackson, ed. (Tuscaloosa: University of Alabama Press, 1983), p. 70.

46   John Shoptaw, in 'The Music of Construction: Measure and Polyphony in Ashbery and Bernstein', p. 214.

47   Bernstein later gives an autobiographical context to reading this line, his father started his business buying and selling 'short-end pieces of fabric rolls ("the

'The seam that binds', echoes 'the notes that ply' and since seams are required to be near invisible giving a form to formlessness, these phrases suggest not only a reference to the act of writing but an extended gesture to the configuration of social relationships.

The poem then approaches notions or relationships of value and consumption. Like participants in an educational quiz, values demand correct answering. We presume that in 'having spelled these names, move on' that the right answer has been given a goal has been reached. But where do we move on to? A conveyor belt of baby products 'toys & talcums' ring pretty hollow as prizes. Having given the correct answer the competitors are then judged themselves. Who is doing the evaluating in this poem, since the members of the panel at the skating contest are faceless and suggest an anonymous corporation of judges?

It would be all too tempting to reduce the poem at this point to a critique or resistance to social conventions and popular culture. Bernstein's 'ideolectical' configuration of the lyric rescues it from such clumsy reductionism. Indeed the final, skewed quatrain of the sonnet strikes a well-judged balance between the impulse towards an emphatic lyric statement and an interpretative possibility through linguistic play. The poem swerves back at this point to an echoing of the first speaking voice who states 'Only the imaginary is real'. Strategically the poem slams together an encryption 'trumps,' possibly the triumphs of success, and an archaism 'beclouding', to create a fusion of humorous linguistic play and romanticism. 'The mind's acrobatic vers/ions' presents thought in a double take which could be a stylised, choreographed performance or indeed a metatextal reference to the process of reading as a feat of high jumps, retracing and evaluation. The poem's self-commentary as it divides into 'vers' and 'ions' suggests that every atomised phoneme counts in the construction of multiple meaning, and this sense of atomisation is reiterated by the closing two lines in an aphorism: 'The first fact is the social body/ one from another, nor needs no other'. What initially appears as straightforward, is an aural trick, the negative destabilises the statement and

trim, the waste") that would otherwise have been discarded', see 'An Autobiographical Interview', *My Way*, pp. 229–52 (p. 234).

thwarts of our expectation. The eye wants to read 'one for another' but in its assertion of differentiation, the singular 'from' complicates the impression of the social nexus as an undifferentiated mass. In this final assertion there is the implication that the lyric's address recognises and respects the plurality of identities which may constitute its public audience.

Clearly Bernstein's ideolectical or erring approach to the lyric is premised on the attempt to reconfigure an understanding of subjectivity as a complex of social relationships. He asserts that the process of reading his poetry activates a mutually dependent engagement: 'I hope the reader does feel implicated because I want to show that *I* as a social construction, a *product* of language and not a pre-existing entity outside it; that *I* is first a *we*. We're implicated in each other from the first.'[48]

48   Bernstein, 'An Interview with Tom Beckett', p. 410.

Chapter Two
Whose Language: Bernstein Reading Cavell, Reading Wittgenstein

The aesthetic premises of Bernstein's early poetry can be aligned to Language Writing's interest in strategies of defamiliarisation. As Peter Middleton has proposed, inherent to a fascination with linguistic strangeness is a commitment to defining new ideas of community. Middleton states that Language Writers 'had to oppose an earlier model of community based on authenticity and individuality ... Charles Bernstein spoke for many poets when he said in 1978 that continuing to write in the mode of the New American Poets would be to merely "describe the conditions of our alienation" without transforming them.'[1] Retracing Bernstein's early poetics enables us to reconsider how his aesthetic of error must be read not only as a challenge to the conventions of grammar and syntax, but as an ambitious claim for the practice of what he calls a socious language. Moreover sourcing Bernstein's reading of language philosophy helps to elucidate the problems faced by the poet in reconfiguring the lyric, and sheds light on the more provocative claims of his poetics. Certainly we need to understand how Bernstein can make an unproblematic correlation between grammar and the social sphere: 'It's NOT that grammar, per se, which is an abstraction, a projection, is repressive, but that societal conditions are repressive and these particular repressions are reflected in grammar, can be spotted in that particular mapping.'[2] A reading of Bernstein's poetics in conjunction with Ludwig Wittgenstein and Stanley Cavell's work, allows us to evaluate the ambitious relation-

---

1   Peter Middleton, *Distant Reading: Performance, Readership and Consumption in Contemporary Poetry* (Tuscaloosa: Alabama U.P., 2005), p. 134
2   Charles Bernstein, 'Socialist Realism or Real Socialism', in *Content's Dream Essays 1975–1984* (Los Angeles: Sun & Moon Press, 1986), pp. 411–27 (p. 418).

ship the poet attempts to set up between linguistic indeterminacy and tangible social structures in his poetry.

Much of the initial impact of Language Writing's defamiliarisation of language and resistance to an unproblematic configuration of realism can be traced to the work of the Russian Formalists.[3] Victor Shklovsky's 'Art as Technique' allows us to consider Bernstein's preoccupation with malapropisms and skewed aphorisms within a broader context of aesthetic defamiliarisation:

> The technique of art is to make objects unfamiliar, to make forms difficult, to increase the difficulty and the length of perception because the process of perception is an aesthetic end in itself and must be prolonged. Art is a way of experiencing the artfulness of an object: the object is not important ... After we see an object several times we begin to recognise it. The object is in front of us and we know about it but we do not see it– hence we cannot say anything significant about it. Art removes objects from the automatism of perception in several ways.[4]

Shklovsky is concerned with how the process of evaluating an artwork establishes a dialogue between the artist and reader. One can see how his analysis of the construction of an artwork and its reception can be related to Language Writing's early preoccupations with a poetics that inscribes the rights of the signifier. This focus upon the 'strangeness of the ordinary', has been read extensively in conjunction with Language Writing's aesthetic of opacity. The strategic defamilarisation of so-called everyday speech in Bernstein's work lends itself to an examination of a Wittgensteinian conceptualisation of language as a shared grammar. Citing Karl Kraus's proposition 'The closer the look one takes at a word, the greater the distance from which it looks back',[5] Bernstein frames an aesthetic of defamilarisation as a pro-

---

3   See for example Lyn Hejinian's extended discussion of the relationship between Russian Formalism and her understanding of realism in 'Two Stein Talks: Language and Realism', *Temblor*, 3 (1986), 128–33.

4   Victor Shklovsky, 'Art as Technique', *Russian Formalist Criticism: Four Essays*, trans. Lee T. Lemon and Marion J. Reis (Lincoln and London: University of Nebraska Press, 1965), pp. 3–24 (pp. 12–13).

5   Karl Kraus, cited in Bernstein's 'Blood on the Cutting Room Floor', in *Content's Dream*, pp. 351–62 (p. 352).

ductive poetic strategy for 'a specific negotiation by a writer that does not appropriate words, but invests them' (353).

In a short poem 'Whose Language', a Bakhtinian analogy of carnivalisation could be applied quite literally to Bernstein's writing since the reader begins to wonder where the next crash may fall: 'Whose on first? The dust descends as/ the skylight caves in ... Doors to fall in, bells/ to dust, nuances to circumscribe'.[6] These images echo a passage from Wittgenstein's *Philosophical Investigations* where the philosopher reminds us that '[t]he results of philosophy ... are the uncovering of one or another piece of plain nonsense and of bumps that the understanding has got by running its head up against the limits of the language.'[7] It was of course Wittgenstein who first gestured to the significance of language as game, and more specifically to our own context of a humorous aesthetic, poetry as word play. Wittgenstein warns 'Do not forget that a poem, even though it is composed in the language of information is not used in the language game of giving information.'[8] This citation appears in Bernstein's seminal essay in verse 'Artifice of Absorption' through his own citing of Veronica Forrest-Thomson's *Poetic Artifice*. In our broader context of an aesthetic of defamiliarisation there is a complex matrix of relations between Bernstein's configuration of error, Forrest-Thomson's examination of artifice and Wittgenstein's philosophy.

Forrest-Thomson's framing of the role of 'artifice' in poetic language, initially helps to establish the parallels between her work and Bernstein's poetics. My opening chapter I have already discussed at length Bernstein's provisional deployment of the terms 'artifice' and 'absorption'. Forrest-Thomson similarly cautions against the dangers of reading poetry purely for its meaning, and identifies this reduction of poetic language to interpretative immediacy as 'naturalisation'.[9]

---

6   Bernstein, 'Whose Language', in *Rough Trades* (Los Angeles: Sun & Moon Press, 1991), p. 25

7   Ludwig Wittgenstein, *Philosophical Investigations*, trans. G.E.M. Anscombe (Oxford: Blackwell Press, 1963), no. 119, p. 48.

8   Wittgenstein, cited by Veronica Forrest-Thomson, *Poetic Artifice* (Manchester: Manchester U.P., 1978), p. ix.

9   Veronica Forrest-Thomson, *Poetic Artifice*, p. xi.

She suggest that 'naturalisation' can be understood as a procedure which:

> Reduce[s] the strangeness of poetic language and poetic organisation by making it intelligible, by translating it into statement about a non-verbal external world, by making artifice appear natural ... Poetry can only be a valid and valuable activity, when we recognise the value of the artifice which makes it different from prose. Indeed, it is only through artifice that poetry can challenge our linguistic orderings of the world, make us question the way in which we make sense of things and induce us to consider its alternative linguistic orders as a new way of viewing the world. (xi)

Evidently we can relate Forrest-Thomson's discussion to Language Writing's early critiques of the workshop lyric, and its configuration of language as an immediate mediation of expression. In arguing for the foregrounding of the artifice of poetic language, Forrest-Thomson's proposition in this passage is remarkably similar to Bernstein's later consideration of the textuality or opacity of poetry in 'Artifice of Absorption.'[10] Importantly, she indicates that the foregrounding of artifice may be linked to a productive way of reconfiguring the way we view the world and how we engage with it. Cast in this light, Forrest-Thomson's treatise corresponds with Wittgenstein's premise of a shared grammar and alerts us to the danger of approaching grammar as merely generating language in terms of rule-governed conventions. *Artifice of Absorption* indicates that these so-called definitive patterns must be viewed as necessarily provisional structures. Bernstein drawing from Forrest-Thomson's discussion in an early essay, suggests that 'there is no natural writing style; that the preference for its supposed manifestations is simply a preference for a particular look to poetry & often a particular vocabulary.'[11] Indeed he adds that 'There is no natural look or sound to a poem. Every element is intended, chosen' (49). This statement once again confirms that the

---

10   For an extended focus on the relationship between Bernstein's poetics and Forrest-Thomson's work see Alison Mark's 'Poetic Relations and related poetics: Veronica Forrest-Thomson and Charles Bernstein', in *Assembling Alternatives: Reading Postmodern Poetries Transnationally*, ed. Romana Huk (Middletown, Co: Wesleyan, 2003), pp. 114–27.

11   Bernstein, 'Stray Straws and Straw Men', in *Content's Dream*, pp. 40–9 (p. 44).

poet's aesthetic of error is not only an adventitious erring, but an intentional strategy to defamiliarise our patterns of reading and interpretation.

Bernstein's approach to a poetics of defamiliarisation linked to his interest in Wittgenstein's philosophy of language. Marjorie Perloff dedicates an entire book, *Wittgenstein's Ladder*,[12] to examining the relationship between the philosopher's work and modern poetics. Her introduction stresses the connection that can be mined between Language Writing and the philosopher's work and she states that Bernstein's volumes *The Sophist* and *Dark City* are amongst those 'written under the sign of Wittgenstein' (6). Wittgenstein's focus on ordinary language and examination of how the same word within differing contexts is not just a repetition of meaning, but a language game, is familiar to the reader of Language Writing. Moreover Wittgenstein's fascination with what Perloff calls 'the strangeness of the ordinary' finds distinct parallels of course with Shklovsky's work.

A section from Wittgenstein's *Philosophical Investigations* illustrates how Perloff's reading of the philosopher in conjunction with the poetics of Language Writing presents an attractive consideration of an aesthetic of artifice. In the following extract the philosopher considers the innocent seeming word 'blue':

> 'Is this blue the same as the blue over there? Do you see any difference?'
> You are mixing paint and you say 'It is hard to get the blue of the sky.'
> 'It's turning fine, you can already see the blue again.'
> 'Look what different effects those two blues have.'
> 'Do you see the blue book over there? Bring it here.'
> 'This blue signal light means ...'
> 'What is this blue called? – is it "indigo"?' #33

Although of course the effect here is not the defamiliarisation of the word blue but a sense of its multifariousness, Wittgenstein illustrates how complex the contextual application of 'knowing' a language functions in practice. The excerpt focuses in effect on the complexities of social discourse and how context is instrumental to each individual

---

12   Marjorie Perloff, *Wittgenstein's Ladder: Poetic Language and the Strangeness of the Everyday* (Chicago: University of Chicago Press, 1996), p. 6.

engagement. Wittgenstein examines the possibilities for a single word, as an adjective or noun in a series of anecdotal sentences, and Perloff in her insightful discussion reads it as a series of child's observations. Her remarks stress the implications of this ordinary seeming paragraph:

> How is it that a child knows that 'blue' is sometimes a fixed descriptor (as in the sentence 'you can see the blue sky again'), sometimes a class comprising various subsets (e.g. shades of blue), sometimes a reference to the ability of manufactured colors to 'match' those in nature ... Because, so Wittgenstein gradually shows us, language has no essence: it is a complex cultural construction, whose variables are articulated according to one's particular intersection with it. (70–1)

Already we can begin to connect Bernstein's focus on error and our earlier examination of his ideolectical approach to poetic language with Wittgenstein's sustained examination of a shared grammar. I will suggest that Bernstein's aesthetic of error in his early poetry invites a similar participation and encourages the testing of our assumptions and interpretations against his text. But before evaluating how effective our conceptual reading of language may perform in the practice of poetry, it is necessary to link a consideration of error with Bernstein's evocation of a socious language. Although we can configure of our understanding of artifice and defamiliaristion in the broader context of Bernstein's aesthetic of error, we need to consider how a poetics of error can viably make a problematic transition from textuality to the establishing of productive relationships in a social and political nexus.

Bernstein's gesture to a socious language can be initially understood in conjunction with his attempt to reconfigure the lyric from a model of emphatic interiority to orchestrate a communal address. Undoubtedly Bernstein's work demands that poetry and poetics have a public function; in his attempt to configure a relationship between aesthetics and politics as a project for poetry he draws on Cavell's conceptualisation of the social contract. The debt to Cavell is readily acknowledged by Bernstein in the essay 'The Objects of Meaning:

Reading Cavell Reading Wittgenstein.'[13] Chapter One's earlier examination of malapropisms in spoken language introduces the concept of provisional meanings within the text. But we need to satisfactorily connect how the indeterminacies in Bernstein's work can be linked to an alternative conceptualisation of a social sphere. Cavell's work presents an alluring possibility for the poet's mapping of an alternative polis. Bernstein's essay focuses upon Cavell's conceptualisation of the relationship between consensus, convention and the social contract and how these seemingly static concepts are reconfigured through the philosopher's conceptualisation of language. Bernstein interprets the philosopher's ideas as an understanding of communication that rests not on legislated conventions, but on provisional guidelines which themselves are in a constant process of actualisation.

In this understanding of Bernstein's reading of consensus and convention in Cavell's work an aesthetic of error can be considered as an ambition to establish a Wittgensteinian grammar in use. Grammar can no longer be read as a determinate fixed standard, but as a method for exploring relations. In 'The Objects of Meaning' Bernstein makes his position explicit:

> Learning a language is not learning the names of things outside language, as if it were simply a matter of matching up signifiers with signifieds, as if signifieds already existed and we were just learning new names for them ... Rather, we are initiated by language into a socious, which is for us the world. So that the foundations of knowledge are not so much based on a preexisting empirical world as on shared conventions and mutual attunement. It is this understanding of Wittgenstein's view of language that leads Cavell to say that our conventions (grammar, codes, territorialities, myths, rules standards, criteria) are our nature, that there is no gap between nature and culture, between fact and convention ... In this context, to speak of absolutes is to speak outside language games, to construct a grammatical fiction– it is to deny the human limitations of knowledge ... Wittgenstein's relation of grammar to 'forms of life', emphasizes that 'human convention is not arbitrary but constitutive of significant speech and activity ... [that] mutual understanding, and hence language, depends on nothing

13   'The Objects of Meaning: Reading Cavell Reading Wittgenstein', *Content's Dream*, pp. 165–81.

more and nothing less than shared forms of life, call it our mutual attunement or agreement in our criteria.' (172)[14]

This is no anodyne attempt at a consensual agreement since Bernstein, through his reading of Cavell and Wittgenstein, insists that the intrinsic characteristic of language use is a continual negotiation with shared rules and conventions. Essential to this configuration is that conventions themselves must be seen as necessarily provisional structures, and ultimately answerable to the demands of their subjects. Bernstein stresses that this process of constant reassessment and negotiation is the basis for all human interaction. Thus Bernstein's configurations of error in his work demand to be read not simply as a reaction against convention, but as an attempt to delineate this process of re-evaluation, testing and contextualizing. The poet stresses that through this process of contextualization and examination one is constantly negotiating our relationships with others.

Integral to this essay is Bernstein's affirmation of presence through language. Early critics of Language Writing have tended to characterise the broad range of this work as merely ventriloquising or at worst, pastiching the investigations of poststructuralist theory. Tom Clark reviewed Language Writing practices as 'the kind of mumbo jumbo you'd hear from a guy who stumbled into a linguistics lecture one day, and walked out an instant expert the next.'[15] Frederic Jameson notoriously read Language Writing as a symptom of a postmodernist aesthetic reliant upon the pastiche of 'dead styles ... the styles of the imaginary museum.'[16] Undoubtedly continental philosophy influences Bernstein's poetics, yet while one can read the linguistic indeterminacies of his work within a poststructuralist frame,

---

14 The final citation embedded in Bernstein's text makes reference to Stanley Cavell's *The Claim of Reason* (Oxford: Oxford U.P., 1979), p. 162.

15 Tom Clark, 'Stalin as Linguist', *Partisan Review* 48.2 (1988), 299–304 (p. 301). Clark's remark was originally made in his review of Barrett Watten's *Total Syntax* for the *San Francisco Chronicle* 13th January, 1985.

16 Frederic Jameson, "Postmodernism and Consumer Society" in *The Anti Aesthetic: Essays on Postmodern Culture*, ed. Hal Foster (Port Townsend: Bay Press, 1983), pp. 111–25 (p. 115).

'The Objects of Meaning' does not want to reduce intention to a phantasmagoric series of differences:

> What Derrida ends up transforming to houses of cards– shimmering traces of life insubstantial as elusive– Wittgenstein locates as *meaning*, with the full range of intention, responsibility, coherence and possibility for revolt against or madness without. In Wittgenstein's accounting, one is not left sealed off from the world with only 'markings to 'decipher' but rather located in a world with meanings to respond to ... The lesson of metaphysical finitude is not that the world is just codes and as a result presence is to be ruled out as anything more than nostalgia, but that we can have presence, insofar as we are able, only *through* a shared grammar. (181)

Bernstein's reading of both Cavell and Wittgenstein presents him with an alluring possibility for situating an aesthetic within a broader consideration of social interaction. Yet how does one voice one's opposition within the polis as it is conceptualised through Cavell's work? Given Bernstein's mistrust of authoritarian rhetoric this seems a pertinent query. Cavell's discussion indicates that individual speech acts should not be relegated to a solipsistic act of complaint or estrangement. As Stephen Mulhall notes in his examination of Cavell's *The Claim of Reason* that in speaking for oneself one is still essentially speaking for a community:

> Possessing a political voice is a matter of claiming to speak for others because it is equivalent to speaking as a citizen, and being a citizen is a matter of being one member of a community of fellow citizens; the extent of that community may be open to empirical exploration but the implication that your speech is representative of some community or other is not. By the same token, one cannot posses a political voice without allowing that others may speak for you, since being a citizen involves consenting to be identified with the words and deeds of one's fellow citizens; once again, their identity and numbers may be open to dispute, but their existence is not.[17]

17 Stephen Mulhall, *Stanley Cavell: Philosophy's Recounting of the Ordinary* (Oxford: Oxford U.P., 1996), p. 62.

William Wordsworth's original incorporation of common speech in poetry as the gesture of 'a man speaking to men',[18] has become in Bernstein's reconfiguration of the lyric a consideration of not whom one is speaking to, but speaking for. After all we are reminded in 'The Kiwi Bird in the Kiwi Tree' that the speaker proposes 'The first fact is the social body.'[19] Bernstein would argue that as initiates into language as a means for exploring relations, the naturalisation of speech patterns need to be dismantled and constantly scrutinised, and this is error's most valuable role. The world in this light is seen not as something external predetermined by language, but as comprising of textuality. Or as Bernstein succinctly states 'the grammars we create in turn create the world' (168).

The Necessity of Speaking to the Public: Bernstein's 'Matters of Policy'

In 'The Book as Architecture' Bernstein suggests that his poetry examines the possibilities for creating an alternative polis. He proposes that 'I prefer to imagine poems as spatializations and interiorizations–blueprints of a world I live near to, but have yet to occupy fully.'[20] With this comment in mind, we can approach Bernstein's early poem 'Matters of Policy'[21] as an attempt to create an architectural/ textual utopia. Certainly this early poem is more successful in reconfiguring the lyric through error and its performance of a socious language, than the more explicit aesthetic of error which dominates his later work.[22]

---

18 Wordsworth's preface of 1800 and 1802 in *Wordsworth and Coleridge Lyrical Ballads*, eds. R.L. Brett and A.R. Jones (London: Routledge, 2005), pp. 286–314 (p. 290, 300)

19 Bernstein, *Rough Trades* (Los Angeles: Sun & Moon Press, 1991) p. 11

20 Bernstein, 'The Book as Architecture' in *My Way: Speeches and Poems* (Chicago: University of Chicago Press, 1999) pp. 56–7 (p. 57).

21 'Matters of Policy', *Controlling Interests* (New York: Roof Books, 1980).

22 For a discussion of later poetry see my opening chapter.

Bernstein sets an ambitious claim for his writing of 'Matters of Policy' suggesting that the poem examines:

> How conventions and language itself induce trances under which we glide as if in automatic pilot ... Certainly the relentless theme of how language socializes us, but so often without a trace of this socialization that would illuminate, like the phosphorescence of an all-permeating world-soul made manifest as a world-body, our self-sameness in being and our communal project that is the socious that shapes not only our thoughts but our very bodies.[23]

Clearly the poet's intention in this poem is informed by Wittgenstein and Cavell's consideration of convention and the social contract. Bernstein similarly proposes that conventions and language must be viewed as provisional structures, informed by a process of contextualisation and a recognition of mutually dependent relationships. A close reading of 'Matters of Policy' evaluates how a configuration of error in conjunction with Bernstein's claims for a socious language can be negotiated with the rupturing of the lyric. The speaker states quixotically in this poem that 'I read somewhere that love of the/ public good is the only passion that really/necessitates speaking to the public' (6). Perhaps we should also bear in mind in approaching 'Matters of Policy' that the poet's engagement with the lyric is premised on an attempt to extend its address without lapsing into abstract rhetorical claims.

The opening of the poem reads as collision of Charles Baudelaire's, 'Invitation au Voyage' with a futuristic city from an architect's design manual:

> On a broad plain in the universe of
> anterooms, making signals in the dark, you
> fall down on your waistband & carrying your
> own plate, a last serving, set out for
> another glimpse of a gaze. In a room
> full of kids splintering like gas jets against
> shadows of tropical taxis– he really had, I
> should be sorry, I think this is the ('I
> know I have complained' 'I am quite well'
> 'quit nudging')– croissants

23   Bernstein, 'An Interview with Tom Beckett', pp. 391–2.

outshine absinthe as 'a plus, plus sans
egal' though what *I* most care about
is another sip of my Pepsi-Cola. (1)

The subjective voice dramatises a process of coming into consciousness 'the glimpse of a gaze' and the movement of these lines establishes a complex chain of relations. Furthermore the slippage, or mala-
propic texture of similes, verbs and adjectives in phrases such as 'kids
splintering like gas jets' and 'tropical taxis', undermines the possibility of a singular reading. Although the French citation gestures
towards a hierarchy of meaning 'the most or best without an equal'
possibly an advertising slogan, its criterion of judgement is quickly
deflated. Grammatical rules are flaunted by parataxis take for example
the gesture of speech which complicates the identity of the speaker: 'I
think this is the ('I/ know I have complained' 'I am quite well'/ 'quit
nudging')'. These speech acts are various articulations of subjectivity
gesturing to self-reflexivity, social politesse and a command or order.
But one might well wonder how to read these citations as parodies of
conversation, or ventriloquism?

Jonathan Culler's study of the lyric draws attention to the citation
of speech in poetry, and provides a useful parallel with Bernstein's
articulation of identity through a matrix of language games. Culler
proposes that traditional criticism's focus upon the lyric 'I' as a voice,
or figure, suggests that writing's primary aim is to 'produce an apparently phenomenal world.'[24] He problematises this assumption suggesting that the gesture of self-reflexivity in the enunciation of the
lyric voice 'opens a gap between the enunciating *I* and the *I* in the
statement' (52). This leads him to affirm that 'a work's self-descript-
ions do not produce closure or self possession, but an impossible, and
therefore open-ended process of self-framing' (52). In a corresponding
light Bernstein's contribution to a symposium 'Characterization'[25]
argues that identity emerges from process and that the self is not
innate nor eternal but an ongoing formation resulting from a process

24   Jonathon Culler, 'Changes in the Study of the Lyric', in *Lyric Poetry: Beyond
      the New Criticism*, eds. Chaviva Hosek and Patricia Parker (New York, Ithaca:
      Cornell U.P., 1985), pp. 38–54 (pp. 50–1).
25   Bernstein, 'Characterization', in *Content's Dream*, pp. 428–62.

of socialisation. Returning to the poem, we could read these articulations of subjectivity in the text as variations of context. If we also approach this opening as a figural clash with the poetics of a high modernism represented ludically by the absinthe and croissants on the revamped ocean liner, there is a further reading to be made. The splintering of these citations may also be interpreted as a retort to a poetics of mastery, or the poetics of an 'ego scriptor'.

Bernstein opens up the lyric to a public address and the mapping of an imaginary metropolis:

> In the summer
> blackouts cripple the city & in the winter
> snowstorms: & yet the spirit of
> the place– a certain *je ne sais quoi* that
> lurks, like the miles of subway tunnels, electrical
> conduits & sewage ducts, far below the surface–
> perseveres. Green leather chairs are easily
> forgotten just as the bath water brings
> only minor entertainment. But we have
> higher hopes. Let me just for a minute
> recount the present standings. There is
> no more white chocolate & all the
> banks are on holiday in Jamaica. All
> the cigarettes have already been lit &
> the mountains climbed & the chills
> gotten over. It is the end of the
> line. Even nostalgia has been used up &
> the moths have been busy making their way
> through all your very favorite attire. True,
> there are still some loose ends, last minute
> details that will never really be completed,
> but in the main there is nothing left to
> do. All the guests have gone home & the
> dishes are done. The telephone is off the
> hook. (3–4)

Returning to Bernstein's earlier evocation of the poem as an architectural construct helps to interpret this section. 'Matters of Policy' reads as an X-ray vision or blueprint of the city; what is most apparent is how the poet attempts to negotiate between a romantic conceptualisation of the lyric and a postmodern affirmation of the mundane. This irreconcilable impulse is accentuated by borrowed idioms of ordinary speech and cliche which read as pastiche: 'the end of the line', 'a certain *je ne sais quoi'*, the pioneering 'mountains climbed' and 'loose ends' left with the inclusion of more lyrical assertions: 'Even Nostalgia has been used up' and the wistful statement 'But we have higher hopes'. One wonders what form of communitas Bernstein is creating in this poem since the figural blueprint given is a grim one given the intimations of industrial action in blackouts that threaten the city's stability. The monuments that Bernstein celebrates for a future civilisation are strangely the 'perseverance' of electrical and sewage systems. Moreover there is a sense of a paralysed present in this city whose citizens have 'nothing left to do.' The poem gestures constantly to a spirit of inclusion, yet the sense of community is increasingly atomised in the close of this passage, communication at its simplest conduit model is severely curtailed 'The telephone is off the hook.'

Many of the passages from 'Matters of Policy' resonate with Louis Zukofsky's attempt and self-declaring failure of a political poetry in *A–9*. This gesture towards the mastery of historical and political subject matter of course finds its precedence in the Poundian ideal of an epic investigation or transhistorical sources. Bernstein's own project does not of course operate within the same ambition as the modernist *il miglior fabbro*, but the parallel with Zukofsky's work has some relevance to a reading of 'Matters of Policy'. Bernstein's ambitions for the public function of poetics and poetry may have been informed by the poet's initial ambition in *'A'* to create a poetry of social document. A further connection can be made between Bernstein's comments on the relationship between poetry and the polis and Zukofsky's evocation of a poetics of sincerity as the necessary acknowledgement of a world that exceeds the self. Bernstein states in 'Comedy and the Poetics of Political Form':

> I know it is almost a joke to speak of poetry and national affairs. Yet in *The Social Contract* Rousseau writes that since our conventions are provisional, the public may choose to reconvene in order to withdraw authority from those

conventions that no longer serve our purposes. Poetry is one of the few areas where the right of reconvening is exercised.[26]

There is a hint of a resistance or even a political coup during 'Matters of Policy,' but confusingly it is immediately followed by a critique of the culture industry:

> Books strewn the streets.
> Bicycles are stored beneath every other staircase.
> The Metropolitan Opera Fills up every night as the
> great masses of people thrill to Pavarotti
> Scotto, Plishka & Caballe. The halls of the
> museums are clogged with commerce. Metroliners
> speed us here & there with a graciousness
> only imagined in earlier times. Tempers are
> not lost since the bosses no longer order about
> their workers. Guacamole has replaced turkey as
> the national dish of most favor. (4–5)

Whether we can relate the reformation of the workplace to Bernstein's earlier remarks on Rousseau's *The Social Contract* remains unclear. Is there a sense of 'reconvening' in this passage? Certainly the opening of the extract gestures to a violent conflict but Bernstein's poem is deliberately ahistorical, occasionally to the detriment of its overall attempt to configure a viable polis. While Bernstein evidently places a stress on poetry as the 'blueprint' of a world he has yet to inhabit, there is a danger that the overall focus on the ludic might undermine the important injustices he is attempting to address. Later in 'Matters of Policy' this idealisation of the workplace dissipates to marshal war and a production line in seizure:

> everyone seemed to go about their business
> in the same old way. Active roll resisting tanks
> pummeling towering carriages, conveyor belts
> incapacitated for several weeks with psychomimetic
> complaints, origami paper oblivious to the needs
> of nuclear families racked by cancer scares. (785–6)

26   Bernstein, Comedy and the Poetics of Political Form', in *A Poetics* (Cambridge: Harvard U.P., 1992), p. 225.

These lines remain ambiguous shielding a complexity of registers. In this passage Bernstein appropriates the jargon of government pamphlets and sociology textbooks to create an effective, if cryptic, political critique. 'Active roll resistant tanks' reads as a catalogue description of the warfare trade, and the clumsy conveyor belts' with their 'psychomimetic complaints' ridicules an attempt to invest news reportage with a psychological spin. Through a process of recontextualisation we can begin to understand 'origami' as a bureaucratic dissemination of facts and figures, and 'nuclear families', once shifted from its conventional sociological definition to an immediate scientific context, can be linked with the malevolence of 'cancer scares'. While these reading might reduce, or naturalise the ambiguity of the poem, the process of interpretation that these examples demand puts into practice Wittgenstein's conceptualisation of a grammar in use.

Candace Lang provides a further way of reading the citational texture of Bernstein's poem. Lang's discussion of humour and irony places a focus on the tactic of unacknowledged citation in texts. She suggests that while the ironist attempts to claim an authentic voice and deploys citation to restrict multiple interpretations of the text, the humourist revels in the indeterminacy of uncited sources. Rather than presenting citations as a discourse of the 'other', the humorist in turn celebrates and welcomes their inclusion. Lang observes that Roland Barthes's suggests that 'irony is the rejection of expression perceived to be Other, the refusal finally of all language as Otherness.'[27]

A reading of humour and irony as noted in the preceding chapter is often complicated quite strategically in Bernstein's poetry. Norman Finkelstein's general evaluation of the poetics of Language Writing provides a further context for interpreting the tone of Bernstein's poetry:

> [T]he real irony regarding language poetry is that the self, despite the massive linguistic displacements it undergoes, proves less subject to fragmentation than has been thought ... Charles Bernstein may believe that 'It's a mistake to posit the self as the primary organizing feature of writing' but in the most intriguing texts by language poets ... the self is a flickering presence of compelling power.

27 Candace Lang, *Irony/ Humor: Critical Paradigms* (Baltimore & London: Johns Hopkins U.P., 1988), p. 60.

However divided or dispersed, it continues its lyric utterance, its language of desire.[28]

Finkelstein makes a useful point, and one that we can apply productively to the tensions that result in Bernstein's attempt to open the lyric to a public address in 'Matters of Policy.' Bernstein's later poetry frequently illustrates a complex interplay between humour and irony. In responding to Bernstein's focus on a socious language there is evidently an irreconcilable impulse in 'Matters of Policy' between humorous play and an evaluative commentary. This tension is the inevitable fall out in Bernstein's attempt to rupture the lyric from a model of an emphatic interiority. Turning prematurely to the final lines illustrates this tension between humour and the desire for an evaluative judgement:

> The surrounding buildings have a stillness
> that is brought into ironic ridicule by the pounding
> beats of the bongo drums emanating from the candy
> store a few blocks away. (9)

Bernstein's close of 'Matters of Policy' displays in its own ludic fashion a desire for an evaluative response. Even in taking the close as a somewhat ironical turn on the lyric epiphany, it still inscribes a desire to comment from a navigable distance.

Returning to the premise of social space and the sense of communitas which preoccupies the poem, thematically the poem wrestles with a prototype of design. An architect's handbook emerges at specific points in the poem. A final remark from Cavell might place Bernstein's claims for a socious language into a sharper focus. The philosopher suggests that:

> The essential message of the idea of a social contract is that political institutions require justification, that they are absolutely without sanctity, that the power over us is held on trust from us, that institutions have no authority other than the authority we lend them, that we are their architects, that they are therefore

---

28　Norman Finkelstein, 'The Problem of the Self in Recent American Poetry', *Poetics Journal*, 9 (1991), 3–10.

artifacts, that there are laws or ends, of nature or justice, in terms of which they are to be tested. They are experiments.[29]

Reading Bernstein through Cavell's remarks, the poet's appeal for a socious language can be considered as an attempt to create an inter-dependent sense of responsibility. This reading frees us from regarding 'Matters of Policy' as merely a circular pattern of self-commentary. Bernstein draws from Cavell's analogy of the social contract as an architectural experiment suggesting that 'the creation of durational spaces in a poem ... produces an internal or negative (in the sense of inverted or inner) architecture.'[30] The following extracts extend the focus on design as an attempt to plot a series of provisional experiments for reconfiguring the lyric's public address. This reading of 'Matters of Policy' may finally allow us to reconsider the humourous texture of the poem as an attempt at re-visioning social relations:

> (1)The use
> of easy & fair surfaces along the general paths
> followed by the water flow. (2) At & near
> the surface of the wave profile. (3) Proof
> of good design. (4) Submerged
> bulbs. I read somewhere that love of the
> public good is the only passion that really
> necessitates speaking to the public. Yet,
> far from that– & distance was by now a
> means of propulsion to theories of design– (6)

> Beyond
> this front is a fair court & in all the corners
> of that fair court fair staircases cast into
> turrets– quarters in which to graze at
> equal distance from each other, surrounded
> by stately galleries & fine cupolas. You take
> the extra moment with exceptional cheer & together we
> begin to shovel away the accumulated dust that blows
> in our eyes & moistens our faces. (8)

29   Stanley Cavell, *The Senses of Walden: An Expanded Edition* (San Francisco: North Point Press, 1981), p. 82.
30   Bernstein, 'The Book as Architecture', in *My Way*, p. 57.

Taking the poem as an investigation of the policies of design, the first excerpt gestures to a historical understanding of form at an evaluative distance; it also foregrounds the politics of classicist rhetoric in its gesture to the address of a socious as a 'love of public good'. The final extract returns to the figure of design somewhat nostalgically. Throughout 'Matters of Policy' the narrative's errant trajectory is attempting to find a centre stage for a communal experience or experiment and this strange quadrangle is the closest one gets to a sense of communication between individuals. The initial glimpse of a gaze which opens the poem is transmuted to become a place in 'which to graze/ at equal distance to one another'. Moreover the poem's close asserts an impression of collective action in 'together we begin to shovel the dust that blows/ in our eyes & moistens our faces'. We could even read these lines as a gentle ridiculing of a tearful nostalgia; a collective *Song of Myself* where the fabled dirt under the boot-soles enacts its humorous revenge.

Bernstein creates an irreconcilable tension between irony and humour in his poetry, and this can be productively understood as the inevitable result of the attempt to rupture the lyric from a model of emphatic interiority to a public address. Approaching his poetics through a configuration or error allows us not only to evaluate how an aesthetic of error impacts upon the lyric, but grants a further insight into the poet's conceptualisation of language as a network of complex social relations. While the ambitious claims of his poetics might frequently falter in the practice of his poetry, Bernstein's remarks on the public function of art suggests that this is the invariable gamble staked by an experimental praxis:

> I believe that artists and intellectuals have a commitment to try to make their work and the work they support available in public spaces, not in the watered down forms that only capitulate to the mediocracy, but in forms that challenge, confront, exhilarate, provoke, disturb, question, flail, and even fail.[31]

---

31   Bernstein, 'The Revenge of the Poet Critic', in *My Way*, p. 15.

Chapter Three
Michael Palmer's Lyric and 'Nobody's Voice'

The Lyric and *Notes for Echo Lake*

Michael Palmer's poetry offers a further approach to an understanding of the lyric as it is reconfigured in contemporary practice. In contrast to Charles Bernstein's 'ideolectical' construction of the lyric and its revision as a polyphonic score, Palmer's ambition is to create a composition that has 'nothing at its center.'[1] Palmer's poetry and poetics gesture to the lyric as 'nobody's voice' and this apparent evacuation is a direct antithesis to Bernstein's multiplicity of ideolects. But 'nobody's voice' is not just the voice of no one; Palmer's explanation posits one directly within a context of European lyricism and a tradition he identifies as 'the analytic lyric'. Paul Celan becomes a key figure in Palmer's consideration of the lyric self in language:

> His response to the discourse of totalitarianism is to create out of the German Expressionist tradition a body of intensely concentrated lyric poetry which addresses the reconstruction of human speech. I was very much moved by the sense of the dispersal of the subject, but also the reaffirmation, the fact that it was nobody's voice and yet it was, also, something– again and again and again.[2]

Palmer's explanation offers several reformulations of lyric practice. The analytic lyric in Palmer's words addresses 'the problematics of purely private utterance' by 'taking over the condensation of lyric emotion and focusing it then on the mechanics of language' (238).

---

1   Michael Palmer, 'From the Notebooks' in *19 New American Poets of the Golden Gate*, ed. Philip Dow (New York: Harcourt Brace Jovanovich, 1984), pp. 341–50 (p. 343).

2   Palmer, 'Interview' in Thomas Gardner, *Regions of Unlikeness: Explaining Contemporary Poetry* (Lincoln: University of Nebraska Press, 1999), p. 239.

This approach produces in turn 'a critique of the discourse of power, to renew the function of poetry' (238). Palmer sees in Celan's poetry a strongly orchestrated conflict between the dispersal of the subject, and its reaffirmation as a 'reconstruction of human speech' (238). Palmer's lyric like Celan's, provides an analysis of utterance and becomes a site for intersecting discourses. The poet reflects upon his own work as being 'almost like building a vocabulary, one whose meanings accrue over time.'[3]

This reconstructive approach presents additional problems in reading Palmer's poetry. There is firstly a danger of imposing upon the poetry a template of meaning and reducing such frequent evocations as 'book', 'echo', and 'voice' to symbolic strategies in his poetry, particularly in the early volume *Notes for Echo Lake*.[4] Palmer's ambition focuses on how an articulation of voice can emerge from the inconsistencies and contradictions in the poetic text. Extracts from his published notebooks point towards this as a possible strategy: 'Feeling now that I need to complete *Notes for Echo Lake* even though it includes sense of itself as a failed work, or work of evasion and inconsistency– are not those two qualities lovely possibilities?'[5] It has also been argued that the recourse to nobody's voice indicates an intense nostalgia for an unproblematic mediation of meaning through language.[6]

Bernstein makes an ambitious claim for a reading of error as a method for establishing a public role for poetry. Palmer by comparison is certainly more circumspect in his claims for the lyric, and resists an understanding of the lyric purely in terms of a workshop aesthetic. Lyric for Palmer is not neutral ground since he affirms that 'lyric poetry– (using that term in quite a broad sense as a poetry that's

3   Lee Bartlett, 'Michael Palmer: "The man by contrast is fixed symmetrically"' in *Talking Poetry: Conversations with Contemporary Poets* (Albuquerque: University of New Mexico Press, 1987), pp. 126–43 (p. 135).

4   Palmer, *Notes for Echo Lake* (San Francisco: North Point Press, 1981).

5   Palmer, 'From the Notebooks', in *19 New American Poets of the Golden Gate*, ed. Philip Dow (New York: Harcourt Brace Jovanovich, 1984), pp. 341–50 (p. 345).

6   See Norman Finkelstein, 'The Case of Michael Palmer', *Contemporary Literature*, 29.4 (1988), 518–37.

personal, again in quite a broad sense, not the lyric poetry of "little me" that is churned out in America)– has a force of resistance and critique.[7] Palmer's lyric is informed by an extensive tradition of both European and American lyricism and our main preoccupation is to find a model for reading the residue of influences and imbricated voices in Palmer's text.

My gesture to a 'residue' in the text points us to Michael David-son's coining of a 'palimtextual' poetics as a method for reading the poetic text as a site for phantasmagorical writings and layering of previous inscriptions.[8] Palmer's claim for his lyric as a configuration of nobody's voice presents pertinent problems, since one is never totally assured that we are reading the poet's work or citations from an extensive lineage of the lyric. Reading these tracings and multiple strata in Palmer's text through an aesthetic of error, provides a methodology for approaching the intertextual impulse of his work. Initially it is necessary to focus on Palmer's lyric and its troubled preoccupation with semiosis and failed communication in *Notes for Echo Lake*. The figure of the book looms large in this volume as both an ideal and threat. Understanding this early work in conjunction with Stéphane Mallarmé's writings will help to evaluate Palmer's later volume *Sun* (1988). *Notes for Echo Lake*'s early preoccupation with a failed or defective language, lends itself to an aesthetic of error. Moreover the often violent rupture of the lyric in Palmer's poetry can be read in tandem with Gilles Deleuze's analysis of schizophrenic writing, bringing to a focus the problematised subject-object dichot-omy of Palmer's lyric. An aesthetic of error will be considered in *Sun* as a series of halts, aberrations and plateaus in the text. This approach enables a consideration of how lyric memory can be presented in Palmer's violently ruptured lyric.

It is tempting to assert that the book in American poetry is an agonistic site where problematic literary legacies can be addressed or

---

7   Palmer, 'Interview: Conducted by Peter Gizzi' in *Exact Change Yearbook #1*, ed. Peter Gizzi (Boston: Exact Change, 1995), pp. 161–79 (p. 169).

8   Michael Davidson, *Ghostlier Demarcations: Modern Poetry and the Material Word* (Berkeley: University of California Press, 1997). This work is discussed in the introduction.

resolved momentarily. While this proposition is an alluring one, recent American poets' continued fascination with the book as both an expansive and liberating site suggests that it is being redeployed as an enabling form. One could claim that paradoxically for Palmer that the idea of a failed book becomes a dynamic field of possibility. The organisation of Palmer's *Notes for Echo Lake* makes for an ambitious formal strategy. The volume is divided into a sequence of twelve notes representing a composite year which alternate with short lyric sections interweaving the myth of Narcissus and Echo through the sections. *Notes for Echo Lake* introduces us to the figure of the book in Palmer's poetry which becomes of key importance in our intertextual reading of the lyric in the later volume *Sun*.

The figure of the book in Palmer's work gestures to a body of early European lyricism, particularly Mallarmé's 'Crisis in Poetry'. Mallarmé interrogates the mediating function of language and take issue with the prevalence of spoken language as the ultimate ambition of a work. He places an important stress on the gestural or suggestive possibilities of language, stating 'Why should we perform the miracle by which a natural object is almost made to disappear beneath the magic waving wand of the written word, if not to divorce that object from the direct and the palpable, and so conjure up its essence in all purity?'[9] Ordinary language serves a mediatory function between a world of objects and a universe of meaning; rather than positioning poetry directly within these two oppositional poles, Mallarmé proposes that poetic language establishes its own reality through a system of pure relations. He refers to this conceptualisation of poetry as the pure idea:

> The poet must establish a careful relationship between two images, from which a third element, clear and fusible, will be distilled and caught in our imagination. We renounce that erroneous aesthetic ... which would have the poet fill the delicate pages of his book with the actual and palpable wood of trees, rather than with the forest's shuddering or the silent scattering of thunder through the foliage ... else the book could not be properly closed. (40)

9   Stéphane Mallarmé, 'Crisis in Poetry' in *Mallarmé: Selected Prose Poems, Essays and Letters*, trans. Bradford Cook (Baltimore: Johns Hopkins Press, 1956), pp. 34–43 (p. 42).

Mallarmé is not designating a transcendental sphere for poetic composition or an idealised space. 'Crisis in Poetry' evokes an alternative to realism and not a hermetic or private language accessible only to initiates. Language he indicates is essentially defective:

> Languages are imperfect because multiple; the supreme language is missing ... the diversity of languages on earth means that no one can utter words which would bear the miraculous stamp of Truth Herself Incarnate ... We dream of words brilliant at once in meaning and sound, or darkening in meaning and so in sound, luminously and elementally self-succeeding. But, let us remember that if our dream were fulfilled, verse would not exist. (38)

Taking a cursory look at *Notes for Echo Lake* it may come as no surprise to see in the opening Note the following formulation:

> Was was and is. In the story the subject disappears.

> They had agreed that the sign was particular precisely because arbitrary and that it included the potential for (carried the sign of) its own dis-solution, and that there was a micro-syntax below the order of the sentence and even of the word, and that in the story the subject disappears it never disappears. 1963: only one of the two had the gift of memory.

> Equally one could think of a larger syntax, e.g. the word-as-book proposing always the book-as-word. And of course still larger. (4)

Notes for Echo Lake dramatises a tension between two impulses which Norman Finkelstein identifies as a conflict between a 'polysemous vision of poetry' and a cabalistic reading of the book as a magical series of initiation rites.[10] Against this process of initiation is the play of semiosis, and the volume expressively situates itself within the context of a failed language and miscommunication drawing on Echo and Narcissus. Palmer's comments provide an interesting pivot to the constant deferral of meaning in the text. He is uneasy with the simplistic cultural coding of the Narcissus myth and its simplification to a mirrorising self-absorption, preferring to treat the myth as a model of discourse. Reflecting on the underestimated role of Echo he suggests:

10   See Finkelstein, 'The Case of Michael Palmer', p. 519.

95

Obviously one version of it being semiotic where you have the decay of the signal over time, in relation to other speakers and in relation to reading the world. Without that semiotic decay and that misinterpretation, there would be no communication. If there were no active interpretation of the signal, we'd just have Morse Code. So the very fact of decay is what is generative of new meanings. This is the act of reading we're talking about also: the text stays alive by virtue of its flexibility, its uninterpretability (or perhaps resistance to interpretation) at times. That was definitely one side of the Narcissus and Echo myth. Then obviously the dilemma of how does a poet move beyond the *moi*, solipsistic self-reflection.[11]

Echo and Narcissus appear throughout the volume, sometimes as figural representations: 'And he sees himself now as the one motionless on the ground, now as the one bending over' (5), 'He-she bends at the mirrored waist/ is seen is visible to a given face/ who drowned in the myth of three crossing four' (37). There are also explicit references to reflective bodies of water, eyes, mirrors, mirror images and doubling. But more complex is Palmer's mediation of semiotic decay in the volume. Failed communication and misinterpretation surface frequently in the work, take the following examples: 'Whose words formed awkward curves' (22), 'The voice/ you hear is your own/ caught in her throat' (44) 'Her stuttering to accommodate a name' (45), 'If if if if if and when if and when/ If if if he is' (48). This final glossolalic explosion suggests an unthreading of the lyric I, and indeed an unravelling of the sign itself. *Notes for Echo Lake* taking its cue from the eighteenth century lyric poet Friedrich Hölderlin, alerts us not only to the 'sign empty of meaning', but 'Sign that empties itself at each instance of meaning' (5). Palmer's comments guide us in this reading and we can relate this loss of faith in the sign to the nostalgia of the idealised 'book', the original work that serves as a template to be imitated or quoted. Palmer makes explicit reference to Hölderlin's phrase:

In Hölderlin's case, he is talking about the metaphysical relationship of the sign, the fact that earth and heaven are no longer connected, that you can no longer talk to God, that our signs do not translate in the literal ecclesiastical sense of *translatio*: the bearing from one realm to another. And equally we

11   Palmer, 'Interview', in *Regions of Unlikeness*, p. 276.

cannot read the signs of God in the world anymore. And it struck me that, in this context, the unravelling of the sign was involved with the unravelling of the subject.[12]

In the section 'A Dream Called "The House of the Jews"' the figure of the book both appears and disappears through a series of disturbing and violent images:

> Many gathered many friends maybe everyone
> Many now and then may have entered
> The ivory teeth fell from her mouth
> The typewriter keys
> Many fell then at the entrance
> Many held them
> Many fell forward and aware
> Various friends gathered at the entrance
> Some held back
> The room contains a question
> Many said now before then this then that
> The room contains a question to be named
> He said *I will tell the book the dream the words tell me*
> The room is not the place or the name (14)

The book is as elusive as the figures introduced in this poem, and the consistent stammerings of the statements make for a continual beginning and reformulation. The referential vectors of the poem are in constant flux; a gruesome physical gesture is made between the 'ivory teeth' falling and the site of composition 'typewriter keys'. Finkelstein in his cabalistic reading of the poem, compares the gathering to a crowd of initiates huddled round the figure of the book. The enforced rhetorical strategy of the poem the many 'gathered' 'now' 'fell' 'held' 'said', sets up a random multiplicity against the search for an ultimate, transcendent meaning. In reflecting upon Mallarmé's ideation of 'the world as book', there is a comparative strategy of 'the pure idea' articulated by the closing speaker of the poem: 'I will tell the book the dream the words tell me.' This line inverts the equating of language with experiential recounting. The impetus in this line is towards a purely conceptual language, the

12   Palmer, 'Interview', in *Regions of Unlikeness*, pp. 257–8.

abolition of objectification and the figure of the book as a code breaking/ translating machine.

This scene of magical initiation is replicated at various points during *Notes for Echo Lake*. Finkelstein astutely suggests that these grand gestures to books, grammar and words in Palmer's work point towards an intensely felt nostalgia:

> These should not be misconstrued as self-reflective language games ... but rather understood as hollow vessels that long ago were filled with a rich tradition of textuality: a tradition which, unlike literature today, affected all the spheres of cultural production. Typically, Palmer's frustration over the loss of such authority results in a determined show of non-meaning. (523)

Finkelstein's point is an important one. In *Sun* a nostalgia for a literary master narrative and a search for origination result in a complex address of literary precursors.[13] Invariably this impetus has implications for reading Palmer's lyric as an agonistic impulse.

Schizophrenic Writing, Lyric Rupture and *Sun*

Palmer's volume *Sun*, reformulates traditional models of lyricism to prove a radical revision of the expressive model of the lyric. The expressive lyric posits the self as the primary organising principle of the work. Central to this model is the articulation of the subject's feelings and desires and a strongly marked division between subjectivity and its articulation as expression. M.H. Abrahams notoriously identified an expressive theory of the lyric as the internal made external:

> A work of art is essentially the internal made external, resulting from a creative process operating under the impulse of feeling, and embodying a combined product of the poet's perceptions, thoughts, and feelings. The primary source and subject matter of a poem therefore, are the actions and attributes of the poet's own mind ... The first test of any poem must pass is no longer, 'Is it true

13   Palmer, *Sun* (San Francisco: North Point Press, 1988).

to nature?' or 'Is it appropriate to the requirements either of the best judges or the generality of mankind?' but a criterion looking in a different direction; namely 'Is it sincere? Is it genuine?[14]

Although Abrahams has in mind primarily the poetry of the nineteenth century, this model resonates as a general impulse in the mainstream lyric of twentieth century American poetry, especially in its evocation of sincerity and authenticity. Furthermore the symbolic use of the external world as a psychic landscape for the subject's state of mind, is one we are familiar with, even in T.S. Eliot's infamous proposal of the objective correlative: 'in other words, a set of objects, a situation, a chain of events which shall be the formula of that *particular* emotion; such that when the external facts, which must terminate in sensory experience, are given, the emotion is immediately evoked.'[15] What is most apparent in the expressive model of the lyric is the immanence of the self, its centrality within the composition as the subject of the writing and the role of language as a transparent medium for communicating intense emotion.

From an initial examination of *Notes for Echo Lake*, it is clear that Palmer's poetry dismantles familiar models of lyricism such as the expressive lyric. But rather than reduce the entire project to an anti-lyrical or oppositional impulse, it is worth investigating what we can recoup from this dismantling in greater detail. A central problem to consider is what model of lyricism can be formulated when the self is displaced from centre stage, and an experience of language takes its place. This shift could be described as a movement away from so-called linguistic transparency to a poetics of opacity. A process which Bernstein characterises as a desire 'to make language opaque so that writing becomes more and more conscious of itself as world generating, object generating.'[16] Axiomatically this reading of poetry argues for a self and experience constituted by, and not mediated through language.

14   M.H. Abrahams, *The Mirror and the Lamp: Romantic Theory and the Critical Tradition* (Oxford: Oxford U.P., 1977), pp. 22–3.
15   T.S. Eliot, 'Hamlet', in *Selected Essays* (London: Faber & Faber, 1972), p. 145.
16   Charles Bernstein, 'Thought's Measure' in *Content's Dream: Essays 1975– 1984* (Los Angeles: Sun & Moon Press, 1986), pp. 61–86 (p. 71).

In an early interview Palmer speaks of inhabiting and being inhabited by language,[17] a general impulse that appears to link him to Bernstein's poetics. But Palmer's focus on what he calls the 'physicality of word as gesture' (129) also suggests that the form which this inhabiting takes differentiates him from the general tenets of Language Writing. Certainly a model of the expressive lyric as mediating the clear distinctions between subject and object, self and world is threatened in *Notes for Echo Lake*. In this volume we are told of 'a man having swallowed his tongue' since 'there is no "structure" to the sentence and no boundary or edge to the field in question. As there is everywhere no language' (5).

Sun in its radical revision of the expressive lyric meditates on the subject as a body comprised and constituted by language. Taken at its most extreme the human figure can only be represented in *Sun* as a sum of dismembered body parts, limbs, mouths and linguistic traces. Words make a violent assault upon the body. The division between the subject and the world is dismantled, and the model of lyricism as an ordering of perceptions and their objectification in the world is radically dissected. *Sun* takes the threat implicit in *Notes for Echo Lake* a step further and examines what form of lyricism is created when the dichotomy between the perceiving subject and world is collapsed. Reading Palmer's *Sun* in parallel with concepts of schizophrenic language enables a consideration of how reminiscence and memory are problematised in Palmer's self-coined analytic lyric. Eventually this difficulty in Palmer's poetry can be addressed by an examination of the relationship between memory and intertextuality in the volume.

When questioned on the nature of language games, autism and the language of schizophrenia Palmer draws specific attention to the work of Deleuze. In his response Palmer focuses upon the grammatical hierarchies which he suggests are the poet's role to scrutinise, interrogate and disrupt:

> There is to some degree a state of linguistic revelation that is involved in the discourse of schizophrenics, the discourse of many people with so-called 'dis-

17   Palmer, 'Interview: conducted by Lee Bartlett', p. 129.

abilities', opened channels of meaning figuration, and metaphor that are outside, that are a kind of minoritarian in Deleuze's sense, which are (and I might add, always have been) very important areas for the poetic to explore. Implicit in that is a certain respect for all manifestations; we have our linguistic hierarchies in which we have our major dialect, and all the sub dialects. And we have been taught certainly by modern linguistics, one of its gifts to us, that none is superior in terms of meaning or grammatical efficacy over the other, and yet politically, the major dialect is the one (so Bob Perelman famously quotes Chomsky) with the army and the navy.[18]

Palmer sees his own work as a continuation of poetry's exploration of how meaning is constituted. He later draws a correspondence with his own work and the more familiar play of logical propositions in traditional nonsense verse. Remarking on the role of nonsense in his poetry, Palmer states that 'in Carroll, there's a fascination with logic/counter logic, syllogism. That logic has trouble permitting itself, but we can have all of it in poetry. The counter-logic of poetry seems to me enormously powerful and not to be ignored. It's dangerous territory.'[19]

Palmer's comments indicate that his poetry provides a complex interchange between the counterlogical play of nonsense verse, and the violence inscribed in schizophrenic language. The equivocation between these two models comes to a forefront in the volume *Sun*. Deleuze's discussion of Caroll and Antonin Artaud, allows us to understand the interplay between these two strategies and the volume's ongoing struggle with what I will later address as 'symmetrical' propositions in *Sun*.

Deleuze distinguishes between two radically different impulses in nonsense poetry through examining what he proposes is Lewis Carroll's language of 'surface' and Antonin Artaud's language of 'depth'.[20] He suggests that Caroll's reliance upon logic and grammar

18   Palmer, 'Interview with Grant Jenkins with Teresa Aleman and Donald Prues', *Sagetrieb*, 12.3 (1993), 53–64 (p. 61).
19   Palmer, 'Interview: Conducted by Peter Gizzi', pp. 175–6.
20   Gilles Deleuze, 'The Schizophrenic and Language: Surface and Depth in Lewis Carroll and Antonin Artaud', in *Textual Strategies: Perspectives in Post-structuralist Criticism*, ed. Josue V. Harari (London: Methuen, 1980), pp. 277–95.

configures a distinct organisation of language; the language of the 'surface' which is comprised of portmanteau words and what he calls 'events' or 'effects'. In this schema 'events' do not designate properties or states of the body but instead 'a manner of being' or a certain 'manifestation', distinguishing action from the physical body. This movement away from the body to its manifestation in language, indicates a duality between what Deleuze calls 'designation' and 'expression'. 'Designation' is linked to the physical qualities of the body and 'expression' to their formulation as an expression of meaning. The movement from designation to expression is 'to enter a region in which language no longer has any relationship to bodies or designated objects (which are always consumable) but only to meanings (which are always expressible)' (283).

We can further clarify the language of 'surface' by considering the function of portmanteau words in Carroll's work. As a neologism, the portmanteau comprises parts of more than one word freighted together and must be read as a semi-grammatical model of writing, always gesturing to the conventions of grammar as a variant or error of 'correct' usage. Far from making no sense, the portmanteau word demands a logical analysis within a grammatical framework. An impetus towards expression in Carroll manifests itself in linguistic games. Paradoxically, the disruption of grammatical conventions and logical propositions in Carroll's nonsense verse, mark an insistent movement towards expression. This distinguishes it from the physical quality of 'depth' Deleuze attributes to Artaud.

Deleuze associates a language of depth with the body. He draws his conceptualisation of schizophrenic language from a clinical study, to formulate a model of language that admits the drives and articulations of the body:

> The discovery that *there is no more surface* is familiar to and experienced by any schizophrenic. The great problem, the first evidence of schizophrenia, is that the surface is punctured. Bodies no longer have a surface. The schizophrenic body appears as a kind of body-sieve. Freud emphasized this schizophrenic aptitude for perceiving the surface and the skin as if each were pierced by an infinite number of little holes. As a result the entire body is nothing but depth; it snatches and carries off all things in this gaping depth, which represents a fundamental involution. Everything is body and corporeal. (286)

The schizophrenic subject experiences the dissolution of set perimeters and boundaries; the puncturing of the body's surface enables a porous exchange between the traditionally set divisions of exterior and interior. Joseph Gabel in a clinical diagnosis of schizophrenic language suggests that schizophrenia can be understood 'as the loss of the dialectic of subject and object, of self and world.'[21] Norman Cameron develops this proposition by suggesting that schizophrenia is indicative of a failure to role-play, a failure 'to learn to react to one's behaviour as others are reacting to it.'[22] In Deleuze's model, the boundaries set in surface language between designation and expression are ruptured, since for the schizophrenic 'Everything is body and corporeal.'

Deleuze examines the implications of this movement away from expression and the rupture of a language order:

> As there is no surface, interior and exterior, container and content no longer have precise limits; they plunge into universal depth. From this comes the schizophrenic way of living contradictions: either in the deep cleavage that traverses the body, or in the fragmented parts of the body, which are nested in one another and whirl around ... In this breakdown of surface, all words lose their meaning ... All words become physical and affect the body immediately. (287)

His analysis explains the radical revision of language as expression and the violent dismembering of words; language is not presented as a conceptual system but as immediate and affective state of the body. In this model of fluid exchange between interior and exterior, decomposed words appear as missiles and not as the carefully orchestrated play of logical propositions witnessed in Carroll. This initial explanation of the terms 'surface' and 'depth' provides a further methodology to examine how Palmer's poetry reformulates traditional model of lyric expression. Eventually this approach may elucidate the vexing question posed by *Sun* 'Is there still an outside, uncancelled as yet by other?' (35).

---

21   Joseph Gabel, cited by Rolf Breuer in 'Irony Literature and Schizophrenia', *New Literary History: A Journal of Theory and Interpretation*, 12 (1980), 107–18 (p. 117).

22   Cited by Rolf Breuer in 'Irony Literature and Schizophrenia', p. 117.

Notes for Echo Lake is a volume dominated by surfaces. The human figure's appearance in this volume is tentative at best marked only by its traces and erasures on the page and as a shattered reflection on water. The volume's fascination with surfaces is approached with some suspicion in *Sun*. At points it is suggested that the earlier volume fails of its initial ambitions: 'Stupid Lake, You were the ruin of a book' (12), 'There are pieces of the lake lie here' (18). What lies behind this sense of failure in *Notes for Echo Lake* and how does *Sun* remedy the obsession with reflection, imitation and echolalia? The problem posed by *Sun* is how can the lyric mediate between the subject and the external world. The lure of mimesis surfaces at intervals during the volume:

> Imitate me says the elm
> Give me an azure sky huge and round
> Give me something in words for a change
> something that fits on a page (15)

These lines enact a poetics of dictation, yet while the model of language as a transparent medium capable of mediating the world is an alluring one, Palmer mistrusts the role of the lyric poem as a mirror held up to nature. Later in the same section, this mirroring of the world is severely problematised as the speaker asks: 'Let's think about this/ Let's consider the lace in neck*lace*/or the turquoise on a *Turk*ish door' (15).[23] These lines focus on the play of phonetic resonance embedded within words. What initially appears to be phonetic duplication or repetition is reliant upon a play of differences. Meaning cannot be reduced to any form of stability, even within the smallest phonetic resonance. Palmer's wordplay bears some similarity to Carroll's use of the portmanteau, yet instead of creating neologisms, Palmer insists on scrutinising the phonetic structure of words.

In *Sun* this mistrust of surfaces is coupled with the fear that the volume will reduce itself to a closed circuit of representation. We are urged in *Sun* 'Don't mirrorise/ Don't be Civil Guard' (29). A direct connection is made here between authority and the lure of mimetic representation. Palmer, in seeking to challenge the expressive lyric

23   Italics mine.

with its duality of inner and outer, is faced with a representational debacle. If the subject becomes instead a site of porous exchange as in Deleuze's conceptualisation of the body-sieve an additional problem emerges, how can the lyric subject evoke or gesture to a process of reminiscence? The volume does not offer us certain solutions to problems of expression, but an intertextual reading of *Sun* consolidates the problem of differentiation.

In a preliminary reading of *Sun* we can see how the text returns obsessively to formulations of this key question, 'How to say I or /we in a rival voice' (70). At times the work expresses nostalgia for the figure of the isolated romantic poet:

> If we're really mirrors in a poem
> what will we call this song
> I want to continue on yellow paper
> like a person in a room
> and like a ladder and like a moth (15)

But even this figure of the subject as attempting to articulate a cohesive 'I' can only be evoked through a chain of descriptive similarities. Palmer wants to dismantle traditional models of lyricism with the self as its primary organizing principle, yet rather than offering us an alternative model, *Sun* establishes an equivocatory dialogue between the language of the surface and a language of depth. The equivocation between designation and expression in his work problematises the lyric as utterance and experiential recounting.

A fear of a closed circuit of representation and the equivocation between a language of surface and depth emerge as *Sun*'s preoccupations. The mistrust of what I suggest are 'symmetrical propositions' appears throughout the volume:

> My name is the word for wall, my head is buried in that wall. (32)

> The world is an object
> Place yourself here as if on a surface
> Replace horizon with an equals sign (60)

> The equation of A with A (61)

105

> I now turn to my use of suffixes and punctuation, closing Mr Circle
> with a single stroke, tearing the canvas from its wall, joined to her,
> experiencing the same thoughts at the same moment, inscribing
> them on a loquat leaf. (83)

These examples illustrate an uncomfortable and claustrophobic sensation of verisimilitude. Roland Barthes's consideration of classical and modern poetry sheds light on the evocation of symmetry in *Sun*. In 'Is there any Poetic Writing?' Barthes distinguishes classical writing as a 'chain of intentions.'[24] Rather than placing a focus on individual words, or the uneven texture of what he describes as modern poetry's fascination with 'semantic accident' in the text, Barthes suggests that the flow of classical poetry is 'a succession of elements whose density is even; it is exposed to the same emotional pressure' (45). Classical poetry, he indicates, focuses on expression: 'The poetic vocabulary itself is one of usage, not of invention: images in it are recognizable in a body; they do not exist in isolation' (45). Barthes develops this proposition by focusing on the construction of the classical poem:

> The function of the classical poet is not therefore to find new words, with more body or more brilliance, but to follow the order of an ancient ritual, to perfect the symmetry or the conciseness of a relation, to bring a thought exactly within the compass of a metre. Classical conceits involve relations not words: they belong to an art of expression not invention. The words here, do not, as they later do, thanks to a kind of violent and unexpected abruptness, reproduce the depth and the singularity of an individual experience; they are spread out to form a surface. (45)

Although Barthes is looking specifically here at the formal rules of classical conceits, his description draws attention to ideas of depth and surface. While the quotations from *Sun* are not constructing the same symmetrical patterns that Barthes outlines in his essay, one can sense a similar anxiety towards formal closure in *Sun*. These instances of an uncomfortable verisimilitude read as a working through of approaches to the subjective 'I' and as a consideration of Deleuze's analysis of language and schizophrenia. Rather than patrolling boundaries be-

---

24   Roland Barthes, *Writing Degree Zero*, trans. Annette Lavers and Colin Smith (New York: Hill and Wang, 1998), p. 44.

tween the subject and world, Palmer's lyric is constantly threatened by the dismantling of differences.

An explicit example appears in the following section from 'Baudelaire Series' in *Sun*:

> You, island in this page
> image in this page
>
> evening's eyelid, silk
> four walls of breath
>
> I could say to them
> Watch yourself pass
>
> Relax and watch yourself pass
> Look at the thread
>
> You, island in this page
> image in this page
>
> What if things really did
> correspond, silk to breath
>
> evening to eyelid
> thread to thread (16–17)

Violence and an overwhelming sense of confinement are suggested by these two short sections, which are effectively presented in the volume on facing pages. The sections initiate a resemblance, a mise-en-abime, appearing at first to mirror one another. In this rewriting of the original lyric evocation 'evening's eyelid', the reader is presented with a threat of lexical violence 'evening to eyelid'. The perceiving subject cannot be said to be the organizing principle at work here; the act of looking becomes an interpenetrative thread between subject and world. Moreover the haunting question 'Is there still an outside, uncancelled as yet by other', seems pertinent to the command 'Relax and watch yourself pass'.

Palmer initially takes issue with metaphoric figures, but these images also suggest a painful attack on the perceiving subject. As the volume progresses the subject is assaulted violently. The following excerpts dramatise a Deleuzian schizophrenic language as Palmer's subject becomes a 'body sieve'. The body is punctured and the surfaces of language break down. These examples illustrate a subject assaulted by acute lexical violence:

> She says, You are counter
> You are degrees only
> and now in summer a mouthful of blood
> and sutured nylon thread (28)
>
> The hood is black with two holes for my mouths (60)
>
> A body disappears into itself
> its mirror self or sister self (61)
>
> enter through the curtain
> and swallow your words (69)
>
> Story of hands abandoning their fingers,
> of an organ emerging from the throat (71)
>
> A word twists backward
> peeling its skin up over its face. (72)

The first example builds upon our initial examination the interpenetrative thread which connects the subject and the world, and results in a gruesome gagging of the subject. In these excerpts the site of the body becomes a gaping depth threatening to consume itself. Words become physical and execute a penetrative assault of the body. Impressions of extreme rupture are reiterated in the intense fragmentation and the dessimation of the whole body into limbs and organs. The final image suggests that the body is not only assaulted by words but becomes a textual body. Elements of Deleuze's essay are evoked figuratively within Palmer's text, but his lyric also attempts to work through Deleuze's conceptualisation of schizophrenic language.

Palmer's rupture of the lyric's dualities of subject and world, results in the testing of both expression and the evocation of memory in the text. *Sun* is marked by a fascination with what cannot be said and this failing or even erasure of expression can be linked to Palmer's interest in Post Holocaust literature. Palmer has consistently

drawn attention to the work of Edmond Jabès as an informing influence upon his poetics, more recently he mentions the format of Jabès's
The Book of Questions as providing an important strategy to his
examination of the lyric. Palmer proposes that for Jabès 'the question
contained a certain conversational generosity, it was an offering to
people, whereas certain dictatorial speech closed off any questioning
and foreclosed the conversation the poem aspires to.'[25] He reasserts
that 'poetry is nothing if not a question, and then a book of questions.
To which the answer is, perhaps, no more than another question.
Poetry in that sense remains open, and without authority.[26] *Sun*
dramatically frames the failing of an expressive lyric voice in elegiac
terms: 'How lovely the unspeakable must be' (37), which later becomes a fascination with the form this 'unspeakable' or unvoiced
writing may take, 'mute flooded paper' (54), 'Unutterable pages' (55),
'Here the poem is called What Speaking Means to Say' (84). This
suggestion of the poem as an unutterable and erotic écriture may well
recall Jack Spicer's assertion 'Where we are is in a sentence.'[27] It is no
accident that the figure of the sentence appears periodically during the
volume, initially linked to memory and a sense of duration 'what
sentence it measures out/ asking after of before' (30). As the volume
proceeds we see Palmer use a partial anagram to imply a formal
restraint: 'We are facing the nets/says a sentence' (44). This trace
mark of the word then re-appears in the more abstract example 'writ
on you/ ilynx and alea/ desire in a net' (76). The focus on the body
'writ on you' and the neologism 'ilynx' which combines both the
ileum' and 'larynx', works as a combined gesture to the violent
penetration of schizophrenic language and an impulse towards expression.

25   Palmer, Radio Interview with Leonard Schwartz on *Cross-Cultural Poetics* (U.
      Penn. Sound) #87: Two From San Francisco. Accessed http://media.sas.upenn.
      edu/pennsound/groups/XCP/XCP_87_Palmer.mp3
26   Palmer, 'Poetry and Contingency: Within a Timeless Moment of Barbaric
      Thought', *Chicago Review*, 49.2 (2003), 65–76 (p. 71).
27   Jack Spicer, 'A Textbook of Poetry' in *The Collected Books of Jack Spicer*, ed.
      Robin Blaser (Los Angeles: Black Sparrow Press, 1975). This line is also cited
      in Palmer's published Notebooks.

This final citation is taken from the section 'Sun' which Palmer mentions as an attempting to erasing Eliot's 'Tradition and the Individual Talent' and *The Waste Land*.[28] It is no surprise that this section's length is exactly that of *The Waste Land*, and 'writ on you/ ilynx and alea/ desire in a net' could be read as a fractured re-write of Eliot's lines 'mixing/ Memory and desire.'[29] Certainly the locus of desire in Palmer's *Sun* is different than the objectification of desire as originating from absence in *The Waste Land*. The ambitions of early modernism, it has been suggested, can be read an aim to successfully objectify the other and Peter Nicholls notes 'in this aesthetic, the self's relation to the other is generally construed as one of domination, and is characterised by discontinuity and separateness. Successful individuation entails the establishing of boundaries which divide the self from others'[30].

Palmer's *Sun* seems less focused on objectifying the other, and the proposition of objectifying memory is an anathema in the poem. The aleatory performance suggested by the throw of the dice or 'alea' indicates that desire especially if it has to be netted, is a flow of energy. This reading of the section provides a connection with Deleuze and Guattari's radical revision of desire in *The Anti Oedipus* where far from conceptualising desire as a lack or loss desire is aligned to a positive and productive activity:

> Desire does not lack anything; it does not lack its object. It is rather the *subject* that is missing in desire, or desire that lacks a fixed subject; there is no fixed subject unless there is repression. Desire and its object are one and the same

---

28 Palmer states 'The first "Sun" is also a kind of erasure of *The Waste Land* ... It's the same number of lines as *The Waste Land*, and I felt it as a typing over the text, erasing this vision of "Tradition and the Individual Talent" that was a primary model for the modernist vision ... At the same time, it was obviously an echo and a homage to that possibility of the modernist long poem. It enacts a kind of ambivalence.' Gardner, *Regions of Unlikeness*, p. 282.

29 T.S. Eliot, *The Waste Land* (London: Faber & Faber, 1940), p. 27.

30 Peter Nicholls, 'Of Being Ethical: Reflections on George Oppen', *American Literature*, 31.2 (1997), 153–70 (p. 156).

thing: the machine, as a machine, and the object of desire is another machine connected to it.[31]

Deleuze and Guattari argue that desire has been mastered for efficient social control and that any excess or recklessness of desire threatens the efficiency of the social apparatus. Julie Rivkin and Michael Ryan suggest that desire in *Anti-Oedipus* is 'innately reckless and inefficient, an energistics without bounds and should be understood as just one segment in the larger flows of energy and matter that constitute the world as a mobile, varying, multiple flux with different strata that make up planes of consistency.'[32] A notoriously provocative argument made by *Anti-Oedipus* is that we are all machines, that there is no independent autonomous self but a web of interconnections. The materialisation of desire into a mass corpus, radically challenges the orthodoxy of the self as the primary perceiver. As Rivkin and Ryan elucidate: 'Thought no longer stands outside matter and understands it as an object of cognition. Thought is a move within matter itself' (346). In this schema representation becomes less a conceptualisation outside of matter, than a body or an amorphous mass and desire is an entity in constant reformulation and revision 'unarticulated into identities or objects or selves' (346).

This cursory reading of *The Anti-Oedipus* provides a useful link to assess Palmer's lyric in *Sun*. The following extract with its direct reference to 'the desiring-machine' marks an explicit connection, yet paradoxically this allusion grants no reprieve from a vociferously enacted 'I' or 'not I' that dominates the passage. Palmer's reference to the 'desiring machine' provides a context for the interrogation of the provisional status of the subject, and examines how memory may be evoked by a distinctly aphasic 'I':

> I was sitting in the dark ivy at the gate
> of the desiring-machine no windshield no

---

31 Gilles Deleuze and Félix Guatteri, *Anti Oedipus: Capitalism and Schizophrenia*, trans. Helen Lane, Mark Seem and Robert Hurley (New York: Viking, Penguin, 1977), p. 26.
32 Julie Rivkin and Michael Ryan, eds. *Literary Theory: An Anthology* (Oxford: Blackwell, 1998), p. 345.

wheels I was sitting in the forest the great
counter-weight I was truly lost I was seated

behind a screen I was aware of things those
things were me amazing the forked branch

spilling names I had been-not I
had been not-lost I had seen you once

and clearly once I had been remembered
only once the boy

shouts Mica and gleams I am in a
versionary state you are in

me as history I fix
and crystal to it

inside the inside once. (69–70)

Far from seeing the social nexus solely as a vast web of energy, this
section dramatises a conflict between two epistemologies. Firstly we
have the description of the poet sat next to the 'desiring-machine'; a
broken down vehicle comically adhering to Deleuze and Guattari's
assertion that desiring-machines 'continually break down as they run,
and in fact run only when they are not functioning properly.'[33] The
attempt to materialise desire into a mass corpus has curious results. As
Palmer attempts to erase the subject 'those things were me', 'spilling
names I had been' 'not lost', the text becomes decidedly logocentric.
Lines bleed into one another, complicating the two positions. Curiously this section combines an epiphanic wonder at the world 'the forest
the great counter-weight', with rudiments of fairy-tale 'I was lost'.
Palmer seems intent on finding a central position to situate the 'versionary' subject in this short lyric. 'Versionary state' should also ring
alarm bells for the reader, is this a subjectivity in flux or the figure of
a visionary romantic?

This initial failure to pin down the subject originates from a loss
of memory and earlier in *Sun* there are masked references to aphasia

33   *Anti-Oedipus*, p. 31.

and even senility: 'Dear George So long/ Will you now have memory again (13)[34], 'I have swallowed this blank' (22), 'He's forgotten his name' (25), 'And each of those letters have a distinctive shape. Or shade. Impossible to remember' (36). An insistent distinction is made between the 'I had been' and the complex 'I had been-not I'. It is only when the other emerges within the text in an intense moment of intersubjectivity that this subjective stalemate is put into relief 'I had seen you once/and clearly once I had been remembered'. A personal history emerges from the hint of a photographic memoir 'once the boy' and the line breaks here are crucial in establishing two different positions. Palmer could be suggesting that while both 'I' and 'you' share a similar 'versionary state', that this perception of intersubjectivity is based on the recognition of difference. A further reading of these lines moves us from the enforced presentness of the writing to reminiscence, 'you are in me as history I fix'. This interpretation indicates a strategy of domination if not appropriation; a few pages earlier there is the command on a wall 'Symbolism died for your sins/ Own the body you desire' (62). To 'fix history' dramatises an attempt to articulate and individuate, which is in direct opposition to the dispersal of subjectivity we encounter in the opening lines. The opening positions an isolated subject 'behind a screen', which further problematises the reading of subjectivity here as an emptying into a vast web of energy. The closing line 'inside the inside once' suggest a highly self-reflexive nostalgia for an expressive paradigm of writing.

Crucial to this reading is the fact that Palmer interrogates two models of thought simultaneously in his lyric. Although the prospect of the desiring machine may initially seem to be an attractive model for rupturing the lyric, in practice it becomes an increasingly difficult position to sustain. The appearance of the other in the text, which establishes a recognition of difference and orchestrates a process of reminiscence, releases the subject from the continual present which threatens to engulf it. Far from privileging an authoritative lyric subject, the closing lines shows us how interdependent the 'I' has become. These lines indicate that the fixing of a personal history is a

34　Gardner in his reading makes specific allusion to George Oppen's 'struggle with Alzheimer's' *Regions of Unlikeness*, p. 260.

provisional, but necessary step to release the subject from the subjective stalemate of the 'I', 'not I' which dominates the opening.

Palmer's engagement with schizophrenic writing enables him to scrutinise the lyric and problematise its role as a straightforward anecdotal recounting. Moreover *Sun's* discontinuous texture works at prompting memory within the text. Examples of a similar prompting appear throughout the volume. Take for example the following: 'A word is coming up on the screen, give me a moment ... Because it's evening I remember memory now. Your English I do not speak' (31). 'Moans can be heard coming from poems ... And out of the head laughter, tears, tiny bubbles of spit. It is a head from another century, the last one or the next' (32). What seems crucial to Palmer's lyric is its deconstruction of the metaphysics of presence, and how this process of deconstruction is executed by the text. Palmer wants to resist the model of the Cartesian *cogito*, and his engagement with schizophrenic language allows him to interrogate and fracture the pervasiveness of the lyric 'I 'as a fixed frame of subjectivity. But problems arise with the attempt to integrate memory within the work since schizophrenic language cannot accommodate the process of recollection which we associate with the traditional expressive lyric. Explicit memories, when they do surface, appear as momentary intrusions in the text. At one point in 'Baudelaire Series' Palmer constructs a mock biographical account of an architect in Vienna. The poem moves through a series of ludic propositions starting with the admission 'I've let go of my practice of the violin' (39), to a statement 'In Vienna there are no musicians'. This is followed by an attempt at informal conversation, 'Call me Eric' (39) and finally a return to statement once more, 'I've designed a circle and a bridge' (40). But the closing line gives a surprising twist to the poem as the trace of an elegy appears, 'My tears are for the person I miss, the down on her lip' (40). The result is that the poem collapses into an evocation of loss. Initially the final line appears to rupture the poem, acting against its texture of impersonality, yet on re-reading this momentary act of reminiscence becomes paradoxically the informing centre of the work.

The keynote difficulty of how to orchestrate memory within the text illustrates the limitations which Palmer faces in his attempt to scrutinise the lyric. As a form of 'counter-lyricism', *Sun* forces us to question the 'I' at different and successive levels. The limitations Palmer encounters are not dissimilar to those faced by deconstruction's critique of the metaphysics of presence. Jonathon Culler points out that 'the Derridean critique of this metaphysics involves, among other things identifying elements, terms and functions which, like difference are difficult to conceive within this framework and which when brought to the fore, work not so much to discredit the framework as to indicate its limits.'[35] Equally Palmer's poetry is unable to offer us a new model of the lyric, and moreover this is not the poet's aim. But this account of the lyric, error and reminiscence remains incomplete until we consider the use of embedded citation in *Sun*.

35   Jonathon Culler, 'Jacques Derrida' in *Structuralism and Since: From Lévi Strauss to Derrida*, ed. John Sturrock (Oxford: Oxford U.P., 1979), pp. 154–80 (p. 163).

Chapter Four
Ungrammaticalities and Intertextuality in Michael Palmer's *Sun* and *Letters to Zanzotto*

'Then ego scriptor gets blotted out': Sourcing *Sun*

A primary difficulty in broaching Michael Palmer's poetry is the frequent suturing of unreferenced citations in the poetry; intertexts are often embedded seamlessly in the text. Introducing extracts from his notebooks, Palmer comments that the citations may well read as a 'game of blind man's bluff played among ghosts' and as a 'kind of thief's journal.'[1] Critical accounts of his poetry have tended to focus on a scholarly sourcing of these embedded citations, which becomes in itself a form of bibliographical errancy. Initially, it will be useful to draw on some of the more explicit correspondences set up by the poems in a tradition of European lyricism, which includes Charles Baudelaire, Paul Celan and Rainer Maria Rilke in *Sun*, and Andrea Zanzotto in the later volume *At Passages*.[2] Yet it is important to note that Palmer's poetry should not solely be read as an anxious dialogue with European lyricism.

A configuration of error as a series of traces, markings and aberrations in the text provides an alternative methodology for addressing the intertextual resonance of Palmer's work. Rather than approaching the intertextual density of *Sun* as an extensive survey of sources, different readings of intertextuality aim to extend an examination of Palmer's lyric through a configuration of error. Initially Mikhail Bakhtin's account of *heteroglossia* in the novel, and his

---

1   Michael Palmer, 'From the Notebooks', *19 New American Poets of the Golden Gate*, ed. Philip Dow (New York: Harcourt Brace Jovanovich, 1984), pp. 341–50 (p. 341).
2   Palmer, *At Passages* (New York: New Directions, 1996).

evocation of the text as 'contaminated' by a plurality of discourses provides a possible reading of intertexts in Palmer's work. Julia Kristeva's discussion of intertextuality as a process of *transposition* and Roland Barthes's evocation of *cryptographie*, extends an initial reading of error in the poetry as a series of aberrations and halts. Finally, the discussion evaluates whether Michael Riffaterre's conceptualisation of intertextuality as a series of 'ungrammaticalities' helps to problematise an understanding of citation as more than the locating of the sources.

Sun is a volume which addresses influence, poetic precursors and a history of the lyric.[3] Even if the reader is not forearmed with this knowledge; the titles of the poems and names mentioned in the volume gesture to a constellation of hidden references in the text. The opening sequence is entitled 'Baudelaire Series'. The names of the following appear within this sequence: 'Paul Celan, Cesar Vallejo, Robert C and Robert D', the last two one assumes are Creeley and Duncan. In the volume's last two sequences (both entitled 'Sun'), there are further names to add to our list: Scardanelli (the pen name of Friedrich Hölderlin), Dante and Bakhtin, coupled with alphabetical shorthand 'G is for Gramsci or Gobbels', 'Z for A'. The latter one refers to Louis Zukofsky and his lifework *'A'*. These are all examples of the more explicit references available in *Sun*.

Palmer has stated that the first 'Sun' is a rewriting or 'erasure' of Eliot's 'Tradition and the Individual Talent' and it is therefore no surprise that the volume functions as a shorthand account of Palmer's influences.[4] Not only are there explicit references to other writers made in *Sun* but lines or fragments of phrases are sutured seamlessly within the text. The temptation for the reader is to try and exhaustively reclaim the primary sources in order to excavate *Sun*. Palmer's publication of poetics, *The Danish Notebook* was written from a request 'to connect the dots' in his work.[5] Moreover the use of em-

3   Palmer, *Sun* (San Francisco: North Point Press, 1988)
4   See Michael Palmer, 'Interview' in Thomas Gardner, *Regions of Unlikeness: Explaining Contemporary Poetry* (Lincoln: University of Nebraska Press, 1999) p. 282.
5   Palmer, *The Danish Notebook* (Penngrove, CA: Avec Books, 1999), p. 9.

bedded or unreferenced citation in *Sun*, creates an anxiety of reading. Is one meant to read the volume as an encyclopaedic homage to high modernism? While the inclusion of citations in the text is something he aims for, it is not a strategy chosen at the reader's expense. Palmer refers to his poem, '*After Rilke, "Orpheus Eurydike Hermes"*' from the 'Baudelaire Series':

> I was interested more in the imbrication, the layering of these things. And I was interested in that gray area. Is that him? 'I'm fine I'm fine I'm really growing blind.' If I frame it as a text from elsewhere, it loses that multidirectionality that it has in relation to the *I* of the poem in here. The sort of counter-lyricism of a poem like this depends, in part at least, on questioning that *I* who is speaking. Maybe we are depriving the reader now in giving a source, but that source will probably disappear again for the reader.[6]

Palmer is clearly not interested in poetry as pedagogy, and suggests that the reader's focus should be on the indeterminacy enacted by the text as opposed to an excavation of intertexts in the poetry. His response places an important stress on contextualisation. An initial consideration of intertextuality and *Sun* requires a sourcing of citations embedded in the text, but one needs to consider the implication of this strategy upon a body of writing. Although inter-textuality can initially be considered as citation in *Sun*, it is integral not to restrict the term to an extensive sourcing of citations. A broader configuration of intertextuality is required to fully address its impact upon the reconstruction of the lyric in Palmer's work.

Citation in *Sun* may be a direct phrase from a poem, occasionally a single word is appropriated retaining a highly localised reference. Palmer indicates that his approach is different from Robert Duncan's strategy of collage. Whereas Duncan alerts the reader to citation as 'a foreign body' (286) entering the text as something to be struggled against or acknowledged, he strives to create a constellation of meaning:

> Occasionally I'll appropriate a source verbatim, but often it will be slightly or radically altered. It becomes altered by the impetus of the poem itself, and the

6   Palmer, *Regions of Unlikeness*, p. 286.

119

demands of the rhythm, the surrounding material, whatever. And so it's not quotation, exactly. It's a form of citation, but it's layered, covered over. (286)

The opening poem of the 'Baudelaire Series', with its italicised typeface, prepares one for another reading of *Les Fleurs du Mal*. Moreover its suggestion of a journey, hints at an examination of the European lyric. Walter Benjamin's reading of the poetics of the modern lyric assert an important revisionary examination for Palmer; 'As Benjamin says, Baudelaire in the strictest sense is not a lyric poet, but we cannot understand the modern lyric without understanding Baudelaire' (283). He adds that this first poem in the series is both an attempt to understand the modern lyric as 'a particularly alienated vision' and unravel its 'complex of voices' (283).

The series begins by tracing and attempting to situate both a literary and historical lineage:

> *A hundred years ago I made a book*
> *and in that book I left a spot*
> *and on that spot I placed a seme*
>
> *with the mechanism of the larynx*
> *around an inky center*
> *leading backward-forward*
>
> *into sun-snow*
> *then to frozen sun itself*
> *Threads and nerves have brought us to a house*
>
> *and clouds called crescent birds are a lifting song*
> *No need to sail further*
> *protesting here and there against some measures*
>
> *across the years of codes and names*
> *always immortal as long as you remain a man*
> *eating parts of him indicated by the prophets*
>
> *stomach skull and gullet*
> *bringing back the lost state*
> *Yes, I just dreamed another dream and nobody was in it*

There are indications of a literary struggle here, yet I hesitate in defining this struggle within an Oedipal frame of anxiety and influence. The poem attempts to navigate a point of origination, '*a spot*', '*a seme*', '*an inky center*', but this site is already always displaced for the writer '*leading backward-forward*'. Palmer's poem is strangely atavistic and the voyage enacted has particular resonance when read in conjunction with Baudelaire's *Les Fleurs du Mal*. Thomas Gardner's reading of the poem directs us to the cited phrases and images taken from Baudelaire's '*De Profundis Clamavi*' and 'A Voyage to Cythera.'[7] The '*frozen sun*' is taken directly from the second verse of '*De Profundis Clamavi*':

> A frozen sun hangs overhead six months;
> the other six, the earth is in its shroud–
> no trees, no water, not one creature here,
> a wasteland naked as the polar north![8]

Palmer's reworking of the citation retains the sense of exile and the binary oppositions enacted in the original. But Baudelaire's psychic landscape of emotional loss becomes for Palmer a self-reflexive site of literary examination. On closer examination Palmer's '*sun-snow*' can be read as an abbreviation or condensation of the Baudelaire's third verse: 'Of all the abominations none/ is half so cruel as that sun of ice/ and darkness worthy of old Chaos itself.' Once more the 'imbrication' of Palmer's text retains the primordial setting of 'De Profundis Clamavi', but the impetus shifts us to a destination '*Threads and nerves have brought us to a house*'. At the very close of the volume we encounter the 'House of Music' (77), which reading backwards suggests that the house Palmer initially writes of is a gesture to the lyric construction in his work.

More complex is the reading of 'A Voyage to Cythera' in the poem. The violent and sacrificial evocation of '*a man/ eating the parts of him indicated by the prophets/ stomach skull and gullet*' works as a shorthand account to the remains of an execution in Baudelaire's

---

7   See Gardner, *Regions of Unlikeness*, p. 256–7.
8   All citations are taken from Charles Baudelaire, *Les Fleurs du Mal*, trans. Richard Howard (Boston: David R. Godine, 1985), pp. 36–7.

voyage poem. The execution is punishment for the worship of the goddess Aphrodite described on the coastline from the ship:

> the eyes were holes, and from the ruined groin
> a coil of heavy guts had tumbled out–
> the greedy creatures, gorged on hideous sweets,
> had peck by vicious peck castrated him. (135)

Palmer's poem builds upon the uncomfortable identification which Baudelaire's poem insists upon at its close, 'On Aphrodite's island all I found/ was a token gallows where my image hung'. Although Baudelaire's speaker asserts that the account is only an 'allegory', the poem's close stresses an overt identification with the scene. Initially the recounting of the event works towards reclaiming memory and strives to differentiate the poet as authoritative commentator. As the poem progresses the clearly demarcated boundary between the subject and the locus of description unravels, since the subject is in fact split. Far from successfully completing a process of individuation the close creates a doubling within the text. Peter Nicholls alerts us to this conflict in Baudelaire's poetry: 'The solitary, then, is in fact always "double": he reacts violently to aspects of himself glimpsed in others only to find in the same moment that it is he himself who is the target of his own violence; he is both victim and executioner as Baudelaire so memorably puts it.'[9] Palmer's appropriation of key images provides more than a citational response to the poem.

The problem of differentiation made so apparent in Baudelaire's lyric becomes, in effect, the shaky ground on which Palmer's 'house' of the lyric must be built. However, the reader must remain wary of approaching Baudelaire's poetry reductively as the originary source for Palmer's sequence. An intertextual reading of *Sun* indicates that such a conception of origination is severely problematised in the volume. Yet it is clear that Palmer's lyric is setting up a series of correspondences with the problems of expression and individuation enacted by Baudelaire's lyric.

9   Peter Nicholls, *Modernisms: A Literary Guide* (Basingstoke: Macmillan Press, 1995), p. 16.

The final statement at the close of Palmer's poem requires further consideration '*Yes I just dreamed another dream and nobody was in it*'. The volume preceding *Sun, First Figure* opens with an epigraph from the poet Paul Celan '*Niemandes Stimme, wieder.*'[10] Translated as 'the voice erased but still sounding',[11] it refers to Palmer's earlier account of a tradition of an analytic lyric and Celan's evocation of 'no-one' or 'nobody's voice'[12] The 'nobody' closing Palmer's poem can be read in conjunction with Celan's volume *Die Niemandsrose*. Palmer's poem in its attempt to find a transcendental '*lost state*' enacts a form of textual cannibalism, moreover the man's consumption of his own body '*eating parts of him indicated by the prophets*' presents the body as a gaping depth. This image severely challenges the self as the primary locus of authority and voice as a metaphysical indication of presence. Palmer's search for origination echoes Celan's poem 'There was earth inside them, and they dug'. The disconcerting excavation within the body finds 'no song' and 'no language' only an empty or evacuated site:

> O one, o none, o no one, o you:
> Where did the way lead when it led nowhere?
> O you dig and I dig and I dig towards you
> and on our finger the ring awakes.[13]

Does Palmer's 'nobody' or 'no one' indicate a complete evacuation of the poem? The insistence of Celan's of 'no-one' suggest that one should consider otherwise. Palmer is aware that this evocation of Celan does present dangers, not least is that of appropriating a Holocaust survivor's testimony. He proposes that the evocation of Celan's 'no one' or 'nobody', is an attempt to create a space for other voices within the text; 'the sense that the poet, by the choice of vocation, gives up his place, is to me a very powerful image. And then the deeper sense of "*Niemandes Stimme*" is reflective, in at least my

---

10   Palmer, *First Figure* (North Point: San Francisco, 1984).
11   Gardner, *Regions of Unlikeness*, p. 287.
12   See opening of Chapter Three for an account of the 'analytic' lyric.
13   Paul Celan, *Poems of Paul Celan*, trans. Michael Hamburger (New York: Presea Books, 1995), p. 157.

practice also, of ceding one's place in a certain respect.'[14] 'The voice erased but still sounding', serves as a fitting evocation for the intertextual density of this opening poem. *Sun* is already alerting us to a trace mark of other presences in the text. Although these tracings are contained by Palmer's poem, they also work as a metatextual comment navigating the reader to a constantly displaced centre where the lyric voice may be recovered. Moreover Palmer's poetry indicates that this act of recovery is an impossible and even an untenable aim.

In a letter to John Taggart, Palmer draws attention to the poetic text as a site of inclusion. Reacting against the ego poetics of Charles Olson's 'Projective Verse' and the insistence upon the authenticity of voice in anecdotal contemporary poetry, Palmer indicates that autobiographical information restricts the reading of his poetry:

> 'I' as an ironized statement– At this point the notion of authorial voice as locus of responsibility seems problematic at best. Too many voicings are left out by this, and too much workshop self absorption let in. There is a projective aspect to it which also seems limiting, i.e. in Oppen's words as if someone had to be limited to the voice with which one was born, and as if we each possessed some natural voice, there for the finding. Not to say that one's voice, whatever may constitute it, is not part of the influence on what comes to be characteristically one's own work ... A further complication of course is that I know full well that certain disclosures of an autobiographical sort would so to speak 'clarify' some of the poems, yet this may be a misleading clarification.[15]

It comes as no surprise that Palmer's prose publication *The Danish Notebook* does not set out to explain his poems or provide answers to the evasions in his work. Although it does offer anecdotal accounts these are frequently linked to a consideration of further texts that have been read. A direct sourcing of material does not grant an instant clarification of the intertextual maze in Palmer's poetry.

Some quotations in *Sun* would remain unavailable as sources without access to Palmer's manuscripts or interviews to even the most informed reader. Take for example the opening of the first 'Sun'

---

14   Gardner, p. 287.
15   Letter from Palmer to John Taggart dated 1st July 1985 MSS 11/17/13 Courtesy of *The Mandeville Special Collections Library* at the University of California San Diego and with author's permission.

section in the volume: 'A headless man walks, lives/ for four hours/ devours himself' (59). These lines could be read as a rewriting and development of the opening poem of 'Baudelaire Series'. Thus it is may be with some surprise and that the reader learns that the first two lines are taken from the front-page headline of *The Sun* newspaper.[16] Palmer mentions that the line 'Neak Luong is a blur' (85) is also taken from a newspaper headline of *The Boston Globe*, referring to a soldier's account of the illegal American bombing of Cambodia.[17] Palmer proposes that the headline's blurring of history somehow legitimised the raid. Turning to the section where the line appears in *Sun*, it is apparent that the broader implications of this reading would not necessarily be lost on an uninformed reader: 'Let me say this. Neak Luong is a blur. It is Tuesday in the hardwood forest. I am a visitor here, with a notebook' (85). Invariably elements of Palmer's poetry demand a scholarly sourcing of the citations but there is a danger that this process overshadows a reading of the poetry. A broader configuration of intertextuality within an aesthetic of error as a series of traces, aberrations and ungrammaticalities offers a less agonistic reading of the lyric in *Sun*.

Error and intertextuality in *Sun*

In his appropriation of Baudelaire, Palmer recognises that the poet's work already exists as a complex of voices. The lyric cannot be considered as a hermetic or self-sufficient whole issuing from a singular authentic voice. An awareness of the text's limitations is clearly mediated by *Sun* and moving beyond intertextuality as a reading of direct citations, the volume as a whole hints at a process of inclusion, citation even plagiarism. *Sun* demonstrates an acute anxiety of how it

16 Laurie Ramey in her paper on Palmer at Southampton 10th May, 2000 showed this as an example from Palmer's manuscripts. The headline date is *The Sun* July 22nd 1986.
17 Gardner, p. 282.

may relate to borrowed sources and how the process of inclusion shifts the citation from its original context.

The evocation of the idealised book, the original work that serves as a template to be imitated or quoted, is a source that for Palmer is always displaced, pillaged or disfigured. In the 'Baudelaire Series' this sense of displacement is indicated in the statement 'Dear Book, you were never a Book' and the admonition to Rilke's poem 'Panther, You are nothing but a page torn from a book' (12). Later the ideal of the book is linked to censorship and a covert dissemination of its contents: 'You is she, a banned book. I have erased its title, something about conversations As for its pages, these I will hand to you one by one' (33). There are further references to the lost or destroyed work: 'The secret remains in the book', 'It is a book you lost/ It is a place from which you watch/ the burning of your house' (22). Later we are told that this house is 'the vacant house / (it will ask you something of song)/ Now it's the liar's burning house' (30). Palmer's reference to the philosophical dilemma of the Cretan liar (a Cretan says all Cretans are liars), and its problematising of truth conditions, is of specific significance for a consideration of the lyric; which becomes a site of site of conflict and contradiction. Rolf Breuer suggests that this dilemma indicates that 'no theory can be proved to be complete or non contradictory within itself; to do this a metatheory is required whose propositions belong to a higher logical level.'[18] Breuer's proposition complements an interpretation of Palmer's poetry as exhibiting a nostalgia for the book as cabalistic site. Since access to this idealised work remains untenable, contradiction and opposition constitute the texture of Palmer's lyric. It is therefore fitting that at the volume's close we are presented with both the destruction and symbolic renewal of the book, 'Pages torn from their spines and added to the pyre, so that they will resemble thought' (85). Although this may be an act of violation, it seems at the close of *Sun* a necessary one to curtail the agonistic impulse of the volume.

Approaching intertextuality as the availability of more than one language system in a text enables a closer examination of the lyric construction in Palmer's *Sun*. It is no accident that the first 'Sun'

18   Breuer, 'Irony, Literature, and Schizophrenia', p. 107.

section refers to 'Bakhtin's Names' (77). Bakhtin's *Dialogic Imagination* notoriously privileges the language of the novel as a site of verbal interaction or *heteroglossia*, in relation to what he indicates is the largely monologic or hermetic language of poetry. Bakhtin suggests that 'The world of poetry, no matter how many contradictions and insoluble conflicts the poet develops within it, is always illumined by one unitary and indisputable discourse.'[19] The novel he suggests is a dialogic site with a diversity of social speech types, and allows for interaction between the multiple voices within the work. Voice for Bakhtin indicates more than an originating source, since it suggests a complex of networks, beliefs and ideologies hence Dostoevsky's novels create a polyphonic score that is 'a plurality of independent and unmerged voices and consciousnesses.'[20] Bakhtin's insistence that the novel accommodates the inclusion of alien discourses, and his evocations of the novel as 'saturated', 'impregnated' and 'contaminated', challenges the conception of a unitary discourse. *Heteroglossic* language for Bakhtin then is not unlike a vast palimpsest, and one can begin to read this resonance as a certain density or opacity in the text.

Contrastingly, Bakhtin states that the poet is unable 'to oppose his own poetic consciousness ... Language is present to him only from inside' (286). He proposes that when the poet incorporates other discourses the effect is one of appropriation. Multiplicity in effect is subsumed by the poet's singular style or language:

> Elements of heteroglossia enter here not in the capacity of another language carrying its own particular points of view, about which one can say things not expressible in one's own language, but rather in the capacity of the depicted thing. Even when speaking of alien things, the poet speaks in his own language. (287)

19 Mikhail Bakhtin, 'Discourse in Poetry and Discourse in the Novel' in *The Dialogic Imagination*, ed. Michael Hoquist (Texas: University of Texas Press, 1981), p. 286.
20 Bakhtin, *Problems of Dostoevsky's Poetics*, trans. Caryl Emerson (Manchester: Manchester U.P., 1984), p. 6.

Bakhtin's criticism of poetry as a hermetic language 'the language of the gods' and the 'priestly language of poetry' (287) is a position that is wryly acknowledged by Palmer at the close of the final 'Sun'. The figure of the poet in this section is not an oracular prophet. Far from being a locus of authority, the lyric poet trades in his lyre and universal truths for vaudeville to become a performing jukebox:

> Let go of me for I have died and am in a novel and was a lyric poet, certainly, who attracted crowds to mountaintops. For a nickel I will appear from this box. For a dollar I will have text with you and answer three questions. (83)

Palmer's sardonic humour is evident the self-congratulatory retort 'I am in a novel' and the commodification of expression 'For a dollar I will have text with you'. However, Bakhtin's direct opposition between dialogic and monologic language raises pertinent issues for addressing the intertextual texture of Palmer's work. While *Sun* does provides citations which could be considered as examples of alien discourses in the text, the overall effect is not the polyphonic score of competing ideolects discussed in Charles Bernstein's poetry.[21] Yet, I would be at pains to relegate Palmer's work to a monologic discourse, since such oppositional poles need to be re-addressed in considering the intertextual texture and density of *Sun*.

There are gestures to multiple voices enacted in *Sun*, but the volume's response to their incorporation is contradictory. Initially *Sun* indicates that citation from other work can be performed as ventriloquism and the multiple sources become: 'dumb words mangled by use/ like reciting a lesson or the Lords Prayer ... and the tribe to show you its tongue. It has only one' (37). Palmer is far from Eliot's ambition to 'purify the dialect of the tribe',[22] since it is suggested here that the lesson leads only to a duplication of initial errors and mistakes. As *Sun* progresses there are gestures to a plurality of discourses and idiolects: 'In tongues books were written, suns/ rose wherever we placed them' (41). Multiple commentators surface dur-

---

21 For a full discussion of Charles Bernstein's 'ideolectical' poetics see Chapter One.

22 T.S. Eliot, 'Little Gidding', *The Four Quartets* in *Collected Poems* (London: Faber & Faber, 1970).

ing the course of the volume. The 'Baudelaire Series' is haunted by a variety of intrusive and competing voices generated self-reflexively: 'Words say', 'The poem says' and a sequence of drafted, anonymous voices 'You say', 'we say 'Someone says'. The final 'Sun' is dominated by a series of repeated commands issued from the margins of the text: 'Write this', 'Say this' 'Name you this'.

Approaching intertextuality as an intrusive polyphonic score does not further a reading of *Sun*. The seamless inclusion of quotations in this volume is closely allied to Palmer's ambition to write a composition 'with nothing at its center.'[23] Palmer's inclusion of citations as a ceding of the poet's place suggests that the strategy has less to do with Oedipal rivalry, than an acknowledgement of difference. Michael Worton and Judith Still's examination of intertextual strategies in Montaigne find that poetic sources remain uncited. Yet unlike Palmer's *Sun*, Montaigne's citations are quoted directly. Worton and Still suggest that Montaigne's approach indicates a mistrust of repetition leading him to 'valorise amnesia as a means of escaping the silencing tyranny of his predecessors.'[24] What is significant is how quotations function in the reading of a text, since Worton and Still suggest that the reader 'strives to incorporate the quotation into the unified textuality which makes of the text a semiotic unit' (11). This assertion returns us to the problem of origination which *Sun* investigates. Worton and Still indicate that:

> [To] quote is not merely to write glosses on previous writers; it is to interrogate the chronicity of literature and philosophy, to challenge history as determining tradition and to question conventional notions of originality and difference. Consequently, to read an explicitly (or even tacitly) quoting text is not to engage in a simple play with and of sources, but to recognise and establish a criterion of difference. (12)

This approach towards contextualisation provides a further understanding of Palmer's lyric. Rather than valorising amnesia, intertextuality in *Sun* strives towards prompting memory in Palmer's

---

23   Palmer, 'From the Notebooks', p. 343.
24   Michael Worton and Judith Still, *Intertextuality: Theories and Practices*, eds. Michael Worton and Judith Still (Manchester: Manchester U.P., 1990), p. 10.

poetry. But before assessing how successful this strategy may be, we need to consider intertextuality as a plurality of signifying systems in the text.

Barthes states that 'the intertext is not necessarily a field of influences: rather it is the music of figures, metaphors, thought words; it is the signifier as siren.'[25] Barthes's celebration of the intertext as a compulsive and alluring strategy draws us away from the text as a site of dogmatic struggle. *Writing Degree Zero* draws attention to the traces of other writing which invariably exist in any new piece of work:

> Writing still remains full of the recollection of previous usage, for language is never innocent: words have a second-order memory which mysteriously persists in the midst of new meanings. Writing is precisely this compromise between freedom and remembrance, it is the freedom which remembers and is free only in the gesture of choice, but is no longer so within duration.[26]

Barthes continues by drawing reference to the text as the site of *cryptographie* or cryptogram. He suggests that all texts work as palimpsestual traces. Barthes's evocation of the trace and cryptogram as a gesture to the formulation of Derridean *différance*. Of particular relevance to a consideration of Palmer's poetry is Barthes's gesture to a density or opacity in the text:

> A stubborn after-image comes from all the previous modes of writing and even from the past of my own, drowns the sound of my present words. Any written trace precipitates, as inside a chemical at first transparent, innocent and neutral, mere duration gradually reveals in suspension a whole past of increasing density, like a cryptogram. (17)

Barthes states that every text inevitably gestures to a history of writing, a proposition already made apparent throughout Palmer's *Sun*. The following examples draw attention to poetic language as inhabited by other texts: 'Desire was a quotation from someone' (37), 'This notebook contains shadows nothing else' (67), 'I want the stolen

---

25   *Roland Barthes by Roland Barthes*, trans. Richard Howard (London: Macmillan 1977), p. 145.
26   Barthes, *Writing Degree Zero*, pp. 16–17.

word here' (68), 'Here whispers collect dust' (69), 'The lines through these words /form other still longer lines' (78).

Barthes's comments alert us to a texture of historicity available in any piece of writing. Julia Kristeva's conceptualisation of intertextuality or *transposition*, provides a way of approaching the text as the 'cohabitation' of more than one sign system. Her discussion of intertextuality as a form of anamnesis furthers a consideration of Palmer's *Sun* as inscribing memory within the lyric. Kristeva interrogates the binary oppositions of monologic and dialogic discourse in Bakhtin which only seem to frustrate a reading of Palmer's lyric. Kristeva notably proposes that the process of signification is underwritten by instinctual drives and desires or the 'semiotic' which exist prior to meaning. She designates the passage from the semiotic into an articulation of meaning or signification as the 'thetic' phase and this passage is strongly modulated by what Kristeva identifies as the *chora*: 'the *chora* is a modality of significance in which the linguistic sign is not yet articulated as the absence of the object and the distinction between real and symbolic.'[27] The *chora* can be understood as a provisional process strongly allied to the semiotic 'which modifies linguistic structures' (88). This uneasy alliance between the semiotic and the symbolic is challenged in poetic language since the semiotic erupts rupturing the thetic border.

Kristeva suggests that signifying practice overlooks the instinctual and generative force of the *chora* by prioritising the emergent signifying system. Paradoxically, the *chora*'s provisional status is the lost component in symbolic signification; 'The process matrix of enunciation is in fact *anaphoric* since it designates an elsewhere: the *chora* that generates what signifies' (100). To focus on the process of signification Kristeva indicates 'would therefore be to break through any given sign for the subject, and reconstitute the heterogeneous space of its formation' (100). Kristeva proposes that 'rhythmic, lexical, even syntactic changes disturb the transparency of the signifying chain and open it up to the material crucible of its production' (101). This textual disruption has particular pertinence Palmer's work is how

---

27   Julia Kristeva, *Revolution in Poetic Language* (New York: Columbia U.P., 1984), p. 26.

Kristeva mediates this eruptive charge to a proposal of a 'subject in process.' Rather than a subject with memories to express, the 'subject in process' is a surge of energy which only forms reminiscences when its passage is traversed by obstacles or forms of resistance. The constant change to this pattern creates memories which are fragmentary and in constant rearrangement. Brief intervals of stasis prevent the process from degenerating into an 'opaque and unconscious organicity' (102) and challenges a fear of the text being subsumed by a continual present. Similarly, we could approach the interrupters in Palmer's lyric as resistances in the text. Such gestures could also be read as necessary intervals of stasis in the procedural pattern of reminiscence and memory in Palmer's poetry. Kristeva's intertextuality or *transposition* focuses on the alternation of the thetic phase in language. It involves the destruction of the old system and the forming of a new one:

> The term *inter-textuality* denotes this transposition of one (or several) sign system(s) into another; but since the term has been understood in the banal sense of 'study of sources', we prefer the term *transposition* because it specifies that the passage from one signifying system to another demands a new articulation of the thetic– of enunciative and denotative positionality ... Poetic mimesis maintains and transgresses thetic unicity by making it undergo a kind of anamnesis, by introducing into the thetic position the stream of semiotic drives and making it signify. (59–60)

Kristeva adopts Bakhtin's chains of binary oppositions, but she emphasises that both the monologic and dialogic poles can be found in any text. Palmer's '*After Rilke, "Orpheus Eurydike Hermes"*' from the 'Baudelaire Series', can be approached productively a 'transpositional' reading of Rilke's poem.

Initially it may seem problematic to situate the reworking of the Orpheus and Eurydice myth in a context of reminiscence, since there are indications in both Rilke and Palmer's poems that the narrative centres on a state of amnesia. Rilke portrays Eurydice as 'deep within herself. Being dead /filled her beyond fulfillment.'[28] Palmer's poem

---

28   Rainer Maria Rilke, *The Selected Poetry of Rainer Maria Rilke*, trans. Stephen Mitchell (New York: Vintage Press, 1989), pp. 49–53.

more problematically gives us these statements: 'I'm not here when I walk/ followed by a messenger confused/ (He's forgotten his name)'. His intertextual treatment of Rilke's poem enacts the three intersecting perspectives of Orpheus, Eurydice and the messenger god Hermes. Eurydice in the opening of Palmer's poem stutters through an elliptical and fragmentary narrative:

> You say
> A miracle from Heaven
>
> You say
> I'm fine I'm fine I'm really going blind
>
> Gay as a skylark today
> You say
>
> I haven't an ache or a pain
> in me in my body inside
>
> I'm fine I'm fine I'm really going blind
> It's a joy to be alive
>
> I had a visitor tonight
> with suit and beard and Malacca cane
>
> climbed through my window
> and entered me
>
> Is this such a bad thing
> Is this a thing at all
>
> Each evening there's a poppy in my brain
> which closes before dawn
>
> Whatever happened then will not happen again
> Please move my arm (23)

There is a carefully constructed anaphoric patterning in these lines and this mnemonic device continues throughout the poem. Against this texture of anaphora several lines function as interrupters, reading as quotations. 'Gay as a skylark today' is incongruous to the poem's subject matter, moreover the aphoristic folk wisdom of 'Whatever happened then will not happen again' is strangely forbidding and could be read as political rhetoric or as a newspaper headline. These interrupters posit a resistance to the mnemonic rhythm of the extract establishing a series of static plateaus in the poem.

Kristeva proposes that the essential operation for the 'subject in process' is 'that of the *appending of territories*– corporeal, natural, social– invested by drives' (104). In explaining what the claiming of territory entails she states: 'It involves *combination*: fitting together, detaching, including, and building up 'parts' into some kind of 'totality.' These parts may be forms, colors, sounds, organs, words etc., so long as they have been invested with a drive, and to begin with, 'represent only that drive' (102). But this process of combination is always then dynamited since the choric drive resists repetition and representation. Equally we can read Palmer's lyric as an accretion of sensations which never form an integral unity. Eurydice's statements start by building upon a sequence of impressions which are then dismantled and reassembled at every turn. In attempting to locate where Eurydice may be situated in the poem Palmer's lyric shifts from the response 'I haven't an ache or a pain/ in me in my body inside' to a sensation of somnambulence and anaesthesia 'Each evening there's a poppy in my brain' and to a final impression of restraint and pain 'Please move my arm'. The figure of Eurydice can only be represented as a sum of body parts since she is reconfigured constantly in the poem.

The competing perceptions of Orpheus, Eurydice and Hermes intersect with increasing rapidity:

> She says, Into the dark–
> almost a question–
> She says, Don't see things–
> this bridge– don't listen
>
> She says, Turn away
> Don't turn and return
> Count no more lines into the poem
> (Or could you possibly not have known

how song broke apart while all the rest watched—
that was years ago)
Don't say things
(You can't say things)
The ground is smooth and rough, dry and wet
Pull the blue coat closer around you
(There are three parts to you)
I'm not the same anymore

I'm not here where I walk
followed by a messenger confused
(He's forgotten his name)
I'm not here as I walk

not anyone on this path
but a figure of walking
a figure projected exactly this far
followed by a messenger confused

(He's forgotten his name)
Don't say his name for him
Don't listen to things
(You can't listen to things)

Some stories unthread what there was
Don't look through an eye
thinking to be seen
Take nothing as yours (24–5)

Palmer's poem is a sustained examination of 'how song broke apart' and focuses on the separate modalities which comprise the lyric, 'There are three parts to you'. These fragmentary statements create a conflicting impression of suspended animation and temporal oscillation. Junctures in the poem such as 'Or could you possibly not have known', 'I'm not here as I walk', indicate that a recalling of events serve only to further disrupt the narrative. Although it relies heavily on anaphoric constructions, the poem shows hostility to naming and representative accuracy: 'Don't say things/ You can't say things', 'Don't say his name for him/ Don't listen to things'. The work mediates an intersection of discourses which in turn perform an unthreading of the lyric 'I'. The complex of subjectivities can be read in the final lines: 'Don't look through an eye/ thinking to be seen/ Take nothing as yours'. These lines read as commentary on the myth of Orpheus and Eurydice, Orpheus of course does look back desiring recognition. But more alluring is a reading of the 'I' in the poem as a subject in process, negotiating memories as opposed to expressing them. Palmer's sustained analysis of utterance provides a reconsideration of memory in the lyric. The discontinuous structure of the poem with its constant interrupters offers a presentation of memory which is procedural. Indications of resistances often read as intertexts, errors or breaches in the text become obstacles that instigate a process of anamnesis in Palmer's poetry.

Reading ungrammaticalities: *Letters to Zanzotto* and *The Promises of Glass*

The use of citation in Palmer's lyric gives rise to an anxiety of reading which can be negotiated by Riffaterre's attention to intertexts as a series of 'ungrammaticalities.'[29] Riffaterre's analysis of grammatical structures dispel some of the interpretative anxieties that can arise from a reading of Palmer's poetry. Using Palmer's sequence 'Letters to Zanzotto' from *At Passages*[30] with Riffaterre's discussion and the poetry of Andrea Zanzotto, develops a further approach to reading a poetics of error and intertextuality. 'Letters to Zanzotto' can be read as a sequence of literary windows, the epistolary framework of this sequence enacts a dialogue between the Italian and American poet. Palmer mentions that the sequence emerged as a series of rhetorical questions to the poet, questions based on a shared preoccupation.[31]

Riffaterre focuses on poetry's application of what he calls 'a deviant grammar' or 'ungrammaticality' to generate meaning. Riffa-

29   Michael Riffaterre, *The Semiotics of Poetry* (Bloomington & London: Indiana U.P., 1978), p. 2.
30   Palmer, *At Passages* (New York: New Directions, 1995).
31   Palmer, University of Luton, 7th March, 2000.

terre's 'ungrammaticalities' designate as a way of alerting the reader to a breach or intrusion in the text. In opposition to the majority of reader-response criticism, Riffaterre attempts to establish how grammatical structures propel the reader towards an interpretative reading and secure an 'orientation imposed on the reader' (12). Riffaterre's 'ungrammaticalities' appear as a certain strangeness in the text, a juncture in the work or as a form of linguistic opacity. He indicates that ungrammaticalities 'thrust themselves forward as a stumbling block to be understood' (6). One can connect this proposal to resistances in the text since Riffaterre emphasises that poetic language is dialectical, what makes the poem 'has little to do with what it tells us or with the language it employs', instead the poem is dependent upon how it 'twists the mimetic codes out of shape by substituting its own structure for their structures' (13).

Riffaterre proposes that the reader strives to accommodate these alien junctures into the body of the text through a process of semiosis, leading to an overarching organising principle or *hypogram*. The *hypogram* grants an overall strategy to reading the poem; it functions to direct us 'under what conditions the lexical actualisation of seimic features, stereotypes or descriptive systems produce poetic words or phrases whose poeticity is either limited to one poem or is conventional' (22). Already 'ungrammaticalities' in the text are gesturing to a linguistic 'trace'. Worton and Still remind us that for Riffaterre ungrammaticalities 'alert the reader to the presence in the text s/he is reading of an (almost hidden) foreign body, which is the trace of an intertext' (26). Riffaterre moreover proposes that 'the only requisite [for reading] may be the presupposition of an intertext.'[32] For Riffaterre the intertext is once more not a direct citation to be sourced:

> When we speak of knowing an intertext, however, we must distinguish between the actual knowledge of the form and content of that intertext, and a mere awareness that such an intertext exists and can eventually be found somewhere. This awareness in itself may be enough to make readers experience the text's

32   Riffaterre, 'Interview', *Diacritics*, 11.4. (1981), 2–11 (p. 16).

literariness. They can do so because they perceive that something is missing from the text: gaps need to be filled.[33]

Riffaterre unwittingly alerts one to the key problem faced in approaching Palmer's work, it is precisely an awareness of the 'text's literariness' that induces readerly anxiety.

One of the criticisms lodged against Palmer's work is the impulse towards hermeticism in his project. Palmer does not necessarily see this as a failure suggesting 'there's an opposition even within hermetic verse ... One remembers the counter-discourse of such work as being enormously powerful, even if it doesn't stop anything from happening. But how *can* you stop things from happening?'[34] It is significant that Palmer's notebooks includes a citation from Riffaterre, 'the arbitrariness of language conventions seems to diminish as the text becomes more deviant and ungrammatical, rather than the other way around.'[35] Palmer hints at a threshold of guidance in his work suggesting that 'the reader completes the circuit',[36] indicating that there is a matrix of meaning to be connected in his work. While Palmer's poetics are not reducible to a paradigmatic plot, he refuses the smokescreen of a humorous errancy encountered in Bernstein's work.[37] Approaching the fifth letter from the Zanzotto series enables a dual reading with Riffaterre's propositions:

> Desired, the snow falls upward,
> the perfect future, a text
> of wheels. You were born here
> between noise and anti-noise
> in first bits of film,
>
> silvers of image, the *of*
> and its parts– particle
> as wave– the perfect

33   Riffaterre, 'Compulsory Reader Response: The Intertextual Drive,' in *Intertextuality: Theories and Practices*, pp. 56–7.
34   Palmer cited in Gardner's *Regions of Unlikeness*, p. 279.
35   Cited in 'from the Notebooks', p. 347.
36   Palmer, 'A Conversation', *American Poetry*, 3.1 (1986), 72–88 (p. 74).
37   For a reading of humour and error in Bernstein's poetry see Chapter One.

future's steps, its thousand lakes
bells, remarks, lunations and dismays

Days were called the speed book
then the scream book, rail
book then the book of rust, perfect–
bound, perfect shadow of a clock,
the photophilographer assembles in negative,

negative sun or negative shade,
negative dust pulled from the ground
and the images negated in ornate frames,
firebricks, funnels and trucks,
figment and testament as one (7)

Riffaterre's *The Semiotics of Poetry* draws attention to 'semes', 'kernel' and 'nuclear' words that poeticise the text in a self-referential process. The focus upon these individual words draws the reader to the overarching *hypogram* which is the poem's organising principle. Correspondingly, in Palmer's poem we there is a focus on 'anti' and 'negative' which indicates oppositions and inversions in the text. In the poem we are given the following binary oppositions; 'noise' and 'anti-noise', 'negative sun' and 'negative shade'. Moreover there is a radical sense of defamiliarisation in the world the poem creates since the 'snow falls upward'. These arresting images can be allied to the idea of 'the perfect future'. Yet if this phrase is taken as its inversion of the grammatical 'future perfect', it also suggests a future finalised or an action complete.

Working through this sense of opposition in the poem Palmer presents us with the neologism of the 'photophilographer' which suggests a combination of both photographer and philosopher, describing one who documents but is aware that the documentation has additional valences and dualities. 'Photophilographer' indicates an epistemological scrutiny combined with a focus on representative accuracy. Building from these dualities and schisms, Palmer's letter also focuses upon what is set between such dualities 'the *of* and its parts'. At the poem's close the concern with documentation and record shifts to filmic precision and analysis appearing to serve or link the imaginary and the real 'figment and testament as one'. The poem indicates that it is within erotic boundary or gap that the reader is born.

These ungrammaticalities are assimilated into a larger matrix of interpretation. But there remain dangers in processing ungrammaticalities to an overriding theme or accessible meaning to be unlocked in the poem. Veronica Forrest-Thomson alerts one to the problems inherent in such an interpretative approach which she characterises as 'naturalisation'. Forrest-Thomson suggests that this critical process is an attempt 'to reduce the strangeness of poetic language and poetic organisation by making it intelligible, by translating it into a statement about the non-verbal external world, by making the Artifice appear natural.'[38] She proposes that 'Good naturalisation dwells on the non-meaningful levels of poetic language, such as phonetic and prosodic patterns and spatial organisation, and tries to state their relation to other levels of organisation rather than set them aside in an attempt to produce a statement about the world' (xi). Artifice could be substituted here by Riffaterre's 'ungrammaticalities.' His insistence that the reader must presuppose the existence of an intertext in any work yet, does not necessarily have to know its immediate location, indicates that he too is sceptical of moving the poem to a definitive interpretation. But Forrest-Thomson's commentary alerts us to the dangers of imposing an all too rigorous grammatical methodology upon the poetic text and not enabling space for further interpretative ambiguities.

Palmer's poem builds upon kernel words, yet the effect is not a totalising conceit or theme. In *Sun*, Palmer's lyric relies on junctures in the text to prompt a shift in the poem. Sometimes a reminiscence that may be prompted or an intentional ceding of the poet's place to other discourses. The fifth letter in the Zanzotto series considers the atomisation of the text and an ambition towards accurate representation. The poem is also alert to the dangers of an overriding strategy or master plan, an anxiety which becomes apparent in the poem's yoking of words usually linked to industry and modernity in a literary context. In the poem we have 'a text made of wheels', 'the speed

38   Veronica Forrest-Thomson, *Poetic Artifice* (Manchester: Manchester U.P., 1978), p. xi.

book', 'rail book' and the 'book of rust'. The poem's close with its 'firebricks, funnels and trucks' points us to how this process of industrial systemisation forms a terrifying link with the practicalities of the Final Solution. Palmer could be criticised for pushing his text dangerously towards overt aestheticization but the resistances in the poem, its stumbling blocks and ungrammaticalities, read as an attempt to report history without recourse to memorialising images.

Palmer's focus on atomisation can be read in correspondence with Zanzotto's work. Consider the opening of Zanzotto's 'The Perfection of Snow':

> How many perfections, how many
> how many totalities. Stinging it adds.
> And then abstractions, astrifications astral formulations
> star-chill, across sidera and coelos
> star chills assimilations–
> I would proceed in the perfected
> beyond the blinding dazzle, of the full and the empty,
> I would search out proceedings
> standing out, avoiding
> the doubtful, the dark; I'd know I'd say.[39]

Zanzotto's poem provides an examination of form and structure. The images of snow create a curious opposition between 'the full and the empty'. The poem simultaneously gestures to the filling in of significant patterns on a blueprint and an obliteration of form. Zanzotto's poem questions concepts of singularity as perfection and a template of the ideal. Acting on a sense of multifariousness, the poem attempts to navigate a linguistic relationship to the world and this opening tract or treatise posits the problem of how to return to the originary and the authentic. The visual pattern of the snow creates not only word substitutions, but also displacements and figurations leading away from snow: 'abstractions', 'astrifictions', 'astral form-ulations', 'star chills assimulations'. The structure of no two snow-flakes are the same and the fractal forms exemplify a series of differences. Even in translation one hears the slant echo or skewed

---

39   Andrea Zanzotto, *Selected Poetry of Andrea Zanzotto*, eds. and trans. Ruth Feldman and Brian Swann (Princeton: Princeton U.P., 1975), p. 211.

design in the string of comparatives, the syllabic embeddings generate a series of differences too. Looking closely at the structure of form generates further abstractions in the poem. Paradoxically the analysis of structure delays the search for the essence of the object, the surface strata of the snowflake only gestures to the formulation of other structures. Similarly the last line from this section is implicated in an analysis of structure and identity, the hesitant 'I'd know, I'd say', indicates that the subject is under examination too. Gino Rizzo suggests that Zanzotto's poetry mines the interstices between *langue* and *parole*:

> Zanzotto assumes as object of his communication the very tension that exists between his unique parole and its reference to la langue of his cultural koiné. This he does at the expense of self-expression, or rather by integrating the expression of the self in the fabric of his work, by making the 'object' of his communication the new (and only 'real') object, which is the work itself. Freeing the sign from any link to a pre-existing 'meaning', the linguistic speculation of the poet becomes the mirror for a heteronomous intelligence of socially conditioned linguistic codes.[40]

The gesture to the intertextual density in Zanzotto's poetry can be applied to Palmer's work. One can see from our brief reading of *At Passages* how Zanzotto offers an attractive counter-lyrical strategy to Palmer's scrutiny of the lyric. Palmer's slightly later volume, *The Promises of Glass*, combines this approach to the lyric with a gesture to rhetorical figures which can be characterised as a slight movement from hermeticism to the ludic.[41]

It seems significant that *The Promises of Glass* features a series of eighteen autobiographical portraits. In this sequence we find Palmer's lyric demonstrating a carnivalesque approach. Palmer suggests that his recent volumes have been drawn to a 'theatricalization of rhetorical figures' and proposes that this shift generates an anti-rhetorical strategy where he uses 'the figures of rhetoric to expose

---

40   Gino Rizzo, 'Zanzotto, "*fabbro del parlar materno*"' in *Selected Poetry of Andrea Zanzotto* (p. 309).

41   Palmer, *Promises of Glass* (New York: New Directions, 2000).

themselves.'[42] In closing upon a reading of the fifth portrait from the sequence, the final space is given to Palmer reading Palmer, a fitting closure to an intertextual study of Palmer's lyric. Initially the poem reads as a stand-up routine commenting on a body of work and even twisting the rhetoric of the journal interview:

> Not exactly a mark, not exactly a trace.
> More like a segment of recording tape.
>
> After I arrived I took a job painting broccoli, cabbage and squash
> on supermarket windows
>
> as I was putting on my face:
> base blusher, mascara, ultra high-gloss lip enamel
>
> when the word *"zurückgehen"* flooded my brain
> as if spoken by the mirror
>
> over the dressing table in which an image
> no longer gathered much light, its
>
> reflecting glaze having decayed.
> We were so close that the way
>
> we came apart was not even visible to the participants.
> Then I became a painter of paintings briefly
>
> then I eliminated paint
> Dear Phil, What a hellish season its been.
>
> For a time I thought I was another
> but now I'm selling shovels and rakes, running a few guns
>
> and awaiting the arrival
> of a photographic apparatus. (17–18)

Reading the opening as a ludic chronology of Palmer's work, the lines present an interview of the poet as celebrity. The modulation of the extract is perhaps camp but not darkly ironic. Reading the intertext of

42 Palmer, Interview: Conducted by Peter Gizzi' in *Exact Change Yearbook #1*, ed. Peter Gizzi (Boston: Exact Change, 1995), pp. 161–79 (p. 176).

the intertext, Palmer in the opening lines is perhaps responding to a critical analysis of his work. Norman Finkelstein's criticism of *Notes for Echo Lake*'s texture as 'an endlessly reproducible synthetic discourse',[43] comes to mind in reading 'a segment of recording tape'. The loaded words 'mark' and 'trace' gestures to the intertextual density of Palmer's writing. Moreover the focus on the German '*zurückgehen*' cannot but satisfy the reader of intertextuality in Palmer's work. Initially the translation points to 'recede' which returns us to Palmer's suggestion of 'the analytic lyric' as a ceding of the poet's place in the poem. But a certain inconsistency if not opposition arises when one considers the valences of this verb: *zurückgehen auf–* to trace back, and *wieder zurückgehen–* to untread. These valences are not lost on Palmer, and suggest an acute awareness of how intertexts in his work are sometimes integrated seamlessly within the text. The 'decay' of the mirror refers us to *Echo Lake's* fascination with the myth of Narcissis,[44] and the humorous 'we were so close that the way/ we came apart was not even visible to the participants' and 'I thought I was another' could refer to Palmer's sustained examination of the lyric subject in *Sun*. The final comment 'awaiting the arrival of a photographic apparatus' draws us to the poet's neologism of the writer as 'photophilographer' in *At Passages*

Possibly I am performing my own interpretative 'naturalisation' upon the poem but Palmer can out manoeuvre his reader quickly. He closes by indicating strategies for new work which pose further problems concerning memory and narrative:

> Perhaps if a face can be recorded–
> but isn't that another story?
>
> Isn't there another story
> consistent with sand?
>
> How it turns to mirror–glass
> when heated in your hand.

43 Norman Finkelstein, 'The Case of Michael Palmer', *Contemporary Literature*, 29.4 (1988), 518–37 (p. 529).
44 See Chapter Three

144

The sounds it makes
make another story.

It is completely silent here
so we hear nothing but high and low tones

constantly
as we take inventory.

The people come in shades of blue.
They take everything from you. (19)

The initial carnival of the poem dissipates into a sombre reflection. Although Palmer begins with a rhetorical flourish, these closing lines indicate unease directed at the critic who reads Palmer's lyric only as an intertextual *bricolage* to be sourced and not transposed to a further reading. Reading the intertextual impulse in Palmer's poetry through a configuration of error as a series of aberrations, resonances, ungrammaticalities and traces in the text, provides a productive methodology for understanding the rupturing of the lyric in his work. Most importantly, this alternative reading of intertextuality enables a reading of Palmer's lyric not as an anxiety of influence' but as demonstrating a responsibility to an earlier tradition of the lyric. Cast in this light, the figurative and often illusive backdrop of the European lyric in Palmer's work allows him to scrutinise his relationship to an earlier constellation of voices, without reducing their inclusion to a pedagogical ambition.

Chapter Five
Erring in Lyn Hejinian's Poetry of the 1980s

The publication of *The Language of Inquiry* offers a position from which to assess the trajectory of Lyn Hejinian's poetics.[1] Collecting most of her essays and papers given over the last thirty years the chronological mapping of the writing reads as a pivotal moment in the poet's critical placing. But Hejinian expresses some concern that the collection may be misread as a pedagogical manual to her poetry:

> It would be a mistake to regard the poetics represented here as a discourse for which poetry is merely exemplary, one for which poetry stands at a distance, objectified and under scrutiny. Rather, these essays assume poetry as the dynamic process through which poetics, itself a dynamic process, is carried out. (1)

The prefaces which introduce the essays are an attempt to update the original enquiry and 'preserve the spirit of provisionality in which they were first written' (4). Hejinian is not only attuned to her own critical placing but indicates that her poetics are subject to revision. The nature of the 'inquiry' which both poetry and poetics embrace is often one of contradiction and epistemological transition. Hejinian's insistence upon a poetics that is neither predetermined nor asserting claims for authority lends itself to a reading of error. Broaching Hejinian's work through a configuration of error helps identify the nature of provisionality which the poet insists, furthering a consideration of an 'open-text' as being more than a poetics of play. Increasingly her essays indicate that the epistemological uncertainty her poetics advocates is strongly allied to an understanding of ethics. Eventually it is necessary to consider whether an ethical claim for the

---

1   Lyn Hejinian, The *Language of Inquiry* (Berkeley: University of California Press, 2000) p.1. Further references to Hejinian's essays will be taken from this collection, unless otherwise noted, and the original dates of publication will be indicated in the footnotes.

poetics can be made, and if a configuration of error has any role in its practice.

Hejinian's proposal of a poetics as 'erring' that is wandering, roaming irregularly and with no apparent itinerary, initially suggests a certain aimlessness But an erring poetics is more than an unproblematic abnegation of mastery. A textual serpentine wandering appears to bypass the problems of rhetorical performance that Hejinian is keen to avoid. Yet, a further understanding of erring focuses on the intentional inconsistencies and the aphoristic texture of Hejinian's poetry. Aphorisms in her poetry are often sabotaged by the substitution of a word or phrase. Far from reading substitutions as malapropisms, this aphoristic tendency staggers the poem's movement towards a phenomenological enquiry. Cast in this light an erring poetics raises useful possibilities and problems for refiguring the lyric impulse in contemporary poetry

Surprisingly, turning to the field of science, commonly associated with epistemological certainty, helps to problematise the initial assumption of error as unequivocal mistake. Robert Kalechofsky's *Knowing and Erring* examines how an evolving mathematical theory must be read as part of a developmental epistemology.[2] Broadening his discussion from a historical understanding of the transitions in mathematical formulae he claims that 'all knowledge is based on knowing structures embedded in a testing and erring process' (13). Most significantly, he indicates that an understanding of error necessitates a reading of context:

> Knowing and erring are two sides of the same coin. To know includes judgment of error and to characterize a belief as erroneous is to assert some new knowledge. Therefore a study of erring should illuminate the knowing process and its structure ... Erring is a relativistic concept. That is, a judgment of error is made from the point of view of the judger but, to repeat, since the individual or cultural group which is said to be in error is not originally in *its* judgement in error, we must say that there is no absolute error, since such a view would depend on everyone's point of view being consonant throughout all time. (39)

2   Robert Kalechovfsky, *Knowing and Erring: The Consolations of Error* (Marblehead MA: Micah Publications, 1997).

Kalechofsky's assertion that there is 'no absolute error' places a focus on an indeterminate passage of erring instead. His proposition that erring offers a form of 'new knowledge', may initially draw some parallels with Hejinian's poetics of transition. But we will need to consider what form of knowledge a context of erring generates in Hejinian's writing particularly later in relation to the poetry's claims for an ethical performance. Kalechovfsky's account enables us to begin considering error as more than a radical disjuncture with the past. Erring in Hejinian's work is also suggestive of a certain accretion, which certainly complicates the idea of error as epistemological certainty.

Hejinian's early essays offer an initial consideration of an erring poetics. A reference occurs in the work 'A Thought is the Bride of What's Thinking,'[3] and her remarks are perhaps more consistent with the initial approach of error as mistake. Usefully Hejinian draws attention to a form of tracing, retreading or repetition informing an errant passage that is by no means a narrative of progress:

> Distortion, or error, To err is to wander, probably in an unanticipated direction, inadvertently. The mistake is not necessarily without advantage, though it may be irrevocable.
>
> Ink, or, the guitar. Returning from the middle distances, to the same points, repeatedly, from whatever direction, one homes, like a nomad or migrant. Perhaps that is a function of thought, nomadic homing– undertaken (consciously or not) in defiance of all narratives of progress. (15)

The identification of 'err' as wandering is consistent with its etymological root– deriving from Latin *errãre*– to stray, wander or rove. Initially Hejinian suggests that the 'mistake' may not be recalled or even memorialised. Paradoxically 'irrevocable' also suggests something which is unalterable or even fixed. Mining this dilemma, the second section presents two contradictory assertions in the oxymoronic 'nomadic homing' claiming that a return to a point of origin is a tenable aim. This section betrays an inflexion of Gertrude Stein's

3   *The Language of Inquiry*, pp. 7–21. Originally published in 1976.

notorious itinerary of 'beginning again and again'.[4] In this understanding, the insistent gesture of 'homing' is not an innocent retreat to a point of origin. Stein declares in 'Portraits and Repetitions' 'there is no such thing as repetition' (100) and continues 'It is not repetition if it is that what you are actually doing because naturally each time the emphasis is different' (107).

Stein's work features as a consistent point of reference for Hejinian's poetics and the parallels with her become clearer if one considers the erring proposed in 'If Written is Writing.'[5] The process of accretion in Hejinian's work is harnessed to an evocation of a Steinian insistence upon a text that is not writing, but 'composition'. She indicates that a focus on the suggestiveness of language generates a self-perpetuating linkage of associations: 'This becomes an addictive motion– but not incorrect, despite such distortion, concentration, condensation, deconstruction and digressions that association by, for example pun and etymology provide; an allusive psycho-linguism ... The process is composition rather than writing' (28). Certainly these propositions can be placed alongside early Language Writing's preoccupation with the viscosity and materiality of language.[6] But Hejinian's gesture to a lateral movement that is 'not incorrect' in the text, coupled with her insistence upon composition rather than writing, draws from Stein's infamous 'Composition as Explanation' and the evocation of a Jamesian continual present: 'The time of the composition is the time of the composition. It has been at times a present thing, it has been at times a past thing, it has been at times a future thing it has been at times an endeavour at parts of all of these things. In my beginning it was a continuous present a beginning again and again and again' (29). This form of temporal folding in Stein's work suggests an accretive measure; the insistence on the 'time of the composition' allows one to consider the text as an ongoing method of

4   Gertrude Stein, *Look at Me Now and Here I am*, ed. Patricia Meyerowitz (London: Penguin, 1984), p. 26.
5   *The Language of Inquiry*, pp. 25–9. Originally published in 1978.
6   See Charles Bernstein 'I want to establish the material the stuff of writing, in order, in turn, to base a discussion of writing on its medium rather than on preconceived ideas of subject matter or form', *Contents Dream 1975–1984* (Los Angeles: Sun & Moon Press, 1986), p. 63.

150

description which is not harnessed to immobilising or objectifying the world. In the later 'Two Stein Talks', Hejinian draws attention to Stein's work as an 'encounter with the world.'[7] This word encounter is significant, and as we will later see, belies an important element in the development of Hejinian's own poetics. Peter Nicholls draws attention to this sense of 'encounter' as a thread between Stein and Hejinian's work in their application of a 'phenomenological literature'.[8] Urging us to understand Stein's work not purely in the terms of self-reflexivity, but as a 'dynamic sense of inherence in the world' (242), Nicholls suggests that the nature of this encounter could be read as 'a refusal of any pursuit of knowledge or truth which would seek to reduce the other to the same' (243). Viewed in a context of erring, the condition of 'knowledge' in Hejinian's work becomes tentative at best, and even ascribes to an erring poetics as the possibility of recognising and acknowledging alterity.

It is significant that Hejinian also gestures to ethics in these early essays. In 'A Thought is the Bride of What Thinking',[9] a tentative sketching of an ethical poetics is indicated by Hejinian's discussion of an 'inclusive art' which performs a certain 'integrity' (20). Characteristically Hejinian re-evaluates and redeploys the word 'integrity' stating that it is not indicative of completeness but instead 'an infinite capacity for questioning' (20). Calling for responsibility and responsiveness, the claim of this early essay is slightly elliptical, and Hejinian's celebration of multiplicity and inclusiveness uncannily prefigures Charles Bernstein's more recent evocation of a poetry of multiple 'ideolects.'[10] Of particularly importance to an inflexion of erring is Hejinian's warning against 'the dangerous purism of a conventional dictionary definition of the ethical '("the condition of not being marred or violated; unimpaired or uncorrupted condition; original, perfect state; soundness")' (20). While this comment does not

---

7   *The Language of Inquiry*, pp. 83–130 (p. 97). Originally published in 1986. .
8   Peter Nicholls, 'Phenomenal Poetics Reading Lyn Hejinian' in *The Mechanics of the Mirage: Postwar American Poetry*, eds. Michel Delville and Christine Pagnouelle (Liège: Université de Liège, 2000), pp. 241–51 (p. 242).
9   *The Language of Inquiry*, pp. 7–21. Originally published in 1975.
10   See Chapter One, particularly the discussion of 'Poetics of the Americas.'

propose an 'erring ethics' per se, it suggests an ethical enquiry which ultimately remains unformulated and not predetermined. Earlier in the essay she proposes that 'to have definite and final opinions, is a matter of doubt to the ethical intellect' (20). There is an equivocal oscillation in this early piece between Hejinian's gesture to the ethical as being non-prescriptive and the closing evocation of the writer exerting a 'moral force of combination' (21).

I will examine a cross-section of Hejinian's poetry from the mid eighties and this chapter focuses on *The Guard* from the volume *The Cold of Poetry*.[11] A primary difficulty is to illustrate how an evolving concern with an ethical, and what I propose is ultimately an erring enquiry, can be linked to a discussion of Hejinian's earlier lyric forms. It is only after this initial mapping of Hejinian's poetics that one can later consider how error may be allied to an ethical enquiry of the lyric and assess overall how effective these claims may be in practice.

The Guard and the lyric dilemma

The writing of *The Guard* is meditated upon at some length in the essay 'Language and "Paradise."'[12] Hejinian indicates that the poem began as a response to the opening Canto of Dante's *Divine Comedy*. This gesture to an epic terrain of purposeful roaming presents a significant cue to a reading of erring. Hejinian remarks that her attraction to Dante's opening lines: ('Midway this way of life we're bound upon/ I woke to find myself in a dark wood /Where the right road was well and truly gone'),[13] stemmed from a proposition of a work beginning in 'the middle' (86). Unsurprisingly, this epic opening appears as a skewed intertext in *The Guard*. Near the centre of Hejinian's poem

11   Hejinian, *The Cold of Poetry* (Los Angeles: Sun & Moon Press, 1994).
12   Hejinian, 'Language and "Paradise"', *Line*, 6 (1985), 83–99. Further references in the text will be to Hejinian's original essay.
13   Dante, *The Divine Comedy: Hell*, trans. Dorothy L Sayers (Middlesex: Penguin, 1974), p. 71.

we find the following evocation: 'When memorized midway this life we lie on/ But there was no reply– my husband/ had gone back to sleep (27). Taken out of context, this appropriation of Dante's line translates the heroic epic into a ludic evocation of everyday life.

Hejinian's intentions are complex, what is taken from this 'beginning' is less an imposition of spatial grid, cartography or itinerary upon the poem than an invocation to consider what the essay points to as 'the lyric dilemma'. The title 'Language and "Paradise"' is drawn from the closing line of *The Guard*. These two words propose a certain lyric aporia which motivating the writing of the poem. A reading of this 'dilemma' appears to return us to Dante's problematic of capturing experience into words:

> Dante says 'I turn the face of my words towards the poem itself, and address it' ... The word 'captives' refers to several things. First and most important, to capturing the world in words. I want to explain to myself the nature of the desire to do so, and wonder aloud if it is possible. The poem opens with a challenge to the poem itself and raises the lyric dilemma. (91)

The impossibility of harnessing experience through language is seen less as inadequacy than a celebration of a desire located within language. More recently Hejinian makes reference to an understanding of 'dilemma' and 'aporia' in the light of Jacques Derrida's examination of the irresolvable doubts and hesitations elicited from the reading of a text.[14] What is most alluring in Hejinian's early account of this problem is the indication that language generates a persistent 'restlessness'. Hejinian frames this characteristic in 'The Rejection of Closure' as a 'Faustian' longing for knowledge and a continual 'curiosity.'[15] The form that this knowledge takes is constantly reviewed in the poetry. 'Paradise' in Hejinian's configuration suggests 'a horizontal or spatial sense of time, eternity being that moment when time is transmuted into space' (86). Against this is the proposal of language as a constant perceptual encounter with the world which exerts a particular temporal 'pressure' upon the work. In a later essay Hejinian

---

14   See Hejinian's 'Reason', in *The Language of Inquiry*, pp. 337–54.
15   *The Language of Inquiry*, pp. 40–58 (p. 49). Originally published in 1985.

refs to the line as establishing a form of 'perceptual rhythm' in her poetry.[16]

Viewed in this light, *The Guard* becomes less the quest for the 'right road' lost, than a focus within a pattern of erring in an attempt to sustain the temporal mobility of the poem. The poem enfolds domestic tableaux, political remarks and self-reflexive commentary within a labyrinthine enquiry of the lyric. These elements combined induce a general sense of accretion and a saturation of the text which frequently 'overspills' into aphoristic observation. The tension in *The Guard* between a constantly shifting process of perception and encounter, and an impulse towards an aphoristic display that frequently slips, generates a thwarted mobility. Hejinian indicates that her intention is 'to set the work in motion against itself, so to speak, to establish the inward concentricity, the pressure, the implosive momentum that stands for the conflict between time and space in the poem' (85).

The opening section *of The Guard* locates the lyric within a passage of erring:

> Can one take captives by writing–
> 'Humans repeat themselves.'
> The full moon falls on the first. I
> 'whatever interrupts.' Weather and air
> drawn to us. The open mouths of people
> are yellow & red– of pupils.
> Cannot be taught and therefore cannot be.
> As a political leading article would offer
> to its illustrator. But they don't invent
> they trace. You match your chair.
>
> Such hopes are set, aroused
> against interruption. Thus–
> in securing sleep against interpretation.
> Anyone who could believe can reveal
> it can conceal. A drive of remarks
>
> and short rejoinders. The seance
> or session. The concentric lapping.

16 'Line', in *The Language of Inquiry*, pp. 131–34 (p. 133). Originally published in 1988.

> If the world is round & the gates are gone...
> The landscape is a moment of time
>
> that has gotten into position.
> Why not arrive until dawn. Cannot be taught
> and therefore cannot be
> what human cunning can conceal. (11)

This extract reads as a constantly interrupted meditation; propositions and aphorisms build up through parataxis. The opening is preoccupied with ideas of restraint, enclosure, focus and even pedagogy. Hejinian comments that *The Guard* is 'about words ... It's words who are guards. And users of words. Do they guard us or do they guard their things? And are they keeping something in or something out?'[17] There are rules and constraints acknowledged in this section, actions are 'repeated', anything that 'Cannot be taught' 'cannot be', and we are told 'they don't invent they trace'. Even the cartoon is prompted, if not guided by the rhetoric of the political leading article. We can re-connect the 'leading article' with the prominence of 'one' 'first' and 'I' in the opening lines. Evidently Hejinian's poetry places a troubled focus on the authority of the static, single speaking subject.

The poem's position on the 'I' or 'whatever interrupts' is am-biguous, and a broaching of a lyric dilemma presents us with a contra-dictory pose of 'hopes' which are somehow 'aroused against interruption'. In 'Two Stein Talks' Hejinian indicates that she resists Henry James's conceptualisation of consciousness as a stream of thought or a certain continuum. Consciousness Hejinian remarks 'often does appear to be broken up, discontinuous– sometimes radically, abruptly and disconcertingly so.' (103). 'Language and Paradise'' proposes that the lyric 'appears to seek to extend the continuity of consciousness' (95). The poem enacts an ambivalence towards this pressure for continuity associated with the lyric form. It is suggested that such a procedure or 'naturalisation'[18] of poetic lan-

---

17   Hejinian, 'Comments for Manuel Brito', in *The Language of Inquiry*, pp. 177–98 (p. 196). Originally published in 1992.
18   See Veronica Forrest-Thomson, *Poetic Artifice* (Manchester: Manchester U.P., 1978).

guage conceals and denies an interpretative freedom. A sense of 'denial' can be extended to the repression of a latent meaning that remains condensed or hidden in 'securing sleep against interpretation'. While the line may not point definitively towards Freud's *Dream-Work*, it evokes a preoccupation with a trace or encryption which the text may 'guard'.[19] This reading could be re-inscribed within Hamlet's notorious equivocation of 'To sleep perchance to dream', to unravel a further aspect of a lyric 'dilemma' as a paralysis between intention and action latent in the text.

The Guard is suspicious of any claim for a lyric continuity and extension of lyric consciousness which might smother the provocative imbrication of meaning in the text. Yet, is it enough to relegate this ambition to a focus on a poetics of play and deferral? The preoccupation with authority in the opening of the sequence indicates that there is an intention at work. Derrida's discussion of Freud's 'Mystic Writing Pad' offers a further perspective on the equivocal dilemma between discontinuity and continuity in Hejinian's poetics:

> Writing is unthinkable without repression. The condition of writing is that there would be neither a permanent contact nor an absolute break between strata: the vigilance and failure of censorship. It is no accident that the metaphor of censorship should come from the arena of politics concerned with deletions, blanks and disguises in writing.[20]

Although Derrida is reading Freud's work as a consideration of a psychic temporality of writing, his discussion draws an interesting link with *The Guard*'s obsessive return to mechanisms of concealment. Hejinian indicates that the lyric's impulse towards continuity must not simply be read as a narrative of progress. A drive towards progress is associated with a display of authority and there are already indications that Hejinian reads this display as a censorial proviso upon the composition.

---

19   At the time of writing, Hejinian is engaged in an extensive work entitled *The Book of a Thousand Eyes*, 'a night work'.
20   Jacques Derrida, *Writing and Difference*, trans. Alan Bass (London: Routledge, 1997), p. 226.

The close of the section returns to more familiar inter-textual territory, we are certainly in a Dante-esque landscape with the indication 'the gates are gone'. There is also an invitation to an errant passage of 'concentric lapping' and the momentum of the poem appears to accelerate in relation to its awareness of a world locatable outside of the poem; 'The landscape is a moment of time/ that has gotten in position'. This 'surplus' or saturation in the text is once more thwarted by the repeated execution of the aphorism 'Cannot be taught'. The gnomic statement is then undermined by the reference to a certain 'human cunning.' Reading the line intertextually allows one to consider an Edenic fall, as human curiosity becomes human error and a banishment outside the 'gates'. This proposition is eerily evoked later in the poem as a resurrection of ghosts 'longing to have their feet fit in boots./ And finish in Eden' (15). Moving away from a purely citational reading, *The Guard* strikes a warning against a predetermined itinerary. The context of pedagogy alerts us to an alternative poetics which is not predisposed to asserting claims to authority or definitive knowledge; a poetics which Hejinian notoriously in 'The Rejection of Closure' draws attention to as an open-text where 'The writer relinquishes total control and challenges authority as a principle and control as a motive' (43).

The Guard, authority and the lyric

Before examining how the errant passage of *The Guard* unfolds, it is imperative to consider what the text is be responding to in its troubled focus on authority. In 'Reason' Hejinian goes as far as to stress that 'what we don't want, of course, is a reason that plows its way to authority.'[21] This suspicion of authority looms large in *The Guard*, and a central question is whether a serpentine wandering in the text counters the problems of rhetorical performance that Hejinian clearly

21 *The Language of Inquiry*, pp. 337–54 (p. 351) Originally presented and published in 1998.

identifies. Moreover the closing lines of the poem 'this is the difference between language and "paradise"' (37), offers a further literary precedent which enables an understanding of *The Guard* as a particular response to the lyric as song or music. The search for an aesthetic which problematises the lyric's claim to mastery is given cryptically by the assertion 'what I wanted was nothing to do with monuments' (29).

The Guard resists an epic ambition by offering an account of quotidian experience within a poetics of defamiliarisation. In assessing the role that erring may play the formulation of these resistances, one needs to consider what *The Guard* may be responding against. The title of 'Language and "Paradise"' in its accounting of a lyric dilemma can also be read as a response to Ezra Pound's admission of failure at the close of *The Cantos*: 'I have tried to write Paradise ... Let the Gods forgive what I /have made/ Let those I love try to forgive/ what I have made.[22] The legacy of Pound for recent American poets is understandably a problematic one, not least in considering the failed political ambitions of *The Cantos*. Pound's politics, coupled with his pedagogical statements on poetic language, provides an antithetical precedent to early Language Writing's broad ambitions to create 'writing as politics and not writing about politics.'[23] Bob Perelman in examining a chronology of conflicts in orthographic procedures in American Poetry draws attention to 'Pound's ideology of accuracy.'[24] An impetus for linguistic precision is certainly inscribed in Pound's statements on poetry, but Perelman's attention to 'ideology' points to the grand scale ambition of a pedagogical instruction which could be organised around the rhetoric of the 'ego scriptor' as Pound called himself in *The Cantos*. Certainly Hejinian does not want to emulate Pound's politics of writing in her own application of a Dante-esque journey in *The Guard*.

22   Ezra Pound, *The Cantos* (London: Faber and Faber, 1990) (CXX), p. 816.
23   Bruce Andrews, 'Poetry as Explanation, Poetry as Praxis', in *Postmodern American Poetry: A Norton Anthology*, ed. Paul Hoover (New York: Norton, 1994), pp. 668–72 (p. 669).
24   Bob Perelman, *The Marginalization of Poetry* (Princeton: Princeton U.P., 1996), p. 88.

In her correspondence with Bernstein, Hejinian explicitly vocalises her disapproval of the Poundian trajectory of *The Cantos*.[25] The following extract responds to Bernstein's paper 'Pounding Fascism'[26] and while Hejinian's remarks do not disavow 'the fact of Pound', she stresses her dislike of the dictatorial impulse of his poetics:

> I'm not sure that you succeed in conveying (to the audience) your disrespect for Pound at the same time that you admit value to certain of his strategies. But of course I see that you want to challenge the positions of both those who would deny the fact of Pound, and those who would accept the entirety of the package. The fluidity of your perspective (which is what he would have wanted to disallow) is the relevant point here, I guess.[27]

Bernstein articulates his abhorrence of the politics inscribed in *The Cantos* and critiques the tendency of commentators to relegate the politics of the work to an attention upon aesthetics. Importantly he examines the curious paradox of *The Cantos*, how Pound's increasingly desperate claims for authority in the work are in fact sabotaged by the complex textuality if not polyvocality of his own creation. As Bernstein puts it 'The authority then is not in Pound's opinions but in *The Cantos* itself ... In the struggle for control, Pound's methods and materials routed Pound's authority and preconceptions' (124). It is precisely this impossibility of denying 'the fact of Pound' which Nicholls examines in his discussion of recent American poetry.[28] He suggests that in responding to Pound's extensive claims for authority, that subsequent generations have mined these textual inconsistencies and interstices to produce a writing of radically different aims and

25   Pound does appear briefly in the following essays by Hejinian, 'Forms in Alterity', 'Barbarism' and 'Reason' but more as a literary point of reference.
26   This paper was originally given in 1984 (the year which *The Guard* was published), and subsequently appears in Bernstein's *A Poetics* (Harvard U.P., 1992), pp. 121–27.
27   Letter to Charles Bernstein dated 29th December 1984 MSS 74/2/10. Courtesy of *Mandeville Special Collections Library* at the University of California San Diego and by permission of the author.
28   Nicholls, 'Beyond *The Cantos*: Ezra Pound and Recent American Poetry' in *The Cambridge Companion to Ezra Pound* (Cambridge: Cambridge U.P., 1999), pp. 139–60.

ambitions. Indeed as Nicholls notes '*The Cantos* retains its Alpine prominence partly because it fails to achieve the kind of coherence Pound desired for it.' (156).

It may appear curious to place *The Guard* in relationship to Pound's poetics given Hejinian's evident interest in a different strand of American Modernism (made prevalent in her writing on Stein and the work of George Oppen).[29] Most suggestive is *The Guard*'s initial attention to music as the project 'Of science for its practitioners' (13). In her complex interrogation of the lyric, Hejinian's work re-routes the precedent found in Pound's statements on poetry to establish an equivocatory relationship with his propositions on music. A focus on music enables a reading of the impression of accretion and saturation prevalent in her poetry and its responsiveness to an analogy of the lyric as song. Moreover Hejinian's attention to an errant enquiry or an enfolding within the text proposes an aesthetic of the everyday. An erring poetics enables Hejinian to gesture to a sense an infinite inclusiveness, which the workshop aesthetic with its focus on the lyric epiphany cannot. As a strategy, erring generates an impression of saturation which in turn complements the aphoristically dense *The Guard*. Cannily Hejinian is already ahead of her critic, quixotically stating 'I'm not opinionated, except with aphorisms' (32). While Hejinian aims to create a work which is neither pedagogical nor predetermined in its ambitions, the tension between a wandering impulse and pithy interjections demands our further attention.

29 See for example 'Two Stein Talks'; 'A Common Knowledge', 'Barbarism' and 'Reason'.

'Of science for its practitioners': music, phenomenology and aphorisms

In Pound's celebrated essay 'The Serious Artist',[30] he draws an analogy between scientific accuracy in poetic composition: 'The arts, literature, poesy, are a science, just as chemistry is a science. Their subject is man, mankind and the individual. The subject of chemistry is matter considered as to its composition' (42). Pound continues stating that the arts contain 'data' to be analysed, 'Bad art is inaccurate art' (43) and '"Good writing" is perfect control' (49). His instructions call for a mastery of technique and scientific enquiry provides him with an analogy of precision. Implicit in Pound's discussion of science and linguistic efficiency is his emphasis on objectivity in writing. The focus on objectivity becomes an explicit process of objectification as the essay develops: 'The serious artist is scientific in that he presents the image of his desire, of his hate, of his indifference as precisely that, as precisely the image of his own desire, hate or indifference. The more precise his record the more lasting and unassailable his work of art' (46). Pound associates precision with the enduring word; we can connect these comparisons with science to our understanding of music and poetry. In 'How to Read', Pound introduces his celebrated configuration of *melopœia* which is identified as a situation 'wherein the words are charged, over and above their plain meaning, with some musical property which directs the bearing or trend of that meaning.'[31] 'A Retrospect' draws a comparison between the artist and the musician, exhorting the writer of poetry to behave as 'a good musician, when dealing with that phase of your art which has exact parallels in music. The same laws govern, and you are bound by no others.'[32]

This essay gestures to a general economy of writing and rules which could be read in the context of musical harmony. Invariably the

---

30 Ezra Pound, 'The Serious Artist', in *Literary Essays of Ezra Pound*, ed. T.S. Eliot (London: Faber, 1960).
31 Pound, *Literary Essays*, pp. 15–40 (p. 25).
32 Pound, *Literary Essays*, pp. 3–14 (p. 6).

relationship between musical harmony, science and social order has an extensive conceptual figuration in western history. John Hollander draws attention to the connection between the early Pythagorean science of 'perfect consonances'[33] and a cosmological order. In this configuration, harmony or the myth of the music of the spheres, could also be reinterpreted 'as a metaphysical notion, characterizing not only the order of the universe but the relation of human lives to this cosmological order' (28).[34] Jacques Attali extends this view by reflecting that musical harmony in the eighteenth century created 'an aesthetic and theoretical base for its necessary order, making the people believe by shaping what they hear.'[35] Attali argues that the preponderance of scientific thought during this period appropriated harmony as a powerful instrument to establish a link between social well-being and science. He stresses that far from imposing a concept of uniformed order, harmony relies on an articulation of differences and rule governed hierarchies within the scale system:

> The harmonic system functions through rules and prohibitions: in particular, what is prohibited are repeated dissonances, in other words critiques of differences and thus the essential violence. Harmony lives by differences alone, but when they become blurred there is a potential for violence. Difference is the principle of order. (62)

Pound's call for an efficient language can be related to a broader conceptualisation of the relationship between harmony and social cohesiveness. In *ABC of Reading* he proposes not only that 'Good writers are those who keep the language efficient', but 'If a nation's literature declines, the nation atrophies and decays.'[36] Characteristically Pound calls on tradition in the attempt to validate his claim of the artist's social and civic responsibility: 'UBICUNQUE LINGUA

33   John Hollander, *The Untuning of the Sky: Ideas of Music in English Poetry 1500–1700* (Princeton: Princeton U.P., 1961), p. 28.

34   It seems a useful coincidence that Hejinian in this light dedicates the volume *The Cold of Poetry* to her husband the jazz saxophonist Larry Ochs under the epithet 'the music of the spouse.'

35   Jacques Attali, *Noise The Political Economy of Music*, trans. Brian Massumi (Manchester: Manchester U.P., 1985), p. 62.

36   Pound, *ABC of Reading* (New York: New Directions, 1987), p. 32.

ROMAS, IBI ROMA Greece and Rome civilized BY LANGUAGE. Your language is in the care of your writers' (32). This enforced impetus on clear articulation in poetic language is linked directly in 'The Serious Artist' to an evolving musical composition:

> You begin with the yeowl and the bark, and you develop into the dance and into music, and into music with words, and into words with music, and finally into words with a vague adumbration of music, words suggestive of music, words measured, or words in a rhythm that preserves some accurate trait of the emotive impression. (51)

Pound succinctly dramatises an evolution of sound into utterance until the music that we hear is fused within language. Music functions as a trace mark regulating rhythm and an emphasis is placed on a developmental hierarchy. The final aim of the poet is to communicate an articulated expression. It is also not unintentional that music in this schema evolves from a certain discordant 'barbarism' to a composition of accuracy.

Unsurprisingly, Hejinian is more circumspect in her remarks on the analogy of music to poetry. In a letter to Bernstein she suggests that the relationship between poetry and music requires serious rethinking:

> I think the analogy of poetry to music is really problematic, by the way. I've thought about it a lot, for obvious reasons, and have to discredit every apparent equivalence. Words just aren't like notes. Poems have rhythm, so do subways, hearts, hoofbeats and chainsaws and the ocean. That's more like coincidence. HOWEVER– there is such a thing as having 'an ear for language'.[37]

It is useful to pause upon Hejinian's suggestion that a musicality can be discerned in the rhythms and momentum of the everyday. While the evocation of music must be reconsidered as a certain inclusiveness and improvisation, she evidently disputes reading language as music. Bernstein's response draws from this limitation of music in poetry as a rigid sign system or determinate rhythmic form. He agrees with

37 Letter to Bernstein 4th March, 1983 MSS 74/2/10. Courtesy of *Mandeville Special Collections Library* at the University of California San Diego, and with permission of the author.

Hejinian's mistrust of the totalising analogy of music and poetry– but significantly draws reference to the work of Louis Zukofsky in his reply:

> It always seems to me that I want to create work where I LOSE count rather than be reminded of it. But I obviously have leaned on the metaphor of music in some essays– music as the sound of words coming into meaning (Byrd on LZ)– as well as the metaphor of song– for what is the element of poetry that relies on the sonorous, not as detachable from the meaning but as establishing the meaning.[38]

Bernstein's response draws an important reference to the two opposite considerations of closure and continuation, pointing towards Zukofsky's *'A'* and its consideration of 'sound in duration'. Rather than approaching music as a method of formal organisation and a momentum towards epiphany, there is the suggestion of music as an epistemology. We are not far here from a Poundian evocation of *melopœia* which appears later in Hejinian's poetics in the context of translation.[39]

The Guard makes a direct reference to music as of the practice of 'science for its practitioners' and the following section furthers an examination of the relationship between the lyric and an erring poetics:

> Painting cannot take captives.
> I remember much the same about all my interests
> repetitious circular interests, of which a roving
> and impressionable mind like that of an hysteric
> seeks disclosure. Of science
> for its practitioners. Of stacked convexities.
> The two notes to the motor
>
> in March the object of the dark
> restricted dirt, not deception nor transparency.

38 Letter to Hejinian dated 21st March 1983 MSS 74/2/10. Courtesy of *Mandeville Special Collections Library* at the University of California San Diego, and with permission of the author.
39 'On Translation: Some forms on Alterity', *The Language of Inquiry*, pp. 296–317 (p. 309).

He sits to piano, it's an attack
on the sound of the lips. Who seem
to be in a cage of parakeets
turning clothes, following a dialogue

made up of science for its practitioners.
The silence fills. Scenes thread bridges.
Such air always flies
to the heart and liver, faces nature
with its changing pan, floating boats on the bay
far from authority, sent truly
speaking in little weights
without knowing French and don't pronounce. (13–14)

Hejinian meditates upon an aesthetic that can captivate the reader
and even the emergent listener in this case. Painting we are told cannot 'take captives' since the work challenges a photographic accuracy,
or a mimetic method. This veiled suggestion of painterly abstraction is
followed by the indication that painting mirrors the 'impressionable
mind' of 'an hysteric'. The lines with their emphatic suggestion of
'roving', perhaps even 'raving' interests pose a challenge to the idea
of art merely as a psychological expression or a therapy which 'seeks
disclosure'. The poem swerves to what would initially seem to be the
opposite approach 'of science for its practitioners'. Science is further
evoked by the analogy 'of stacked convexities'. This elliptical line
suggests a convex lens or a precision optical instrument. One could
relate the 'stacked convexities' of Hejinian's poem to Zukofsky's 'An
Objective'. Zukofsky memorably states that an objective is *the lens
bringing the rays of an object to a focus. That which is aimed at.*[40]
And the gesture to music in 'two notes to the motor' allows one to re-
read this image as the curved line of a slur on the composer's score,
denoting that notes of varying pitches to be played without separate
articulation. This reading of the text problematises the accuracy
implicit in Pound's dictum on poetic language and music. Hierarchies
of harmony are threatened by the dissolution of their differences, a

40   Louis Zukofsky, 'An Objective', *Prepositions: The Collected Essays of Louis
      Zukofsky* (New York: Horizon Press, 1967), p. 20.

dissolution which is enacted graphically on the strophes of a modern composer's score.

The call to science in *The Guard* is a problematic one. Indeed there is something distinctly inhuman to the 'motor' of notes and the 'attack on the sound of lips'. Against the initial impression of hard resonance there is a suggestion of organic regeneration. The section is possibly pointing towards the atonality and chromatic melodies of modern and contemporary classical music. Given the context of this music 'the motor in the dark/restricted dirt', Igor Stravinsky's *The Rite of Spring* comes to mind. The notoriously negative response given to the first performance of *The Rite of Spring* grants a consideration of the reception of music which informs *The Guard*. It is suggested that a challenging of existing forms creates hostility since 'People like the lock of a pattern' (23). Similarly a distaste for the reverential awe that an audience approaches a composition– 'It's to listen piously/ to music' (33).

Stravinsky's challenge to tonal structure is meditated upon in his *Poetics of Music*. Although tonality still informs his work he suggests that the centre of compositions are formed by 'poles of attraction, no longer within the closed system, which was the diatonic system'.[41] In this blurring between the hierarchies of harmonic execution, we find a link with Hejinian's errant enquiry of the lyric as a latent desire or 'restlessness' inscribed in language. *The Guard* appraises a medium which allows a compositional materiality to come to the fore since we are presented with a visual evocation of quavers and semiquavers on the musician's score 'sent/ truly speaking in little weights'. But the centre of this composition appears to be an inclination to perform 'far from authority'. In a later section *The Guard* indicates that the role of the reader as interpreter is a central one: 'Ear, the already hollow, mouthpiece./ Perfection defeats the world/ for inspection. There's a poem/ with anything in it' (33). Curiously the ambiguous response to the dialogue of 'science for its practitioners', stresses that the dissolution of a ruled governed harmony does not result in either heinous barbarism or dissonance. Indeed the final stanza stresses a spatial,

---

41   Igor Stravinsky, *Poetics of Music*, trans. Arthur Knodel and Ingolf Dahl (Cambridge Mass.: Harvard U.P., 1947), p. 37.

even utopic freedom that a somewhat restrictive or pedagogical commentary could be guarding against.

The Guard cannot be characterised as acting purely against rule-governed conventions in its attempt to counter didacticism and authority. The text responds to a tradition of modernist mastery through a phenomenological enquiry of the lyric. The inflection of phenomenology in the section accounts not only for the pervasive saturation in the text, but for the system of linkages in Hejinian's own score. Understanding the wandering impulse of Hejinian's work as an attempt to situate a 'sense of dynamic inherence in the world',[42] has relevance to our reading of music. Drawing on Maurice Merleau-Ponty's philosophy Hejinian notes in 'Language and "Paradise"' that *The Guard* strives towards a 'phenomenological' investigation (83) and that her poetics generate a 'rhythm of attention.' Indeed as she later indicates the line becomes a form of 'perceptual rhythm' in her poetry.

The Guard proposes a different path to the strongly demarcated subject-object relations inscribed in the more conventional expressions of mid-eighties lyrics. Merleau-Ponty's introduction to his *Phenomenology of Perception*[43] helps to elucidate the phenomenological inflexion in Hejinian's lyric. He states that phenomenology is a philosophy 'for which the world is already there' and is an attempt to achieve 'a direct and primitive contact with the world' (vii). Merleau-Ponty maintains that phenomenology is a 'rigorous science' (vii), but an investigation which has at its core 'a matter of describing and not analysing' (viii). Understood in this light, a phenomenological impulse has as its aim not the objectification of the world into reducible knowledge but 'an account of space-time and the world as we live them' (vii). This has a pertinent link to Hejinian's insistence on a poetics which is neither pre-determined nor making claims for authority. How do these phenomenological claims work in practice? Certainly we can see how a perceptual rhythm is established in this section with the evocation of 'Scenes thread bridges' and 'faces nature

42   See Nicholls, 'Phenomenal Poetics Reading Lyn Hejinian'
43   Maurice Merleau-Ponty, *The Phenomenology of Perception*, trans. Colin Smith (London: Routledge, 1999).

with its changing pan'. Yet dangers remains that inexhaustible attempts at description threaten to jettison the lyric towards perceptual indulgence.

Hejinian proposes that this conundrum is countered in her work by harnessing description to a condition of 'strangeness'. Her poetry challenges the reduction of description to a realism harnessed to a retrospective account of the perceiver. The world becomes not a related experience of objects of knowledge, but an attempt to reconnect a relationship with the world through description. Hejinian's explanation echoes Merleau-Ponty's assumption that 'in order to see the world and grasp it as paradoxical, we must break with out familiar acceptance of it' (xiv). Moreover Hejinian states that description is 'phenomenal rather than epiphenomenal, original, with a marked tendency towards effecting isolation and displacement, that is towards objectifying all that's described and making it strange.'[44]

Strangeness although it may envelop the comic and the quirky, has in Hejinian's work a serious intention since it creates an intersection in the poem's compositional field between writer and reader. Yet is Hejinian's argument completely reassuring; does the formulation of strangeness in the poem necessarily circumvent the troubled locus of authority in *The Guard*? There is possibly a danger of losing sight of the initial lyric aporia which opens the poem. However much Hejinian stresses her affiliation to a poetics of improvisation, a reading of erring in *The Guard* is informed by the foregrounding of the tensions between a descriptive impulse and a lyric form that somehow 'contains' this gesture. In this understanding of erring, a phenomenological impetus towards description is occasionally thwarted and derailed in Hejinian's work.

Pound's 'The Serious Artist' provides a surprising thread to the poetics of transition associated with the erring impetus of *The Guard*. Pound presents *melopœia* as a musical device which establishes meaning in poetry and also works as an access to the unconscious. *Melopœia* becomes 'a force tending often to lull, or distract the reader from the exact sense of the language. It is poetry on the borders of

44   'Strangeness', in *The Language of Inquiry*, pp. 135–60 (p. 138). Originally published in 1989.

music and music is perhaps the bridge between consciousness and the unthinking sentient or even insentient universe' (26). *Melopœia* works in tension with *logopœia*, the intellectual or emotive association of the words themselves. This simultaneous gesture to accuracy and distraction, forms a useful connection with erring as a tension or friction between phenomenological description and the lyric form in Hejinian's text.

Building from this reading, Roland Barthes's essay 'The Grain of the Voice'[45] enables us a further way of reconsidering the lyric aporia which propels the erring enquiry of *The Guard*. Barthes adopts Julia Kristeva's terms *phenotext* and *genotext* to an application of understanding music and its performance. The genotext in Kristeva's account lends itself to melodic devices an ecstatic drive closely allied to the semiotic while the phenotext suggests the communicative level of language, structures which underpin grammatical rules and conventions. Kristeva states the phenotext 'obeys rules of communication and presupposes a subject of enunciation and an addressee.'[46] In 'The Grain of the Voice', Barthes transposes Kristeva's configuration to *pheno-song* and the *geno-song*, the former becoming the impulse towards articulation, expression and performance and the latter delighting in the *jouissance* of linguistic materiality. As Barthes elucidates the geno-song has 'nothing to do with communication' instead it is:

> That apex (or that depth) of production where the melody really works at the language– not at what it says, but the voluptuousness of its sound-signifiers, of its letters– where melody explores how the language works and identifies with that work. It is, in a very simple word but which must be taken seriously, the *diction* of the language. (182–3)

Barthes places a particular emphasis on the display of the geno-song in the recital, as a form of writing and the recital through its heightened performance of the geno-song becomes in turn a text. Barthes is categorical since he states 'The song must speak, must *write*– for what

45 Roland Barthes, 'The Grain of the Voice', in *Music Image Text*, trans. Stephen Heath (New York: The Noonday Press, 1977), pp. 179–89.
46 Julia Kristeva, *Revolution in Poetic Language* (New York: Columbia U.P., 1984), p. 87.

is produced at the level of the geno-song is finally writing' (185). The emphasis on the 'grain' forces us to reconsider how one applies the analogy of music to poetry; as an element of resistance in the recital the grain raises a challenge to the idealisation of closure and perfection.

The insistence of aphorisms in *The Guard* not only staggers the poem's impulse towards phenomenological description but strikes a reminder of the lyric form that Hejinian is working within. The following section bears a striking resemblance to the performance of an operatic aria:

> Loosely a bullfrog exits a pond.
> My heart did suck... to fidget, soothed
> ... by seawater, restless... against
> the unplugged phone. Barking up the street
> in a rainstorm as a rose
> with ardent jiggling stands. A jackhammer
> shatters the pavement– was this repression
> radiant with static and a single dog.
>
> However the lawnmower is idling
> outdoors... it is like slowly throwing oneself
> ... as if simply to walk into arms... so much
> restlessness because one is hungry. The tongue
> becomes observant and the tongue gets tough
> inevitably, like a fruitskin. Now it migrates
> (I hear the pen pat as I come to the end
> of the phrase and make a comma) in G-minor.
>
> Spring and convention... the ringing
> in my ears is fear of finishing...
> in a bus, but the rhapsodic rider-driver, springing
> invention... (poetry is not solitude).
>
> So she tells me she loves adjectives
> ... that love is emotional restlessness...
> it mobilizes in modesty... bathed in modesty...
> (the window is waterish)... we are reserved
> in vehement strings, retraced, retracted
> and sometimes reversed exclusively for it. (28)

The opening of this section is overwhelmingly dense with phonetic resonance and glossolalia; there is an onomatopoeic wallowing in the poem. Reading the geno-song in the resonance of sound signifiers an evocation of an instinctual drive is built up through associations of the bodily and the sensual. Scanning the poem an association is formed from the membrane of the bullfrog's skin to the beating heart and the physiological implication of speech as the tongue thickening– 'the skin gets tough'. One can add here Barthes's distinction of the grain as a physical manifestation, the grain 'is in the throat, place where the phonic metal hardens and is segmented, in the mask that *significance* explodes, bringing not the soul but *jouissance*' (183). There is a similar reciprocative awareness of the phenosong within the performance of this piece. Indeed *The Guard* proposes that the ardent 'jiggling' and 'restlessness' is working against the implied 'repressive' rules of the genre, suggested by 'Spring and convention' and 'the fear of finishing'. The humorous dramatic portrait of the lawnmower 'idling outdoors' and the emotive response it elicits 'it is like slowly throwing oneself' conforms to the narrative of the tragic heroine in a libretto. This scene of erotic love is transposed to an insatiable desire for linguistic description, 'so much restlessness because one is hungry.' The tension between the geno-song and pheno-song reaches its apex in the references to technique and a simultaneity of composition: '(I hear the pen pat as I come to the end/ of the phrase and make a comma) in G-minor.'

The simultaneous examination of composition within the confines of the pheno-song or governing rules can also be extended to intrusions of slipped aphorisms in the text. It seems significant that Hejinian in her revision of 'Language and "Paradise"' for *The Language of Inquiry*, adds to her original discussion a pertinent note on the aphorism:

> I wanted to resist the synthesizing tendency of the syllogism and the aphorism; I wanted to subvert the power of 'therefore' and, wherever one of a series of terms (sentences) might threaten to subsume others (the sort of sacrifice that the

dialectical tend to make in its quest for categorical clarity), to deny it the capacity to do so.[47]

This is an important gesture, Hejinian attempts to protect her own work from the reading of aphorism as pedagogy. One cannot read the aphorisms 'straight', as proverbial or common-knowledge epithets. In the later essay 'Strangeness' the criteria for the aphorism is the communication of knowledge 'in a mode that condenses material' (154). The impetus for delivering knowledge is skewed in the design of Hejinian's own aphoristic impulse. There is also a contrariness and a wilful defiance in *The Guard* towards the totalising import of its own aphoristic texture. In this section we are told with a flourish that 'Poetry is not solitude', although the opening draws attention to the 'unplugged phone'. Hejinian's playfulness cannot be underestimated and the appropriation of aphorisms generates humour. Take for example the line that *almost* echoes a popular ballad– 'she tells me she loves–' but what does she love– 'adjectives'? This undercut aphorism is further punctured by the self-aggrandising statement 'love is emotional restlessness'. Bearing in mind that this scene is played out in a backdrop of 'vehement strings', what we have is a troubadour's lament in a suburbia of jackhammers, circuit traffic and barking dogs.

'Language and Paradise' confirms that the tension between the phenotextual perimeters of the lyric and phenomenological description is a deliberate strategy. There are however often dangers to be acknowledged within this orchestration. In moving beyond the humour of domestic particulars *The Guard* occasionally leans on a borrowing of gnomic epithets. Hejinian's erring aphoristic impulse generates humour, and on occasion the tenor of the statements are Confucian-like in their authority. Quixotic examples include 'Vulgarity is tender in its own complexity' (19), 'Hysteria is soul voyaging' (25) and 'A cell of graffiti is aphoristic' (33). One could argue that these phrases err on the side of witty repartee rather than extending the responsibilities of the poem towards a social intervention. Although Hejinian proposes that 'I have many social thoughts' (29), it becomes

---

47   'Language and "Paradise"', in *Language of Inquiry*, pp. 59–82 (p. 68). Revised edition.

apparent that towards the close of *The Guard*, that this impetus is occasionally frustrated into recreational social commentary. Indeed we are told rather soberly in *The Guard* 'but mere table talk unites us' (31).

In Hejinian's aesthetic of erring a central locus of authority is avoided with the aim of opening the text to broader implications of political responsibility and a devolution of mastery. It is also important to note that there are hints in *The Guard* that Hejinian's concern with an art of integrity is performed through an inflexion of 'generosity' and 'altruism'. A reading of Hejinian's lyric must exercise caution since it raises the issue of whether a sketching of a provisional ethics can be animated spontaneously in the lyric. Hejinian is fully attuned to this problem since it is suggested in *The Guard* that there is a safeguarding or mechanism of concealment which insures the work from political naivety; 'there is a way of saying things that is insurance, so to speak in stock ... now I'm saving up to tell' (34). Hejinian's 'telling' in *The Person* and *Happily*,[48] enables us to consider how an erring poetics can accommodate a sustained ethical enquiry and propose a viable site for an intersubjective lyric.

---

48   Hejinian, *The Person* in *The Cold of Poetry, Happily* (Post Apollo Press, 2000).

Chapter Six
'There is no one correct path': Lyn Hejinian's Prepoetics

Altruism, erring and *The Person*

A consideration of poetry as an ethical enquiry is given considerable focus in Hejinian's recent poetics; indeed the essay 'Barbarism' retrospectively stresses that the intersection of aesthetics and ethics is 'one of the basic characteristics of Language Writing.'[1] This reciprocal relationship proposes that 'aesthetic discovery is congruent with social discovery. New ways of thinking ... make new ways of being possible' (322). Hejinian's configuration of an ethical enquiry is related to situating the praxis of poetry in the everyday. For Maurice Blanchot the everyday resists formulation or predetermination: 'It belongs to insignificance; the insignificant being what is without truth, without reality, and without secret, but also perhaps the site of all possible signification. The everyday escapes.'[2] Hejinian's mapping of an ethical poetics extends a consideration of the everyday beyond a fascination with the strangeness of the ordinary; moreover the provisionality associated with the everyday has a particular correspondence with her suspicion of a predetermined ethical investigation.

'Barbarism' provides a useful summation of Hejinian's recent poetics, and indicates that a responsible aesthetics could be configured as a 'poetics of encounter'. This phrase, earlier linked to Gertrude Stein's writing, is extended to a consideration of the poem as a 'social

---

1   Lyn Hejinian, 'Barbarism', in *The Language of Inquiry* (Berkeley: University of California Press, 2000), pp. 318–36 (p. 322). Originally presented in 1995.
2   Maurice Blanchot, 'Everyday Speech', in *The Infinite Conversation*, trans. Susan Hanson (Minneapolis and London: University of Minnesota Press, 1993), pp. 238–45 (pp. 239–40).

text' and Hejinian suggests such a politicised poetry 'will engage the poet in her affiliations– her attachments to others and through which she, too is other' (330). Her remark points us towards a sense of responsibility and acknowledgement of alterity inherent in a poetics of encounter. The essay in responding to Theodor Adorno's infamous statement that 'To write poetry after Auschwitz is an act of barbarism', suggests that this evocation of a lyric 'encounter' is drawing on a deliberate lineage. Significantly Paul Celan describes the act of the poem as 'the mystery of an encounter'[3]:

> The poem wants to reach an Other, it needs this Other, it needs an Over–against. It seeks it out, speaks towards it.
> For the poem making towards an Other, each thing, each human being is a form of this Other. (409)

The parallels seem striking, and while Hejinian does not mention Celan by name, she states that characteristics of Language Writing are attributable to 'certain Post Holocaust themes' (325). In attending to a lineage of theorists and philosophers including Emmanuel Levinas, Hejinian is grappling with an ambitious precedent and takes the linking of poetics and ethics to be of tantamount importance.

The invocation of barbarism in the title is examined firstly as a consideration of *barbaros* or strangeness, which is then developed to an examination of the Greek word 'xenos', suggestive of foreigner or stranger. Hejinian meditates upon the figure of the border as both a point of reciprocity and differentiation. Borders she asserts are 'by definition addressed to foreignness' (326). The figuration of the border is suggestive not only as a meeting point or encounter but an overlap which Hejinian points to co-existence or *xenia:*

> The *xenos* figure is one of contradiction and confluence. The stranger it names is both guest and host ... The guest/ host relationship is one of identity as much as it is of reciprocity... The guest/ host relationship comes into existence solely in and as occurrence, that of their meeting, their encounter. Every encounter produces, even if for only a flash of an instant a *xenia*– the occurrence of coexistence which is also an occurrence of strangeness or foreignness. It is a

3   Paul Celan, 'The Meridian', in *Selected Poems and Prose of Paul Celan*, trans. John Felstiner (New York: Norton, 2001), p. 409.

strange occurrence that, nonetheless, happens constantly; we have no other experience of living than through encounters. (326)

One is not far from the initial consideration of the lyric 'dilemma' which opens *The Guard*.[4] Beginning to understand the figure of the border as a meeting point which signifies an excess or irresolvable overspill, provides a significant thread to an examination of erring. Calling upon the figure of this encounter as *xenos*, Hejinian states that it is the 'inquirer, dislodged and dislodging, in a transitive rather than intransitive poetry' (333). The foregrounding of transition in Hejinian's poetics, has more than a passing resonance with *The Guard's* focus within a pattern of erring as sustaining the temporal mobility of the poem. Yet, whether this patterning can be translated to an understanding of the ethical import of Hejinian's work needs some consideration. Hejinian's reference to Levinas in conjunction with Zukofsky's poetics of sincerity,[5] indicate that issues of responsibility and altruism may broached through a dual reading of *The Person* and the philosopher's work.[6] While there are dangers in this 'retrospective' account of *The Person*, Hejinian's early concern with an art that performs a certain integrity indicates that the preoccupations of 'Barbarism' are not new considerations.

Jeffrey T. Nealon's understanding of the recent fascination with the 'other' in philosophical discourse, draws a neat argument for the recent intervention of ethics in current debates over identity politics. He suggests that ethics 'necessarily concerns itself both with general theoretical structures and specific concrete responses', and adds 'one might argue that its ability to bring together the theoretical and political is one of the reasons ethics has re-emerged so centrally in recent critical discourse.[7] The emphasis on a practical ethics, places some

4   For a full discussion of *The Guard* see Chapter Five.
5   See 'Barbarism', p. 332. Here Hejinian indicates that her reference to Levinas is informed by Peter Nicholls's article 'Of Being Ethical: Reflections on George Oppen', *Journal of American Studies*, 31.2 (1997), 153–70.
6   Hejinian, *The Person* in *The Cold of Poetry* (Los Angeles: Sun & Moon Press, 1994).
7   Jeffrey T. Nealon, *Alterity and Politics: Ethics and Performative Subjectivity* (Durham and London: Duke U.P., 1998), p. 2. For a recent study of the

added demands on our consideration of Hejinian's poetry and attempts to mesh aesthetics and ethics provides a useful response to an examination of the lyric and its address. Hejinian in her endeavour to circumvent a didactic rhetoric is not interested in proposing a definitive ethical grammar. We need consider whether the gesture to 'altruism' in the poetry is entirely self-sacrificing, or if it also betrays the irresolvable complexities created by the attempt to move beyond an authoritative lyric 'I'.

The Guard states that 'Altruism suggestively fits' (14) which can be read as 'selflessness', abnegation and even generosity towards the reader. But are generosity and altruism necessarily the same practice in the configuration of an ethical enquiry? The Guard proposes that they are decidedly different: 'Generosity is all over the place/ invited to politics, weeping witticisms /with a speed that resembles improvising. (15). 'Generosity' hijacked by political rhetoric suggests that it may be nothing more than an aphorism or sound bite. Against this reading we can parallel The Guard's evocation of sincerity as a'deference' (31). The earlier and suggestive phrase 'Memory meaning physically, expository, generous with substitution (16) hints that there is a relationship to be mined between altruism and generosity through processes of substitution. This early suggestion in The Guard is developed in The Person, where an evocation of altruism reads calls for an ethical consideration of the subject and its responsibilities to recognising and acknowledging alterity.

In Hejinian's lyric an erring poetics creates a strategic wandering and the raising of irresolvable aesthetic dilemmas in the text. In The Person erring can be extended to address Hejinian's poetics of encounter and mobility. 'The Person and Description' proposes that the subject is less a fixed entity than 'a mobile (and mobilized) reference point.'[8] Writing specifically on The Person, Hejinian states that the work developed as an attempt to show the 'persistent experiences of a

intersection of ethics and poetry see Tim Woods *Poetics of the Limit: Ethics and Politics in Modern and Contemporary American Poetry* New York: Palgrave, 2003).

8   Hejinian, 'The Person and Description', *Poetics Journal*, 9 (1991), 166–70 (p. 167).

person, drawn into the world by perception, implicated by language and unwilling to give up attempts at description' (168). Once more there is a phenomenological import to Hejinian's construction of the person. Rather than seeing the self in a stable opposition to the world or to other subjects and establishing boundaries through a process of objectification, 'the person' constantly constructs and overrides boundaries. Hejinian proposes that this is occasioned through a process of radical introspection which 'establishes the relationship between self and other ... then transgresses the borders which it has established– a transgression which by the way, might be expanded and rephrased in the context of the boundaries (or blurring of the boundaries) between art and reality– to describe a person' (170). These ideas of transgression gesture once more to a reading of erring. Examining *The Person* in conjunction with Levinas's work enables us to consider erring as a sequence of serial traces which are reinscribed within each encounter in the trajectory of Hejinian's mobilised subject. While Levinas's discussion does not provide a definitive solution to an understanding of altruism in Hejinian's text, it offers a provocative correspondence with the key tenets of the poet's enquiry whether such claims can be realised in the practice of poetry.

Levinas's *Otherwise than Being*[9] approaches subjectivity as an acknowledgement of difference and an obligation of responsibility to the other. He seeks an approach to subjectivity that enables the subject to make contact with the other and places an emphasis on 'sensibility' as a passive but sensuous enjoyment of the world. Levinas's evocation of a sensuous appetite also gestures to an egotistical drive; the subject desires to incorporate these sensations. This process of incorporation is thwarted by the appearance of the other or *l'autrui* and the other resists consumption. The initial approach of the other may be described in terms of astonishment or surprise and Levinas states that the response elicited by the subject is one of responsibility, or what he designates as substitution:

9   All citations from Levinas, unless otherwise noted will be taken from *Emmanuel Levinas: Basic Philosophical Writings*, eds. Adrian T. Peperzak, Simon Critchley and Robert Bernasconi (Bloomington and Indianapolis: University of Indiana Press, 1996).

It is this summoning of myself by the Other (*autrui*), it is a responsibility toward those whom we do not even know ... It is *already* a summons of extreme exigency, an obligation which is *anachronistically* prior to every engagement ... To be a 'self' is to be responsible before having done anything. It is in this sense to substitute oneself for others. In no way does this represent servitude, for the distinction between master and slave already assumes a pre-established ego. (94)

Being a social subject in Levinas's work means to exist primarily for the other person. Importantly, substitution is not merely substituting oneself in the place of the person, since Levinas stresses that his account of substitution occurs before conceptualisation, or what he draws attention to as 'an obligation which is anachronistically prior to every engagement'. Obligation is a paradoxical demand in Levinas's discussion and his reading does not provide a schema or configuration of ethics within a pre-existent grammar. To an extent his work proposes a pre-philosophy, it is a radical attempt to approach ethics as a demand that cannot be predetermined only contextualised within each encounter.

A provisional intersubjective ethics can be understood as an instant or encounter that does not return a need to the self. Levinas's encounter is not the epic wandering of an imperial or Odyssean self that seeks to appropriate the other to a form of knowledge. There is moreover a resonance between Levinas's articulation of an obligation towards the other, and Hejinian's evocation of *xenia* as a moment of co-existence. The meeting or summoning of responsibility in the philosopher's work is prompted dramatically as a dialogic 'face to face encounter.' An insistence on the immediacy of the encounter privileges spontaneity and the necessity of a performative response to the other since the face-to-face meeting with the other is evoked as a moment of epiphany. Subjection is an obligation to respond, a movement outward to a necessary exteriority. This response elicits a marking or tracing which informs all other responses within an infinite series of substitutions. In *Otherwise than Being*, this resonance or trace mark in the trajectory of subjection, is developed as a distinguishing of the terms the *saying* and the *said* which are imbricated in a process identified as *reduction* (a form of inhabitation within expression). The 'saying' must be understood as the direct address to an

180

interlocutor designating a shared space and proximity. By contrast the 'said' is a statement of identifiable meaning. This cohabitation is evoked as a reduction within expression, a residue that marks an awareness or obligation to the other.

We can identify a particular resonance between Levinas's implication of residue or tracing within a performative expression, and the guest/ host relationship Hejinian draws attention to as *xenos* in 'Barbarism'. In case these terms appear too ponderous or esoteric, it is important to note that Levinas stresses in *Otherwise than Being* that this imbrication is taken for granted within communication since it is woven into our cultural fabric:

> A testimony is borne by every saying as sincerity, even when it is a Saying of the Said and the Said dissimulates; but a dissimulation that the saying always seeks to unsay (*dédire*)– which is its ultimate veracity. In the game that activates the cultural keyboard of language, sincerity and testimony signify through the very ambiguity of every said, through the greeting it offers the other. (107)

Can we accord this impression of immediacy with an obligation which is '*anachronistically* prior to every engagement'? Although Levinas stresses that the obligation to the other works outside a pre-existent ethical grammar, it is a highly ambiguous phrase which can evoke a moralising response. The ambiguity becomes clearer, once the process of subjection is considered within a context of transition or erring. Levinas absolves his discussion from a prescriptive morality through the necessity of substitution to propel the subject into being. Within this transitional patterning there is no singular identifiable ethical position. Nealon clarifies the rejection of a static appropriating subject in the philosopher's work:

> It is precisely this subjected predicament (where there is no outside ground, and I am thereby called to respond) that makes possible the articulation of my identity– which is of course never 'mine' but rather a 'saying' that consistently exposes me to a network of serial substitutions out of which the 'I' emerges. (51)

Questions remain over whether *The Person* delineates 'a network of serial substitutions' and if a prospect of altruism in poetry generates added complications to conceptualising the lyric.

181

Certainly *The Person* alerts the reader to a certain 'love of life'. There are gestures to sensuous enjoyment and satisfaction which occur during the volume: 'A person puts meals in its head' (145), 'Audible, visible, or tastable form/ Speaking only to concentrate instability/ I recognize that tone, the words/ are straight from life (152), and 'do the body/ with food, physique and action' (157). It is best to focus on the first appearance of the word 'altruism' In *The Person* and how it is consolidated in poem:

> Altruism in poetry
> Such is huddled in all audible life
> Why do I say this?
> Are there perpetual experiences and do we have them?
> Nature washed her hands in milk in many years
> What of the blotting power?
>
> Each sensation is witness to the congestion of its glance
> It is very specific to say this
> The person goes up to a perfect stranger in an enclosed
> public space (for example, a bank, or supermarket, or
> department store) and there belts out some aria
> It's a wonderful thing
> Love wants to be more so
> The personification in branches gesturing from the
> desperate trees
> It will rain this afternoon, but I do not believe that it will
>
> Elation can manifest itself from time to time in finding
> like a seashell on a beach things of no great conse-
> quence perfect, and then–
> The skin itches at a restless nerve end
> Like a child with a bunch of keys then went down to the street
> She knocked with a two-penned hand below the storm-punched trees (146)

Language is essentially 'altruistic' since it makes a concession to the other. Yet this 'huddling' in what the text calls 'audible life', is challenged by the consideration of 'perpetual experiences'. The phrase refers us once more to an indication of subjectivity as sensibility indicating a site where boundaries between subject and addressee are in constant relocation and improvisation. The second stanza aids a further reading of 'altruism' in the light of Levinas's account of substitution. The complex line 'Each sentence is witness to the congestion of its glance', not only indicates recognition of a face-to-face encounter, but 'congestion' enforces a sense of impenetrability even a refusal of assimilation. Similar evocations are meditated upon during *The Person*. On the facing page Hejinian refers to 'Large organizing faces' which elicit a response of 'lavish wakefulness' (147). Most useful perhaps is the later statement on the duration of this rather hesitant encounter:

> Ellipsis is strong, and I can't absorb it
> with love
> (the selfishness of continuity)
> of the uncut (150)

These lines cause the reader to halt momentarily, 'the uncut' can be related to a desire for continuity within a pattern of transitional erring. In applying a reading of substitution in these lines the obligation to the other could be read as a form of 'love', which enables a reading of the 'ellipsis' as a recognition of difference or alterity.

Later in *The Person* a recognition of difference is celebrated by a further meditation on altruism:

> You yourself could generate the aesthetic heat
> of globes and stops, of shore and drone
> This makes for altruism—
> the generosity of the poem
> If you know what to want you will be free (177)

It is clear that Hejinian is advocating a certain response to altruism in her text. The 'globes and stops' once more evoke a momentary halt an elliptical transition but is an 'aesthetics of altruism' a feasible project for poetry? Hejinian suggests that it is, but then again how do we read the aphorism 'If you know what to want you will be free'? This is a provocative gesture in the poem; altruism is linked here to passivity. While Hejinian's work champions a non-prescriptive ethics, there is an ambiguous response here to an ineffectual aimlessness. This ambiguity is highlighted in *The Person* and echoes the passivity inherent in Levinasian ethics. Hejinian comments:

> The body is used impenetrably for flopping around
> with compassion
> So that it isn't perhaps discontinuity to exit and deploy (163)

While it may not be feasible to harness Hejinian's entire project to Levinasian subjection, there is a considerable irritability in this extract towards a person 'flopping around with compassion.' A redemptive value is given to an aesthetic of erring in the meditation upon 'exit and deploy' and we are faced with a lyric aporia, even an ethical dilemma for the poet. These 'resistances' in Hejinian's text are performed to indicate a transitional pattern of encounter and mobility. Earlier we noted how *The Guard* performs a lyric dilemma in its conflict between a desire for continuity and discontinuity.[10] In approaching *The Person* as an ethical performance, the reader is made aware of the instability of the poem's claims. The poem wants to practice 'altruistically' and we are given conflicting remarks on how this may appear in practice. Take for example this later remark:

> Pedagogic love
> Learning is like poetry– an uncalm practice
> It makes the promise of unlikeness and discipline (167)

'Unlikeness' here demonstrates an evocative relationship to 'strangeness.' Hejinian suggests that the seduction of an authoritarian rhetoric may betray the aesthetic integrity of the poem. Given Hejinian's early consideration of a poetics of integrity as a practice which is necessarily incomplete, doubtful and deliberately questioning, this tension is a familiar one. Usefully one can begin to consider Hejinian's own erring enquiry as a deliberate attempt to mar any danger of a totalising and prescriptive moralising.

Returning to our initial opening section, the poem attempts to translate ideas of altruism into practice. The realisation of these propositions surfaces in the playful vignette of the person entering a public space and serenading the stranger. The humorous practice of altruism occurs in a recognisable public domain 'a bank or supermarket or department store'. This extremely lyric person 'belts out some aria'.

10   See Chapter Five.

184

The Person proposes that this gesture is less an ethical obligation to the other than a desire for expression: 'Its a wonderful thing/ Love wants to be more so'. The evocative serenade reads as an exaggerated lyric epiphany, the appearance of the stranger in this light offering transcendence. Certainly situating a performance of subjectivity in a shopping mall punctures any danger of an inflated or highly esoteric discourse.

The close of the section offers a phenomenological approach to the person. Initially the line 'The skin itches at a restless nerve end' evokes an impression of restlessness which hints at an awareness of engaging with the world. Later in *The Person* it is stated that 'There is no outside position' (148) indicating that 'the world is relevant/ as the medium of recognition' (168). The greatest clue to reading this line is Hejinian's earlier proposition in *The Guard* that 'The skin contains endlessness'[11]. Returning to Levinas, we can approach these lines as an encounter which betrays vulnerability or passivity towards the other, taking place in the philosopher's words 'on the surface of the skin, at the edge of the nerves' (63). Levinas returns us to an understanding of subjectivity which is prior to conceptualisation. In *Otherwise than Being* Levinas suggests that:

> The ego is *in itself* not like matter is in itself, which perfectly wedded to its form, is what it is. The ego is in itself like one is in one's skin, that is to say cramped, ill at ease with one's skin, as though the identity of matter weighing on itself concealed a dimension allowing a withdrawal this side of immediate coincidence, as though it concealed a materiality more material than all matter. (86)

It could be argued that applying this proposal of vulnerability and unease to *The Person* assumes too much of a correspondence between the poem and *Otherwise than Being*. Yet, looking forward to Hejinian's later volume, *The Cell*,[12] there is an uncanny echo of Levinas's description of an ego 'ill-at-ease':

11   Hejinian, *The Guard* in *The Cold of Poetry* (Los Angeles: Sun & Moon Press, 1994), p. 18.
12   Hejinian, *The Cell* (Los Angeles: Sun & Moon Press, 1992).

> The body taken from the
>   mind
> Where are your shoulders and
>   your hands, your color, face,
>   and, while I speak your
>   ... everything?
> The skin is the only
>   possible means of keeping the
>   different pieces together (98)

The poem's insistent questioning 'where are your hands, your colour, face... your everything', evokes an anxious enquiry to situate a relationship of proximity to this person. It is not insignificant that the initial locating of this other person 'taken from the mind' reasserts itself as a corporeal proximity, as an embodiment of the skin.

Reading Levinas in tandem with *The Person*, provides an opportunity to scrutinise how a poetics of altruism can be configured from the hints in Hejinian's poetics. Clearly *The Person* orchestrates a complex account of the consideration of an ethical enquiry in poetry. Inconsistencies in the text extend the lyric dilemma dominating *The Guard*, to an examination of how the person is constantly recontextualised. In *The Person* Hejinian is actively flirting with different conceptualisations of intersubjectivity and ethical obligation. Moreover transitions in the work create a serpentine wandering to counter the temptations of rhetorical performance, and motivate the complex sense of encounter in the poem. But does this patterning of transitional encounter and hesitation occasionally frustrate a sustained ethical enquiry and threaten to jettison the poem to a paradigm of post-structuralist play?

In Hejinian's defence *The Cell* emphasises that tactics of delay and diversion cannot be equated with a reverence for playful textual possibilities. *The Cell* warns its reader 'I hate a person's sentimental/ use of the word "play"/ as a substitute for subjectivity' (27). The following section from *The Person* illustrates how these contradictions may finally be extended to a further reading of intersubjective relations:

> We reproach ourselves for the heroism
> of the person in the episode body

We are filled with scruples
about beauty

and individualism
Spouse, Child, Citizen
A composition
Cheerfulness is indelicate

as a separate body-part
The incriminating contents
of the portrait-bowl
The person is the form

it determines
with a porous advantage
One can shudder without understanding
with chronic ideas

Good– an intuition
But isn't that merely preknowing
–and one can remain
in a state of preknowing indefinitely

Entertainment in poetry
We reproach ourselves for enthusiasm
It's unthinkable
that my skull would turn out

to be empty
if it were opened I feel
my brain
At first I didn't fasten

           this feeling to words
Adorable Subject-Object
A moment of intense orientation
as it swings. (173–4)

Hejinian illustrates the difficulties in countering prescribed cultural assumptions of the traditional lyric subject. Although Hejinian's poetry cannot be read merely as an oppositional impulse, there are indications here that the work is striving against prescriptive conceptualisations of 'heroism', 'beauty' and 'individualism'. The position of *The Person* is once more flirtatious; although these assumptions are reproached they appear temptingly seductive for the poet. In attempting to configure a different proposal to a transitional responsibility, Hejinian is testing different propositions through an erring process.

Taken at its most critical the person in this section functions as a series of serial portraits or personae. Evidently the poem moves from pre-determined role-play 'Spouse, Child, Citizen', to an indeterminate state of 'preknowing'. Hejinian's critical tone here is useful; the enquiry indicates a scepticism in its consideration of 'Good– an intuition/ But isn't that merely preknowing'. Yet if one can 'shudder without understanding' what exactly is the text attempting to pinpoint in its examination? There is retaliation against an intersubjective encounter constructed as passivity, the text reads as a rhetorical polemic against initial assumptions of a passive altruism. The person even flexes a degree of Cartesian muscle in the exclamation 'Its unthinkable that my skull would turn out to be empty.' The close of this section draws us to reconsider how an intersubjective impulse may be enacted in *The Person*. Hejinian's gesture to 'The adorable subject object', betrays the difficulties inherent in construing a poetics of altruism that does not return a need to the self. Reading this elliptical line in tandem with the pragmatist thought of George Herbert Mead, indicates how Hejinian's construction of the person is not consistently self-sacrificing.

Mead proposes that the human self is both the subject of experience and thought, and also the object of experience. In considering subjectivity he states that the essential problem must be, 'How can an individual get outside himself (experientially) in such a way as to become an object to himself?'[13] Mead maintains that the answer to the problem of selfhood can be located in the relation of the self to its community 'its solution is to be found by referring to the process of social conduct in which the given person or individual is implicated' (138). Therefore it is only through being a member of a community

---

13   George Herbert Mead, *Mind Self and Society*, ed. Charles W. Morris (Chicago: University of Chicago Press, 1962), p. 38.

that one's self, can become the object of one's thought and experience:

> The individual experiences himself as such, not directly, but only indirectly, from the particular standpoints of the other individual members of the same social group ... he first becomes object to himself just as other individuals are objects to him. (138)

Mead's account of the relationship between self and society as a proposition of co-operative action draws some useful correspondences with Hejinian's altruism. In order to co-operate with others, he proposes we must at least be capable of responding in the same ways to the same things as others. This proposition also places an equal focus on anticipating how others are likely to respond to our own actions. Mead illustrates that this process of 'give and take' has implications for a construction of the self and its relation to society:

> The self is not something that exists first and then enters into a relationship with others, it is so to speak, an eddy in a social current, and so is still part of the current. It is a process in which the individual is continually adjusting himself in advance to the situation to which he belongs, and reacting back on it. So that the 'I' and the 'me', this thinking, this conscious adjustment, becomes part of the whole social process. (182)

In Mead's configuration society, or community, is seen as an undifferentiated mass that is there invariably to reflect back to the individual what she namely desires, that is the objectification of her self. This conceptualisation of co-operative action places a focus on responding to others as satisfying a responsibility to one's self, as opposed to a responsibility generated by some altruistic drive. In re-reading Hejinian's line, we are given a reminder that there may be a strategic and self-serving inclination in this intersubjective encounter: 'Adorable Subject-Object/ A moment of intense orientation'. Although the serpentine erring in Hejinian's *The Person* affords a certain 'Entertainment in poetry' an anxious problem is raised by an early statement in the poem, 'I'm going to write lest my other behaviour contradict my words' (169). In reading Hejinian's later volume

Happily[14] we need consider how the conflict between proposition and practice is placed into relief by Hejinian's recent sketching of what she calls 'a responsible prepoetics' (340).

Happily and a prepoetics

Hejinian's essay 'Reason' offers an opportunity to reconsider the inconsistencies which are set up intentionally in her poetry. The essay considers how an ethical enquiry that is neither predetermined, nor prescriptive, may operate without recourse to an all-encompassing aesthetic of spontaneity. In my earlier reading of *The Guard* I have noted that harnessing a phenomenological impulse within the perimeters of the lyric threatens to prioritise a poetics of descriptive immediacy.[15] This impulse threatens to overwhelm the poetry and paradoxically may even affirm the authority and primacy of the perceiver. Hejinian's early poetics indicates that a formulation of 'strangeness', serves to purposely halt and momentarily sabotage an aesthetic of spontaneity. 'Reason' examines a 'poetics of encounter' within a configuration of specific 'context' to highlight an ethical dimension to a gesture of 'strangeness'.[16]

Philosophical terms are often adapted and redeployed in Hejinian's poetics and we are required to translate how these amended concepts perform in the poetry. 'Reason' begins with the consideration of an irresolvable 'dilemma' or 'aporia' that motivates the writing of poetry and the essay focuses upon what Hejinian coins a 'prepoetics'. Understanding this dilemma as a 'pressure of doubt', Hejinian maintains that a prepoetics functions 'not as a condition either logically or chronologically prior to the formulation of a poetics but as a condition necessary and simultaneous to it' (340).

14   Hejinian, *Happily* (Sausalito: Post Apollo Press, 2000).
15   See Chapter Five for a full discussion.
16   Hejinian, 'Reason' in *The Language of Inquiry*, pp. 337–54.

190

An unformulated poetics in this schema refutes an authoritative impulse, even suggesting an erring provisionality or a trajectory which is constantly reconfigured and reamended. One might question how this proposition moves beyond an aesthetics of contingency and most importantly how can a prepoetics claim to perform 'responsibly'? The answer proposed in 'Reason' is a consideration of each encounter as a specific and singular establishing of 'context'. At the heart of Hejinian's evocation is the consideration of context as a mediatory inter-subjective ethics: 'The context, in other words, is the medium of our encounter, the ground of our encounter, the ground of our becoming (i.e. happening to be) present at the same place at the same time' (342). For Hejinian context suggests not only a meeting point of two different positions but also the affirmation of a shared commonality what she terms 'a moment of incipience' (343).[17] In this constant con-figuration of context, reason is presented not as a rational figure of causation, but as a suture or linkage. Hejinian's essay affirms that the situating of context continually establishes a shared recognition and a proximity that is not burdened by a preconfigured ethical grammar. The form that this perpetual beginning takes is evoked as an acknowl-edgement of the sensation that *'this is happening'* (343).

While the proposal of a prepoetics resists a foundational ethical grammar, it is also non-arbitrary. This may seem paradoxical, but Hej-inian's enforced recourse to an evocation of 'context', suggests that each and every response must be taken in the singular. In this way we can begin to read the ethical in 'Reason' as a poetics of constant reinvention. Each context generates not only a different response, but the invention of a new rule or approach in relation to each specific encounter. Hejinian's prepoetics advocates a highly localised con-sideration of ethics and what one might even be tempted to coin a micro-ethics.

This yoking of singularity to a conceptualisation of an ethical enquiry is an important step to take. One could propose that the underlying intention in this essay is to redress the problems inherent in

17   Hejinian acknowledges in her essay a debt to Hannah Arendt's work *The Human Condition*, and that her configuration of the phrase is drawn from Arendt's discussion of 'the condition of natality'.

a polyphonic poetics overt reliance upon an aesthetic of multiplicity and contingency. Reliance upon multiplicity and contingency as a strategy for avoiding the spectre of an authoritative, if not to say authoritarian rhetoric, threatens in Hejinian's words to reduce poetics to 'a directionless pluralism' (348). It is evident that Hejinian attempts to distance her work from a post-structuralist paradigm of purposeless play. 'Reason', in its evocation of an encounter as a 'moment of incipience', draws a different perspective to the configuration of a community than is proposed in Bernstein's work. Bernstein's 'ideolectical' approach with its recourse to a mutable conceptualisation of community, threatens to collapse his poetics into a routine of ventriloquism or role-play.[18] While Hejinian's poetics assert that a conceptualisation of community must be seen as a transitional locus, there is a grave suspicion in this essay that an affectation of plurality gestures only to a vague possibility as its political vantage point. Instead 'Reason' proposes that one needs to consider how sustainable relationships can be formed in a poetics of multiplicity. The essay stresses that recourse to possibility alone threatens to engender 'a dangerous immanentism' (348).

Does Hejinian's essay satisfy concerns of privileging a poetics of immediacy and indeterminacy? It is crucial to a study of erring and the lyric that we consider how memory and history can be evoked in a configuration of a prepoetics. I have already suggested that a focus on erring in the poetry does generate a sense of accretion, and that the perpetual 'beginning' in the work is highly deceptive. Hejinian resists the evocation of experience as a demand for authenticity and asserts that there can be no context without history:

> One cannot meaningfully say 'this is happening' *out* of context. At the very moment of uttering the phrase, 'natality' occurs. And from that moment of incipience, which occurs with the recognition of the experience of and presented by the phrase *along comes something– launched in context* through the phrase *this is happening*, we are *in* context, which is to say, in thought (in theory and with critique) and in history. (345–6)

18 See Chapter One.

This is a radical re-evaluation of how one configures ideas of history and memory in poetry. Rather than presenting history as a disengaged narrative, the focus on context promotes a constant re-memorialisation of each encounter, not unlike the passage of serial substitutions in Levinas's work. Hejinian wants to situate this idea of context within history. Similarly, we have noted how the configuration of the lyric can only be enacted within a pattern of erring; how her poetry intentionally stakes a conflict between the perimeters of the lyric form and it's impetus towards descriptive mobility. Hejinian emphasises that these relations in the poem generate a sense of history not only as 'a descriptive and explanatory account of what has happened, but it also gives *something* a history with a future. Context is a past with a future' (347). A gesture to a setting of relations is emphasised in 'Reason' by the affirmative refrain '*this is happening.*' Hejinian's phrasing draws from Jean-François Lyotard's probing of '*is it happening?*' in his consideration of contingency and linkage in *The Differend.*[19]

Most ambitious is the final supposition of Hejinian's essay where she suggests how a responsible pre-poetics may be enacted:

> Faced with the notorious gap in meaning, we may ask, 'What should we do?' But we already know what to do. And this knowing what to do is neither derived from nor does it produce guidelines– either prescriptive, proscriptive, or even descriptive. It is, rather, intrinsic to living in context. (352)

The closing comments echo the earlier problem faced in Levinas's work with its understanding of responsibility as 'an obligation which is *anachronistically* prior to every engagement'. This sense of 'knowing' in Hejinian's work is equally provocative. Whereas in the parallel reading with Levinas this obligation can be understood as a necessary exposure to propel the self into being, it remains unclear in 'Reason' whether this responsibility is a demand imposed upon the subject, or

---

19 For an extended discussion on the relationship between Lyotard's *The Differend* and Hejinian's essay see Peter Nicholls 'Phenomenal Poetics: Reading Lyn Hejinian', in *The Mechanics of the Mirage: Postwar American Poetry*, eds. Michel Delville and Christine Pagnouelle (Liège: Université de Liège, 2000), pp. 241–52.

an action given altruistically. Peter Nicholls's assessment of this pronounced ethical turn in Hejinian's poetics strikes a note of caution in approaching the poetry. He indicates that the expansive trajectory of the poetics and the execution of these claims place a considerable demand on the practice of the poetry. In particular he notes that a reliance upon an aesthetic of strangeness as a method for articulating these claims, generates a pressure 'on the capacity of poetic form to translate a quotidian and "homely" content into something other, something productively "unhomely"' (251).

Read in this light Hejinian's *Happily* presents some final dilemmas to a study of erring in Hejinian's poetry. A conflict of positioning is maintained throughout the text, the poet seeks to situate the poem in an unfolding linkage of encounter. At times there is temptation to establish a broader overview. This temptation to somehow step 'out' of context is enacted by Hejinian's texture of aphoristic call and response, and the desire for an omniscient commentary.

Happily's opening echoes 'Reason' and is an attempt to situate its claims into momentum. Hejinian does not advance a prescriptive trajectory. The poem works against the presupposition of a pursuit of 'happiness' by insisting on the momentum of linkage. *Happily* affirms that 'What I feel is taking place, a large context, long yielding' (3). The formation of this extensive context emerges in the text as a form of nomadic wandering, reminding one intermittently of the pattern of erring in *The Guard*. The journey in the text is 'no straight line' (8), its movement is consistently thwarted 'We go no more than a couple of feet before we come upon the obstacle punctually' (24). There are even remnants of a cartography in *Happily* since the day aims at 'the future fork' (24). This evocation of a tentative trajectory is frequently dispelled or disbanded 'North, east, south and west, the four directions turn in play away' (29). Most telling in this literal reading of erring in the text are the statements and questions posed in the poem. We are that 'There is no one 'correct path'/ No sure indication' (28). Importantly the work also interrogates a reliance upon an aesthetic of improvisation and spontaneity 'Does it all come to a distinction for accidental wanderings' (38).

It is possible to dwell too literally on the figural map of erring in *Happily* and one needs to consider how the claims for a prepoetics are orchestrated in the poem. A main consideration is how Hejinian's evocation of serial contexts can be launched into a sustainable momentum, and whether a conceptual reading of erring in the poem provides a way of partially deploying the ethical claims configured in Hejinian's poetics. In the poem there are evident attempts to claim an ethical enquiry, happiness is initially configured altruistically as 'what we volunteer' (6). There are references to a configuration of 'good' in terms of an encounter 'The good is the chance with things that happen that inside and out time takes' (10). Later this abstract conceptualisation of the good is linked with an unconfigured ethical grammar: 'A store of intellect, a certain ethical potential, something that will hold good' (16). Situating this 'ethical potential' is a difficult task. Analysing an extended passage gives a clearer impression of how *Happily* attempts to sustain what Hejinian draws attention to in her preface as 'the shapes of thinking'[20]:

> It is midday a sentence its context– history with a future
> The blue is sky at all high points and the shadow underfoot
> moves at zero point
> Someone speaks it within reason
> The one occupied by something launched without endpoint
> Flaubert said he wanted his sentences *erect while running–*
> almost an impossibility
> Nonetheless, though its punctuation is half hoping for failure,
> the sentence makes an irrevocable address to life
> And though the parrot speaks but says nothing this has the
> impact of an aphorism
> Are you there?
> I'm here
> Is that a *yes* or a *no*? (7)

The passage begins by unravelling and retracing the mechanics of a proposition and statement, 'It is midday' is subjected to an extended descriptive analysis. Links between these sentences emerge from a stress upon a highly localised spatial evocation. The pattern of these observations is placed in opposition to an extended linear journey 'without end point.' This countering of a linear trajectory is further

20   Hejinian, Introduction to *Happily*, in *Language of Inquiry*, p. 384.

emphasised by an anecdotal account of spontaneous writing. One wonders how a conceptualisation of 'context' operates within the extended linking of these reflections. The interjections of Hejinian's 'accordioning sentences' (384) can threaten to overburden the passage and dissipate into unsustainable rhetorical claims. If indeed the sentence is conceived as an 'address to life', it offers scant relief since it is immediately reconfigured as ventriloquising a claim of concern. The thrust of this passage seems less focused upon establishing an intersubjective context than abnegating claims to responsibility. Invariably the passage's position is notoriously ambiguous and customarily diffident; there is a line here that Hejinian is eager to overstep. But paradoxically the indeterminacy created by these rhetorical interjections rather than promoting a shared navigable space, or 'moment of incipience' lean towards an ironic commentary on the text. One could question where these claims for reciprocation may be performed– in the interstices of the text, or beyond it?

Happily stresses that the performance of this encounter is syntactical and as a result there pressure is placed on Hejinian's text. Can the poem actually perform these claims, or just thematise them into self-reflexive conjecture:

> From something launched we extract our sentences
> Altogether written, writing everything, writing mockery (of
> vague physical complaints, political cliches, silence)
> beautifully in a follow-up writing (rejecting self-
> containment, without fear of standing face-to-face) as if
> we were ephemeral we are here and we mark out our
> place in it (29)

The performance of a prepoetics is pulled towards analytic reflection. Moreover the parenthetical and digressive structure of this extended sentence lends itself to a reading of erring, yet making the sudden transition from an evocation of the 'ephemeral' to the concrete claim of 'we mark our place in it' is a difficult task. How credible are these moments of assertion and do they advance Hejinian's desire to situate sustainable relationships in the work moving it beyond a paradigm of play? There are indications of an underplayed heroism 'without fear of standing face-to-face', but one wonders whether the localised situating of this brave gesture remains isolate in the enfolding sentence structure.

Happily states that 'To another human one acts one intervenes' (21), yet in spite of the text's frequent recourses to 'we' and 'our', the terrain of this volume seems surprisingly depopulated. Hejinian's pursuit of establishing some the claims of 'Reason' in the poem creates a texture of doubting in the poem. Doubt and contradiction are of course the necessary pre-requisites of Hejinian's enquiry, yet the enforced appeals to context can make responsibility a point of reference as we are told: 'Not proving but pointing ... I admit to being sometimes afraid of the effort required for judgment, afraid of the judgment required (21–2). This inability to judge is induced by the text's focus on a highly localised evocation of encounter and the proximity this establishes generates an 'impression of something short lived we can't retreat, can't know where we are' (23). When the poem shifts its position to an omniscient overview a sense of a viable trajectory is revealed and the rhetorical claims of the text are thrown into a sudden relief:

> In summer a city below a clock in wormy progress plays a
> prominent role in what might otherwise be hampered by
> sincerity but that wouldn't arrive for hours
> Come winter I see the particularly foreshortened perspective
> disguise retreat and in no way get arranged
> Come spring
> The inevitable fall then is not now an admirable representative
> time though it once eagerly served
> But there was such a beginning happiness at it that I could
> hardly be calm I blurted and then held my position like a
> statue in moonlight when comment comes slowly and
> must be read likewise (37–8)

This 'held' or elevated position in *Happily* stands out from the rest of the poem, particularly when one considers that earlier in the poem Hejinian asserts 'we're closer to the ground to see one another clearly (21). What is presented is far from a static panorama of the city since this halt establishes a point of reflection from the inexhaustible premises of encounter in the text. With considered reflection, Hejinian comments that the progress of the city would be 'hampered by sincerity', implying that the practical application of these thematised claims is at odds with the infrastructure below. Hejinian's commentary on the seasonal shifts establishes a complete stepping out of context, but the position of the speaker as a 'statue' creates a distinct impression of a civic monument. While there is no evident rhetorical embellishment in this passage, there is a veiled implication of legislative power or mandate in 'when comment comes slowly and must be read likewise.' Hejinian may be gesturing to the poet here as a figuration of Shelley's 'unacknowledged' legislator.

Michel de Certeau's distinguishing between the panoptic vision of the city and the pedestrian experience of its inhabitants, offers a way of considering the different perspectives set up in *Happily*. In *The Practice of Everyday Life*, de Certeau suggests that the desire to view or map the city from such a height betrays a desire to theorise, the panoptic spectator becomes a 'voyeur-god' whose overview is comparable to Icarus's flight over Daedalus's maze.[21] This position allows not only a cartographic reading of the city, but threatens to establish a totalising fiction. In opposition, the practitioners of the city live 'down below' (93). Certeau's commentary draws an evocative description of the labyrinthine and the frequently illegible passage of daily encounter:

> The paths that correspond in this intertwining, unrecognized poems in which each body is an element signed by many others, elude legibility ... The networks of these moving intersecting writings compose a manifold story that has neither author nor spectator, shaped out of fragments of trajectories and alterations of spaces: in relation to representations, it remains daily and indefinitely other. (93)

One can see how the indeterminacy promoted by Hejinian's evocation of a prepoetics resonates with a trajectory which defies incompletion and mapping. Although Hejinian's own allusion to the poem as 'a map of its own imperfections' (35) defies a totalising logic, there is the veiled indication that the lure of addressing a polis, however tentative it may be, does inhabit *Happily*. Hejinian's imaginary legislator is

21 Michel de Certeau, *The Practice of Everyday Life* (Berkeley: University of California Press, 1998), p. 63.

often a ludic and momentary commentator, but we can retrospectively assert that it is within these breaches in the text's trajectory that any form of 'ethical potential' may be sourced.

Viewed unsympathetically Hejinian's juggling act of ethical claims on one hand and aesthetic indeterminacy on the other, could be read as projecting a vague 'possibility' as its political vantage point. But if one contextualises the doubt in her conceptualisation of a pre-poetics as a necessary prerequisite to the questioning of consensus, one finds redemptive claims to a poetics of indeterminacy. Possibly Jacques Derrida's comments in the *Politics of Friendship*,[22] indicate how instrumental the concept of possibility may be in motivating any broad claim towards an ethical engagement:

> It is indeed a *perhaps* that cannot as yet be determined as dubiative or sceptical, the perhaps of what *remains* to be thought, to be done, to be lived ... Now this *perhaps* not only comes 'before' the question (investigation, research, theory, philosophy); it would come, in order to make it possible, 'before' the originary acquiescence which engages the question in advance with the other. (38)

I stake that we can translate the 'perhaps' of Derrida's discussion to the 'doubt' of Hejinian's prepoetics. Certainly a reading of erring in Hejinian's poetics highlights that the poet's enquiry is willing to embrace error and dispense with the certainties inscribed in an 'ideology of accuracy.'[23] Moreover, the 'doubting' of Hejinian's erring poetics can only encourage the reader's agency to engage with, and act upon the questions the poet invariably prompts.

---

22   Jacques Derrida, *Politics of Friendship*, trans. George Collins (London: Verso, 1999).

23   It should be noted that Hejinian is acutely aware of the problems faced in the would-be extolling of aesthetic indeterminacy. She states 'Recently in my own classroom experience I have noticed that students are increasingly troubled by uncertainty ... They find even the authoritative (and sometimes authoritarian) certitude of high modernism preferable to the postmodernism that worked so hard to overthrow that certitude and achieve uncertainty.' 'Stages of Encounter with a Difficult Text' in *Poetry and Pedagogy: The Challenge of the Contemporary*, eds. Joan Retallack and Julian Spahr (New York: Palgrave, 2006), pp. 205–11 (p. 211).

Chapter Seven
Lyric from L=A=N=G=U=A=G=E
into the 21st Century

In the last two decades there has been an alert and inherently sceptical examination of Language Writing's legacy to a younger generation of poets. Emerging from current scholarship is a strong sense that Language Writing must be viewed as the last of the American avant-gardes. If the appropriation of the avant-garde into mainstream culture denotes the invariable commodification of a radical aesthetics, it could be argued that Language Writing has already been disseminated into a texture of writing. Yet in adhering to a chronological pattern of emerging schools, there is the risk of fetishising poetic style as an adherence to what Alan Golding refers to as 'New Newer and Newest Poetries.'[1] Within this chronological framing there is also the temptation to view how a 'post' Language poetics may be shaped. Since Language Writing refused to view literature as a site of agonistic struggle, a 'post' Language poetics entertains ideals of critical continuity in a lineage of experimental writing. One productive view of the recent emerging poetry of the last twenty years, has been Steve Evans's proposition that readers should consider generation 'as a verb.'[2] This statement was given in 1993 as part of the introduction to *New Coast Writing*, a two-volume anthology originating from a conference at SUNY Buffalo dedicated to a younger generation of contemporary poets. Evans's comment indicates that generation should mean activity and action, and he delights in the absence of a formulating discourse which surrounds a new poetics: 'The most direct evidence concerning the existence of a "new coast" may be that

---

1   Alan Golding, 'New, Newer and Newest American Poetries', *Chicago Review* 43.4 (1997), 17–21.
2   Steve Evans, 'Introduction', in *Writing from the New Coast: Technique*, eds. Peter Gizzi and Juliana Spahr (Providence: Oblek, 1993), pp. 4–11 (p. 4).

so many have found themselves washed up on it. Crevice mongers, impercipients, mistakes, squatters, singular constellations of the minor and miscellaneous, the oblique and the near obliterated, so this emergent collectivity appears even to itself.'[3] Recently, Evans makes an emphatic claim on the relationship of the dissemination of the avant-garde writing practices: 'Ever since the mid 1990s when a host of forces conspired to drive the rigid designator "Language poetry" out of credibility for all but the professoriat, avant-garde poetry in the US has proliferated without benefit– or detriment– of a shared conceptual horizon, agreed-upon situation definition or common archive.'[4]

However, Evans's open-ended response is in conflict with a more deliberating evaluation of contemporary poetry 'post' Language Writing. The *Village Voice* reviewer of Jennifer Moxley's *The Sense Record* declares that the trajectory between Language Writing and recent poetry is clearly mappable and indicative of a reactionary response: 'With an iron fist, avant-gardists soundly thumped poetry of lazy sentiment by scrabbling verse into Steinian fragments. Now with these poets manning the academic mothership rather than hastily stapling chapbooks, a younger generation is imploding invention by returning to the lyric.'[5] The suggestion is that the lyric form cannot be investigated in an experimental praxis. Moxley's contemporary, Kim Stefans comments upon the general reception of her first volume. He states that *Imagination Verses* 'sent a useful signal to many writers that it was time to write "lyrics" again, poems that are spontaneous, subjective (i.e. autobiographical and emotive) and "musical," discarding for the meantime whatever discoveries in form, rhythm and vocabulary that such movements as Dada, Objectivism, Projective Verse and Language Poetry have put forth.'[6] Some thirty years

3   Evans, 'Introduction', p. 7.
4   Evans, 'The Resistible Rise of Fence Enterprises'. Accessed: http://www.third factory.net/resistable.html
5   Cathy Hong, 'Oppen Sesame: *The Sense Record* and Other Poems', *Village Voice*, October 2–8 (2002). Accessed: http://www.vilagevoice.com/books/0240, hong,38873,10.html
6   Brian Kim Stefans, 'Jennifer Moxley's *Wrong Life*', *How 2*, 1.5 (2001). Accessed: http://www.scc.rutgers.edu/however/v1_5_2001/current/alerts/stef ans. html

following the emergence of Language Writing the critical argument (for some commentators) remains that it is an inherently 'anti lyrical' tendency. Following this line of thought a consideration of lyric subjectivity, form and musicality would seem to be at extreme odds with the proclaimed status of Language Writing as a recuperated avant-garde. Werner Wolff in a recent study of the lyric remind us of the necessary digressive nature of the lyric enterprise. He states that 'no distinction between "the lyric" "poetry" and "poems" seems to be appropriate any longer ... As a consequence of this terminological situation, the lyric covers a vastly heterogeneous text corpus that is moreover in a continuous process of development.'[7]

Hopefully, the preceding chapters on the poetry of Charles Bernstein, Michael Palmer and Lyn Hejinian demonstrate that the lyric retains an important focus to writers affiliated with early Language Writing. Throughout *Reading Error*, I attempt to show that the consideration of an erring poetics enables us to revise the role that lyricism establishes in the work of the three poets. To broach a comprehensive survey of a recent generation's writing as evolving from Language Writing, would be to embark upon a problematic pursuit of continuities and discontinuities. Yet, it is evident that the tenor of scholarship is shifting towards a more sustainable understanding of how lyricism may be understood in recent writing. One could suggest that Palmer's proposal of an 'analytic lyric' and the sense of lyric as an oppositional force not the lyric of 'poor little me' are propositions that have been eagerly adopted by a recent generation of American poets.[8] This final chapter considers how the interaction of Language Writing and the lyric emerge in the work of contemporary poet, Jennifer Moxley. Moxley has been given the somewhat dubious honour of reinventing, rereading or reconfiguring lyric practice in recent American poetry. Before examining how a conceptualisation of an

7   Werner Wolff, 'The Lyric Problems of Definition and a Proposal for Reconceptualisation', *Theory into Poetry: New Approaches to the Lyric*, eds. Eva Muller-Zettelmann and Margarete Rubik (Amsterdam: Rodopi, 2004), pp. 21–56 (p. 23).

8   Michael Palmer, 'Interview' in Thomas Gardner *Regions of Unlikeness: Explaining Contemporary Poetry* (Lincoln: University of Nebraska Press, 1999), p. 238.

erring poetics enables a reading of lyricism in her poetry, it is necessary to note how an anxiety concerning 'post' Language poetry has been chronicled thus far.

'Post' Language or 'After' Language?

In 2001 ten younger American poets were asked by Swedish magazine *OEI* where they saw their work in relation to Language Writing. Entitled 'After Language Poetry', their responses were uploaded and disseminated on the UBU website.[9] Two questions were asked: 'How do you conceive of innovative poetry in America after Language Poetry?' and 'How do you define your own practice in relation to Language Poetry?' Invariably the responses are varied and suggestive of considerable differences in which a younger generation conceptualise Language Writing. There is however one broad consensus; for the majority of younger poets Language Writing is now read as a historical phenomenon, contextualised at a certain point in literary chronology. This understanding reasserts Bob Perelman's proposition in *The Marginalisation of Poetry*, that there is a history of Language Writing to be written. In 1997 he states that 'Language Writing can be placed in a sequence ... but while it can be subsumed within a readerly literary history it holds out the possibility for new social possibilities for writers who might find literary history less burdensome, more useful.'[10] We could add to this Steve Mc Caffrey's earlier admission in 1986 when republishing 'The Death of the Subject' for *North of Intention* that the essay has been superseded by writing practices. McCaffrey states: 'A decade later I can safely speak of this concern as

9   Co-editor, Jesper Olsson, *OEI*, 7–8 (2001). Accessed: http://www.ubu.com/pap ers/oei/intro.html

10   Bob Perelman, *The Marginalization of Poetry* (Princeton: Princeton U.P. 1997), p. 37.

an historical phase with attention having shifted to a larger aspect.'[11] These citations challenge a convenient reading of an already emergent second generation of Language Writing.

For many of the poets questioned, Language Writing is conceived as the most recent act in a sequence of American literary experimentation. Stacey Doris proposes that it is 'the last avant-garde of the twentieth century,'[12] Moxley adds that Language Writing is certainly a historic movement since it was 'the last credible avant-garde in the US to be critically assimilated.'[13] Kenneth Goldsmith is even more definitive, stating that as a movement its 'work has been done.'[14] However, the ten poets interpret the processes of assimilation, recuperation and dissemination in conflicting ways. There is general agreement on the relationship between Language poetics, a commitment to scrutinising the power invested in linguistic structures and a politicisation of poetic form. Yet there is considerable variation on whether this can be conceived as a continuing project for younger writers. Christian Bök suggests that there is a definitive end point to the investigations of Language Writing and that its formal preoccupations require enervation by other disciplines. For him Language Writing 'pushed poetry as far as poetry on the page can go; now poetry must find new avenues of thought beyond poetry itself, seeking inspiration, for example, in the work of architects and musicians, scientists and engineers.'[15] For others there is a continued momentum to be followed and further investigation to be taken to addressing race and sexuality. Juliana Spahr proposes that there is a 'new exciting writing coming after Language Writing.'[16] She adds that Language writers have 'done much to politicize writing, to break down hierarchies between readers and authors, and to investigate subjectivity in terms of class and gender,' yet they have curiously 'avoided doing much investigation around race or sexuality.' Race and ethnicity is one of the key considerations that

11   Cited by Marjorie Perloff, *Differentials: Poetry, Poetics, Pedagogy* (Tuscaloosa: Alabama U.P. 2005), p. 157.
12   Accessed: http://www.ubu.com/papers/oei/doris.html
13   Accessed: http://www.ubu.com/papers/oei/moxley.html
14   Accessed: http://www.ubu.com/papers/oei/goldsmith.html
15   Accessed: http://www.ubu.com/papers/oei/Bök.html
16   Accessed: http://www.ubu.com/papers/oei/spahr.html

Stefans takes up in his discussion. He poses that Language practices were initially caught in a conundrum 'Since one of its early premises was the critique of "identity" and the self, it never had the language for dealing with minority issues that attempted to legitimize "identity" as a central subject of discourse.'[17] The result he proposes is that Language Writing was often seen as 'elitist.'

The sense of a shared trajectory following Language Writing is greeted with considerable opprobrium. Doris states that as younger poets her generation have been faulted 'as incoherent, indefinite; lacking a program.' The dissemination of writing practices in itself, raises crucial issues about the recuperation of any aesthetic project. There is a general fear that Language centred practices may only be viewed as formal techniques. Bök for one, proposes that the writing's challenge of generic conventions and referentiality has paradoxically 'spawned a younger generation of dedicated imitators.' Paradoxically Doris holds to the credo that 'poetry can be revolutionary; that by reinventing syntax, opposing and questioning grammar, and so on, we open language and thereby society to new organizational alternatives.' This would suggest a return to the Marxist materialist imperatives of early Language Writing poetics. For the majority of the poets the influence of Language Writing upon their work is similar to Robert Duncan's 'place of first permission.'[18] Language Writing's questioning of established lyric forms offers alternatives to what Spahr refers to as forms of 'individualism and idiosyncrasy', pointing instead towards 'unexpected and yet intimate pluralism.' Usefully she considers this momentum as a shift from ideas of confessionalism to 'Language Writing's self-aware roots in modernism.' Equally Jena Osman associates Language Writing techniques as a challenge to 'the big pay-off: the epiphanic "ah!"'[19] or the predominant mode of the eighties.

For many the continued development of hybrid forms would appear to emphatically move the future of poetry from the page and into cyberspace. Stefans sees his own work as a direct descendent of

17   Accessed: http://www.ubu.com/papers/oei/stefans.html
18   Robert Duncan, 'Often I am permitted to return to a Meadow', *Opening of the Field* (New York: New Directions 1973), p. 7.
19   Accessed: http://www.ubu.com/papers/oei/osman.html

Language Writing but he proposes that the next step for a poetry focussed upon the materiality of language is web-based experimentation. Karen Mac Cormack echoes this position suggesting that any future writing will 'make use of visual, sound, performance, and cyber media in order to bring the materiality of language (and thus the reader) into a more activist position.'[20] The continued dissemination of web poetics would also appear to further the positioning of a 'post' Language poetics in global terms. Mac Cormack asserts that she cannot 'conceive of post-L=A=N=G=U=A=G=E Writing solely in American terms.' Equally Stefans makes connections between the poetics of Language Writing and poetry that has not been readily adopted by the movement such as 'non-American' concrete poets Ian Hamilton Finlay and Haraldo de Campos. Moreover Stefans challenges the reading of post Language poetics as advancing the ambitions of European modernism. In querying this immediate associative lineage he seeks to disrupt the established narrative of an evolutionary poetics, and hopes that his own poetry will never 'be marred by a critic's misguided attempt to place it back into the box of continental modernism'. Contrastingly Peter Gizzi proposes that the shared connection is an interest in modernism: 'we share common texts. Whether it be the Writings of Emily Dickinson or Jack Spicer. Ezra Pound or H.D. Gertrude Stein or John Cage. George Oppen or Lorine Niedecker. It is about listening to a tradition that provides method and ground in our present.'[21]

A critical consensus regarding the affiliations of Language Writing with an early tradition of modernist poetic experimentation has already been established.[22] Stefans proposes that for many poets of his generation the ambition is to integrate ideas put forward by Language poetics, with more traditional poetic values. Other poets recognise the danger of treating Language Writing purely as an aesthetic instead of a writing that inscribes political, conceptual or philosophical claims. For Chet Wiener the poetics of Language Writing

20   Accessed: http://www.ubu.com/papers/oei/maccormack.html
21   Accessed: http://www.ubu.com/papers/oei/gizzi.html
22   See for example works by critics such as Marjorie Perloff and Peter Nicholls in Bibliography.

provide a link with the tenets of Russian Formalism, and this sense of interdependence is emphasised as borrowing from different traditions. Wiener suggests that poetry 'after' Language must focus on the inter-relationship not only of different media, but also multiple competing conceptual claims: 'I find the most innovative American writing and the most interesting projects are those that motivate their work with complex conceptual systems and/or intensely developed views of the world ... I'd add those that combine looking at the present with divulging historical recurrences while at the same time somehow or other displaying awareness of the history of poetic forms.'[23] While ideals of a postmodern multiplicity remain an important feature, the survey emphasises the importance of understanding how aesthetic premises can be translated to a possible political mapping of the world. Mac Cormack emphasises that the relationship between poetics and political realities is of tantamount importance. Her aim is to create a poetry of 'socio-political existence' which reveals 'how our private intimacies have public obligations and ramifications, how intimacy has a social bond with shared meaning.'

These responses complicate any simplistic reading of a definitive 'post' Language generation, and most certainly the sample answers from the ten poets do not present a retreat to the lyric as a rejection of the 'Language mother ship'. Marjorie Perloff's long established readings of the lyric texture of Language Writing grant a nuanced perspective on the emerging characteristics of post Language Writing. In considering what can we expect of American poetry, her answer maps a similar consensus of ideas:

> We can anticipate (1) a return to narrative– but a highly fractured variant; (2) much less resistance to the lyric 'I' as operative principle, (3) enormous care for the materiality of words; the look of language as well as to the asyntactic, disjunctive modes we have learned to expect from Language poetry, and (4) a return to literary allusion, scorned in the seventies and eighties as too well-bred, together with a new interest in Beauty, the aesthetic, the pleasure of the text. It is an exciting moment for lyric poetry.[24]

---

23   Accessed: http://www.ubu.com/papers/oei/wiener.html
24   Perloff, 'Yang Introduction to Younger American Poets.' Accessed: www.epc. buffalo.edu/authors/perloff/yang.html

Moving from some of these assumptions, it will useful to understand what reading of the lyric can be configured from Moxley's work. Her poems provide a sceptical and attentive analysis of the early propositions of Language Writing, and establish a productive correspondence with a definable lyric tradition. Possibly her poetry evinces what Mark Wallace refers to as the collaborative processes of a younger generation: 'Post Language poets need to be aware, I believe, of the insights of Language poetry, and their practice therefore becomes to varying degrees a creative collaboration with the productions of Language poets, although that collaboration includes many writers who are not Language Writers at all.'[25]

Jennifer Moxley and the lyric

In Moxley's words she is often considered a 'lyric poster child'[26] of her generation. Her first volume *Imagination Verses* was published by Tender Buttons in 1996, and has since published two volumes of poetry *The Sense Record* (2003) and *Often Capital* (2005).[27] The preface to *Imagination Verses* addresses the lyric in no uncertain terms; Moxley declares that the volume was written 'out of a desire to engage with the universal lyric "I", as well as the poetic line, with all of its specific formal artifice.'[28] More recently, she questions whether the information she gave in this early preface was in fact 'disingenuous' (49). Moxley's poetry is densely musical, incorporating citation, digression, meditation and a provisional self-reflexive testing of the lyric. The more evident references in her poems consciously display

25 Mark Wallace, 'Definitions in Process, Definitions as Process/Uneasy Collaborations: Language and Postlanguage Poetries.' Accessed: http://www.flashpoint mag.com/postlang.html
26 Moxley, 'Lyric Poetry and the Inassimilable Life', *The Poker*, 6 (Cambridge, MA: 2005), 49–58 (p. 49).
27 Moxley, *Imagination Verses* (New York: Tender Buttons, 1996), *The Sense Record* (Cambridge: Salt 2003), *Often Capital* (Chicago: Flood Editions 2005).
28 Moxley, *Imagination Verses*, p. x.

an affiliation towards a lyric tradition ranging from the Romantics to the New York School. Moreover her relationship to Language Writing can be seen less a commitment to its formal investigations than the attention Language poetics placed upon less acknowledged poets. Responding to the survey on 'post' Language Writing she situates herself specifically within a lineage of modernist poetic practice. She admits that 'as a set of theories about writing Language poetry ceased being of any help to me about 1989,'[29] but that the writing was important in its insistence 'on keeping poetry political' and its contribution to a tradition of small magazines and presses. She adds 'more significantly still, it was through Language poetry that I was introduced to many of the writers I continue to hold very dear, poets such as Zukofsky, Oppen, Duncan and Creeley, to name only a few.' Moxley is keen to indicate that there is a tendency to focus on textual methods as exclusively deriving from Language Writing without distinguishing between periods and earlier experimentations with parataxis or field forms. She adds that all the characteristic devices associated with the poetics of Language Writing, 'get subsumed under the category of Language poetry not unlike when everything strange becomes "surrealist."'

Turning to the poems from *Imagination Verses*, one is aware of the citational density of Moxley's lyric. Moxley unabashedly engages in a dialogue with 19th Century Romanticism in her two page opposing lyrics, 'Duet #1 Wordsworth' and 'Duet # 2 Keats'. Her reading of Romantic lyricism functions as both a conversation and a musical responsiveness to key phrases from the two poets. The 'duets' that Moxley performs are an investigation in poetic translation; the sensation of these brief poems is not unlike a literary condensation. Both poems transform fragments of phrases from William Wordsworth's 'Intimations of Immortality', 'Tintern Abbey', 'Lucy Gray' and John Keats's 'Ode to a Nightingale' and 'The Eve of St Agnes' to impressions of literary ventriloquism. Reading these two poems produces a similar sensation to the deliberation of Bernstein's malapropisms, Hejinian's failing aphorism or the intertextual resonance of Palmer's work. Take for example the following variations: Moxley's

---

29   Accessed: http//:www.ubu.com/papers/oei/moxley.html

'Seal my fits with grey immortality' (62) combines Wordsworth's three titles; 'A slumber did my spirit seal', 'Lucy Gray' and 'Intimations of Immortality'. Further into the poem the phrasing 'reaper slumber among the ruined/ world ways' (62) echoes Wordsworth's 'She dwelt among the untrodden ways.'[30] Moreover, Moxley's pronouncement that 'the ode/ is a lyrical joy, a morning's march/ among spirit lines' (62) proposes a continuation of lineage and compositional movement. It is tempting to read Moxley's poem as haunted by tradition's 'spirit lines' or as evoking a form of textual uncanny, the poem provides a degree of familiarity which is simultaneously unnerving. Equally her 'duet' with Keats enacts a synopsis, indexing or even condensation of the poet's works. The following are the more explicit references: 'O Nightingale how many bards have I', 'St Agnes I laugh the ode into me/ once again tiptoe on the sitting sea' (63). The poem also incorporates the explicit titles *Hyperion*, *Endymion* and *King Lear*. 'Living poetry was drear' (63) reminds the reader of the difficulty which thwarted Keats's completion of *Hyperion* and his admission of an over reliance upon the Miltonic epic. Returning to the curious closing line to 'laugh the ode into me once again' (63) hints at Moxley's relationship to a tradition of the lyric. The intense subjectivity traditionally associated with lyric practice and its epiphanic highs becomes a physical wish for internalisation– the reader's desire for textual incorporation of the lyric into the body.

There is the temptation to read Moxley's work merely for its intertextual resonances, 'Duet #1 Wordsworth' and 'Duet # 2 Keats are taken from a volume entitled *Imagination Verses* which refers us to Wordsworth's own *Poems of the Imagination* (1815). While Moxley's poetry does not enact a derivative poetics, her writing explores what may constitute a sense of a tradition. Stefans proposes that Moxley's evocation of tradition does not establish a lineage in a chronological sense, but rather the 'texture' of a tradition:

---

30   William Wordsworth, *The Poetical Works of William Wordsworth*, ed. E. de Selincourt (Oxford: Oxford U.P., 1944), John Keats, *The Complete Poems*, ed. John Barnard (Middlesex: Penguin, 1973).

Moxley's tradition is not The Tradition– the European canon, the centrality of 'clear expression' in lyrics, hierarchical moral values resting on patriarchal dominance, Oedipal altercations with the Masters, etc. ... It has more to do with the feel of a 'tradition,' or a personal tradition which one controls and occupies, which is a fairly fresh concept these days.[31]

Moxley examines her affiliation to the lyric in a recent essay in *The Poker*.[32] Initially she admits that her perception of lyricism was coloured more by 'a phenomenon of my reception,' she adds that she has 'Never to my memory consciously setting to revitalise lyric practice' (49). In responding to the premise of a reinvigorated 21st Century lyric, Moxley is adamantly opposed to the fetishisation of the new: 'I didn't feel that there was any such thing as the "new lyric." The lyric had neither vanished nor been made obsolete just because there was a brief period in the 70s and 80s when formally progressive poets coming out of Modernist tradition stopped thinking about it' (53). Instead she places a focus on lyricism as a dissenting practice with a social conscience. Reminiscent of Theodor Adorno's claims for the social implication of the lyric, Moxley makes a claim for the 'social lyric' as a voice 'which has been excluded from the political power of dominant narratives', and that the lyric poem can approximate an experience of "presence"– thereby providing relief from both longing & regret' (50). Cast in this social context, the lyric becomes an antidote to the heroic ambitions of epic poetry. Once situated within history the lyric assumes a powerful dissenting role and 'Via the lyric alternative the articulate of the inassimilable individual structurally barred from the epic it comes forth. This voice is not perforce "anti social" in fact it may even feel a passionate connection and investment is the very history from which it is excluded' (50–1). Turning to Adorno's 'On Lyric Poetry and Society' one can see the emerging parallels more clearly:

The highest lyric works are those in which the subject, with no remaining trace of mere matter, sounds forth in language until language itself acquires a voice. The unself consciousness of the subject submitting itself to language as something objective, and the immediacy and spontaneity of that subject's expression

31   Stefans, 'Jennifer Moxley's Wrong Life'.
32   Moxley, 'Lyric Poetry and the Inassimilable Life'.

as one and the same: thus language mediates lyric poetry and society in their innermost core. This is why the lyric reveals itself to be the most deeply grounded in society when it does not chime in with society, when it communicates nothing, when, instead, the subject whose expression is successful reaches an accord with language itself, with the inherent tendency of language.[33]

Notoriously, far from seeing the lyric as a purely solipsistic enterprise or a voicing of estrangement, Adorno approaches lyric voicing as simultaneous with social articulation. The essay posits great force on the lyric's resistance to social integration. The lyric's withdrawal into subjectivity cannot be separated from the social realm, since it is an action, which implies critique or even opposition in itself. It is this very resistance to reification and incorporation that Moxley celebrates: 'That which cannot be easily assimilated not only provokes frustration and astonishment its very existence can serve as a radical critique of things as they are ... Thus through the lyric what *fails to be* in social space –*IS*' (52). As Moxley's essay continues her discussion mirrors Adorno's assessment of the lyric as a reflection of a social unconscious. Moxley's discussion moreover echoes Hejinian's earlier investigation of the lyric dilemma in 'Language and "Paradise."' In Hejinian's essay the impossibility of harnessing experience through language is seen less as inadequacy than a celebration of a desire located within language as a sequence of irresolvable doubts and hesitations elicited from the reading of a text. Moxley comments on this sense of failure in the lyric text as indicative of a social and political possibility:

> We see how the social becomes more visible at its point of failure. The same might be said for the experience of the temporal present ... Lyric poetry and indeed all literature which employs a similar syntactical density, while stopping short of altering the laws of physics, is yet able in its best manifestations, to approximate the experience of 'presence' Once again through the lyric what *fails to be* – the experience of temporal presence–*IS*. (52)

33 Theodor Adorno, 'On Lyric Poetry and Society' in *Notes to Literature Volume One*, trans. Shierry Weber Nicholsen (Columbia: Columbia U.P., 1991), 37–54 (p. 43).

Moxley's interrogation of a lyric tradition is evident in her referencing of Wordsworth in both *Imagination Verses* and *The Sense Record*. Invariably one is drawn to reflect upon the call to common speech presented by Wordsworth and Samuel Coleridge's *Lyrical Ballads*, in conjunction with Moxley's poetics. Wordsworth's preface asserts the political leverage of individual speech as the utopic possibility of poetry. He infamously suggests that the primary purpose of poetry is to analyse the mind's operation or 'the primary laws of our nature' and that a poet is 'a man speaking to men.'[34] But Wordsworth adds a proviso to his statement of a democratic poetics by emphasising the importance of lyric artifice: 'To these qualities he has added a disposition to be affected more than other men by absent things, as if they were present; an ability of conjuring up in himself passions, which are indeed far from being the same as those produced by real events' (300). In *The Sense Record* Moxley questions her own fear that metaphorical and comparative poetic language might be seen to do violence to her subject. 'Grain of the Cutaway Insight' she questions the Romantic tradition directly asking: 'For what old law/ reputes to this, or any other/ chain of inept similes, vague images/ "the general Truths"?/ Those bold beliefs that Wordsworth's/ spirited Grasmere Boyhood/ never seemed to/ lack for' (3). Behind this questioning also lies Shelley's treatise on poets as 'the unacknowledged legislators of the world' in his 'A Defence of Poetry.'[35] Poetry he suggests is central to human life because it is the creator of culture; the poet creates a broad vision that transcends the poet's time and place to create a dialogue with past and future generations. Shelley not only associates poetry with melody but also harmony since poetry has a belief in the principles of the good and the true, the perfect, the ideal, the eternal and the infinite. The poem is 'the very image of life expressed in its eternal truth' (281) and poetry 'strengthens that fac-

---

34   Wordsworth's preface of 1800 and 1802 in *Wordsworth and Coleridge Lyrical Ballads*, eds. R.L. Brett and A.R. Jones (London: Routledge, 2005), pp. 286–314 (p. 290, 300).

35   P.B. Shelley, 'A Defence of Poetry' (1820) in *Shelley's Prose*, ed. David Lee Clark (Albuquerque: University of New Mexico Press, 1954), pp. 275–97 (p. 297).

ulty which is the organ of the moral nature of man in the same manner as exercise strengthens a limb' (283).

'Grain of the Cutaway Insight' strives to assert a connection with Wordsworth and Shelley's conceptualisation of poetry as the highest order of perception, mediating ideas of political and ethical responsibility. Shelley indicates that the ordering of perception and expression of 'the good' is not limited to the practice of artists. In his 'A Defence of Poetry' a broader social and political nexus is asserted:

> But Poets, or those who imagine and express this indestructible order, are not only the authors of language and of music, of the dance and architecture and statuary and painting: they are the institutors of laws, and the founders of civil society and the inventors of the arts of life and the teachers who draw into a certain propinquity with the beautiful and the true. (279)

The qualities that Shelley associates with poetic thinking, the visionary and ethical, extend to political and social spheres. He does not distinguish between the vision exercised by the poet and the vision necessary for those that would be teachers of the highest order, individuals in civic office and lawmakers. It is, however, the rhetoric associated with civic institutions and a political poetry which troubles Moxley in a later poem 'The Occasion' from *The Sense Record*. The poem questions the rhetorical ambition and idealism of speaking for those who have no power and no voice: 'Does the permission to silence others /come with the authority to speak? Is the authority to speak the authority to condescend those without authority /who by definition cannot speak?' (89). It is precisely this ongoing interrogation of situating a lyric sensibility in the late 20th Century and early 21st Century which enervates Moxley's reading of tradition. Moxley's comments build upon concepts of voice, articulation and communality from Adorno's 'The Lyric and Society'. Adorno considers that 'A collective undercurrent provides the foundation for all lyric poetry ... this undercurrent that makes language the medium in which the subject becomes more than mere subject' (45). He adds that Romanticism practices a 'programmatic transfusion of the collective into the individual through which the individual lyric poem indulged in a technical illusion of universal cogency without that cogency characterizing it inherently' (45). Hence we can begin to associate the lyric artifice that

Moxley points us to as an attempt to decentre an ambition of explicit pedagogy in contemporary poetics. In 'The Open Letter' series Moxley reiterates her belief in a community of readership; that the solitary reader of poetry is in face interrelated to a network of other readers, a presupposition which is not so far from the Wordsworthian ideal of 'common' language and Shelley's ideation of the imagination as the 'great instrument of moral good' and poetry as 'acting upon the cause' (283). Moxley comments that:

> Poetry continues to manifest its necessity through individual experience–people alone in rooms reading, each recognizing that certain something that leads them to dream of an universal, a language, a truth or whatever word we use to signify that place that leads us out beyond the boundaries of ourselves and into the larger concerns of existence that unique and glorious feeling that steals our minds away from the trivial so that we might partake of something important.[36]

The association of reading, tradition and agency is a pertinent one– further into the essay Moxley draws a parallel reading of Palmer's poetry as urging the poem to bear witness to the atrocities of the 20th Century. In a recent paper Palmer comments upon the network of associations and configuration which make the poem; and how a poem must be read with as retaining a degree of mobility and momentum at the time of its reading. His analysis of poetry's response to 'a moment of Barbarism' re-establishes the relevance of contemporary poet's ongoing engagement with society:

> The poem is altered by events that it cannot possibly foresee ... The point is not simply how work responds to current events, but how previous work is altered by and alters, them.) ... Poetry as something happening among other things happening. As something happening in language, and to language under siege. Poetry as memory, sometimes memory of the future. Poetry as both fixed and in process, ever a paradox. Above all, poetry as experience, as Philippe Lacoue-

36   Moxley 'To Whom It May Concern "sphere of generality"/on content', *OPEN LETTER* 11.3 (2001). Accessed: http://slought.org/ files/downloads/publications/openletter/04a.pdfshelley

Labarthe would put it. (He would add, poetry as interruption of the 'poetic,' but that's for some other time.)[37]

Palmer's configuration of poetic agency is reminiscent of Hejinian's examination of a prepoetics in *Happily* and her setting of relations in 'Reason' as the affirmative refrain '*this is happening*'.[38] His gesture to poetry as both fixed and also in process, draws us to reflect upon the self-reflexive awareness of an erring momentum that has determined our reading of the lyric so far. Moreover, the combination of his reflection upon poetry as 'happening in language' and Lacoue-Labarthe's proposition of poetry as 'interruption of the poetic', also causes one to consider how the lyric itself may perform against its own artifice. Moxley's own conditions for the lyric draw striking parallels for the consideration of individual agency, the configuration of memory and an erring momentum that challenges sequential movement:

> The lyric can provide a literary approximation of those fleeting moment of experience through which the present comes into being. In the lyric, where syntactically digressive devices work against narrative, the word both *is* and *is not* temporally fixed, and thus through lyricism, the past and the future along with the affective frames proper to each, namely longing and regret become presentized. (53)

The emphasis on the simultaneity of past and present indicates that lyric memory becomes the traditional complex of a present tense evocation of the past. Moxley's reference to what she calls 'digressive' strategies points us to interruptions in the text, resonances that hamper poetry's assimilation into an immediate narrative. In considering lyric language as a language of immediate enquiry, Moxley also makes reference to the palimtextual density of lyric poetry. Although Moxley's engagement with the lyric differentiates itself from Hejinian's labyrinthine enquiry, it is integral that we consider the framing of Moxley's lyric as concerned with constructing a certain artifice. There are indications in Moxley's poems that lyric artifice is linked to

---

37   Palmer, 'Poetry and Contingency: Within a Timeless Moment of Barbaric Thought', *Chicago Review*, 49.2 (2003), 65–76 (p. 75,6).
38   For a discussion of *Happily* see Chapter Six.

a sense or simulation of a tradition. Artifice in Moxley's *Imagination Verses* and *The Sense Record* can be linked to ideas of error and errancy as a form of poetic language that wanders, challenges and interrupts the lure of narrative.

Lyric Artifice and Lyric Errancies: *Imagination Verses* and *The Sense Record*

Reflecting on the poetry of the 1980s Moxley comments that 'the dirty word back then was not lyric but NARRATIVE' (55). She adds that 'I have no recollection of this term ever being conflated with the word "lyric". In fact I don't remember the question of lyricism ever coming up. And yet somewhere along the line lyricism and narrativity had ... become conflated' (55). Importantly she stresses that there was a curious reversal of genre identities in the poetics of this time. In Moxley's estimation 'Language poets were writing a kind of new prose which was far more heavily indebted to non-narrative lyric devices than anyone cared to admit' (55). Contrastingly, in her view 'the mainstream poets were writing a very dull prose in the approximate shape of lyric poems' (55). Moxley's statement should not be misread, she is not making the case for the valorising of non-narrative poetry– as evinced by her own self proclaimed narrative poem on 9/11 in 'The Occasion.'[39] But her focus on ideas of narrative continuity, transparency and opacity returns us to the key claims in Bernstein's notorious essay in verse 'The Artifice of Absorption' which was delivered as a talk

---

39   Moxley states that 'The Occasion' is 'a long narrative poem I wrote following 9/11 about the impossibility of finding "common ground" in the wake of that event and in the military campaigns that followed. While arguably this poem addresses questions of the state the self and the citizen, it is decidedly not lyric but a narrative' (p. 54).

during this time.[40] Bernstein gives both key terms 'artifice and absorption' provisional interpretations; while one would intuitively associate the 'transparency' of the workshop aesthetic with a certain narrative 'absorption', and the 'opacity' of more innovative poetry with a certain 'artifice', Bernstein problematises these categories by suggesting that a poetry of 'impermeability' can also be 'absorbing'. Moreover Bernstein suggests that interruptions, discontinuities, resonances and densities in the text are key tactics for maintaining narrative interest:

> interruptions also
> function like Brecht's framing devices, to situate
> the reader at an alternative vantage point, an
> additional attentional field, rekindling interest
> in a narrative that might not hold the interest
> without this supplement.[41]

This fascination with narrative digression, inconsistency and errancy in the poetic text is of course mirrored in 19th Century lyric practice. Michael Collings revisits Wordsworth's poetry as perambulating texts to provide cultural re readings of the 19th Century. In *Wordsworthian Errancies*, Collings useful proposes that ideas of erring in Wordsworth's narrative poems can be read as solitary excursions in which the poet errs from the proper path and cannot indicate the difference between truth and falsity.[42] Collings's examination of the erring impulse in Wordsworth's poetry provides us a way into considering the lyric artifice which Moxley stresses is integral to her understanding of lyricism. The study moves from a sense of momentum and obvious perambulation in Wordsworth's larger narrative poems to a conceptualisation of poetic language as 'a duplicitous poetics' (3). Collings comments that the erring impulse is initially 'the wandering male solitary who in straying from the proper path may or

40　The essay was initially delivered as a talk on August 25th, 1985 as part of the New Poetics Colloquium of *The Kootenay School of Writing*, Vancouver Canada.

41　Charles Bernstein, 'Artifice of Absorption', in *A Poetics* (Harvard: Harvard U.P., 1991), pp. 9–89 (p. 69).

42　David Collings, *Wordsworthian Errancies The Poetics of Cultural Dismemberment* (Baltimore and London: Johns Hopkins U.P., 1994).

may not arrive at the goal of his quest. In rhetorical terms this figure is errancy or hyperbole' (3). In framing his discussion Collings quotes Jean-Pierre Mileur's analysis of hyperbole as a form of linguistic errancy. Milleur proposes that hyperbole is 'not just the language of heights aspired to and depths fallen to; it is also the language of detours of exaggeration, errancy, extra vagrancy. And just as ... hyperbolic depths are perceptively indistinguishable from hyperbolic heights, so are wanderings from the true path indistinguishable from true quests.'[43]

Reading 'Kalypso Facto' from *Imagination Verses* enables us to initially consider the rendering of lyric artifice and its relationship to error in Moxley's poetry. Taking as its central narrative the figure of the stranded Odysseus on Kalypso's Ogygia, the poem evokes a sentiment of anti-uxoriousness. The poem's subject already invokes the ultimate errancy narrative– *The Odyssey*. Moxley's poem in articulating Kalypso's perspective creates a sonorous linguistic patterning in which mythic and domestic, ancient and contemporary clash spectacularly. The poem's linguistic density creates an impression of archaism and a sensation of a tradition. Moxley's writing generates a conflict between the established 'facto' of Kalypso's narrative and the mundane details that overlay events to create a palimpsestual text. Susan Vanderborg comments that there is an evident relationship between the palimpsest and issues of originality and authenticity. By using a source from history or literature 'the palimpsest allows even a marginal author to claim a place among canonical works. The contemporary palimpsest is a plagiaristic reproduction so detailed moreover that is seems to collapse the distinction between source and revision.'[44]

The dominance of domestic detail in 'Kalypso Facto' detracts the reader from the underlying narrative, there is certainly the 'sense' of a tradition, but one whose impression is built upon synthesis, simulation and linguistic density. Kalypso berates Odysseus: 'The matrix of your

43   Jean Pierre Mileur, *The Critical Romance: The Critic as Reader, Writer, Hero* (Madison: University of Wisconsin, 1990), pp. 31–2.
44   Susan Vanderborg, 'The Communal Lyric: Palimpsest in the Corpus of Susan Howe', in *New Definitions of Lyric: Theory, Technology and Culture*, ed. *Mark Jefferys* (New York: Garland, 1998), pp. 99–125 (p. 99).

hamstrung home life/ is undercutting all my generous gifts' (58). Not quite a neologism, the near compound description creates a graphic if not violent impression of immobility, magnified by the sense of 'undercutting' or disabling in the text. Words and phrases such as 'bedlamite', 'othered lands', 'jilted memory' create a text of conflicting temporal styles and languages. Moxley's poem is a curious melange of emphatic hyperbole at points. The poem is also guided by sonic affiliation and translation of aphoristic phrases, the following have a sense of familiarity and yet are new formulations of existing phrases: 'hopped up interventionist', 'dress-up progress' 'curb your second guessing' and 'jilted memory' (58). On Zeus's arrival Kalypso's remarks: 'His loud armaments have been making petits fours of continents for far too long' (58). This combination of war, violence, mannered social interaction and dainty patisseries is jarring, but also enforces the implied 'domestication' of Kalypso's analogies. Ostensibly Moxley grants Kalypso's articulation and also politicises her narrative. At the close of the poem Kalypso retorts that Odysseus is leaving her for Enyo (the Goddess of war and the waster of cities). Yet Moxley's politicisation of Kalypso is not the overtly self-aware re-writing or gendering of mythic narrative. The patterning of the poem with its hesitations and slipped aphoristic paraphrasing, enforces an acute examination of phrasing and critical observation. These resistances in Moxley's lyric paradoxically enable a more fulfilling examination of gender definitions. Moxley comments that the lyric with 'its non-narrative syntactical knots is the form most suited to examining the complexity of human subjectivity.' (56)

In considering these linguistic errancies in Moxley's poetry there is the temptation to link her methods to strategies of defamiliarisation for interrogating more expressive language practices. Certainly we have seen how Hejinian's phenomenological lyric uses techniques of *ostrananie* in her negotiation of the everyday. But Ron Silliman emphatically challenges situating Moxley as a direct 'inheritor' of Language Writing practices. Instead, he proposes that her work must be placed in the context of other 'post-avant' writing: 'Moxley associates with and publishes in the journals of the newer generation of post-avant writing, which allegedly eschews direct address.'[45] In his recent study David Caplan proposes that 'Moxley self-consciously writes not only after modernism but also Language Writing and formalism.'[46] Wallace warns that while for many recent poets Language Writing would not be a pivotal influence, that the post Language poet 'who pays no attention to the theoretical insights of Language poetry does so at the risk of misunderstanding how poetry is related to cultural production.'[47] We could add that Moxley is responding to Perelman's challenge in 'The Marginalization of Poetry', for more discursive language practices less focused on the politics of reference and signification. His analysis of the future of Language Writing as an avant-garde practice calls for 'a more/ communal and critical reading and writing' where 'margins are not metaphors, and where readers are not simply there, waiting to be liberated.'[48]

It has been suggested that a distinctive feature of poetry 'after' Language Writing is a willingness to further the investigations of hybrid poetic forms; yet for Wallace the hybridity practiced includes 'elements rejected by Language poets narrative, lyric, spirituality, and a poetics of the every day.' This general comment threatens to lead one down the wrong road of antithetical genres. Moxley's lyric is aware of an existing practice of the lyric in Language Writing, but it is her responsiveness and dialogue with a lyric tradition that informs the texture of her work. Rod Menghan's attention to ideas of linguistic transgression in *Imagination Verses* furthers this perspective of poetic artifice in Moxley's lyric and its relationship to error:

A Connoisseur of mistranslations, both between languages and cultures and within them, the poet insists on a parallactic gesture, not just to offset damage, but also to find an equivalent means of countering the potential for cultural and emotional wiliness and misconstruction. Gerrymandering syntax, discourse and

45   Ron Silliman's Blog Monday, December 9th 2002. Accessed: http://ronsilliman. blogspot.com/2002_12

46   David Caplan, 'Prosody after the Poetry Wars', in *Questions of Possibility Contemporary Poetry and Poetic Form* (Oxford: Oxford U.P., 2005), pp. 127–37 (p. 135).

47   Wallace, 'Definitions in Process'.

48   Bob Perelman, 'The Marginalization of Poetry' in *The Marginalization of Poetry* (Princeton: Princeton U.P., 1996), pp. 3–10 (p. 10).

the tradition, Moxley is engaged in a continual reconstitution of her American-ness, one of whose verges, perhaps the largest, is clipped by an English accent.[49]

Menghan's remarks focus on the transatlantic passage and transcription of a poetic tradition, as well to acts of deliberate misreading and an errant narrative momentum. His attention to the erosion of distinct cultural boundaries and their constant dismantling and transgression draws on 'gerrymandering' (which historically describes the deliberate rearrangement of the boundaries of congressional districts). Clearly Mengham reads error as a deliberate cultural strategy in Moxley's poetry, a challenge to what Veronica Forrest-Thomson identifies as 'naturalisation' in poetic language. Syntactical disruption and strategies of error defy the reduction of poetic language to interpretative immediacy. Forrest-Thomson states 'Poetry can only be a valid and valuable activity, when we recognise the value of the artifice that makes it different from prose. Indeed, it is only through artifice that poetry can challenge our linguistic orderings of the world.'[50]

Historically not all critics have engaged in such a positive light to concepts of artifice or the digressive patterns of hyperbole in lyric poetry. Alexander Pope infamously addressed ideas of linguistic density and error as 'bathos' in his mock and parodic treatise *Peri Bathous, or The Art of Sinking in Poetry* in 1728. Keston Sutherland pertinently draws attention to ideas of the bathetic and their recuperation into normative strategies of defamiliarisation in contemporary poetics. On the emergence of bathos, Sutherland states that 'Pope uses the word to describe the prolific misuse of poetical language by his contemporaries.'[51] Pope states that far from advancing ideas of transcendence or the sublime, Bathos is 'the Bottom, the End, the Central Point, the *non*

---

49   Rod Mengham, 'Reading Jennifer Moxley's *Imagination Verses*', *How 2* 1.6 (2001). Accessed: http://www.scc.rutgers.edu/however/v1_6_2001/current/alerts/mengham.html

50   Veronica Forrest-Thomson, *Poetic Artifice* (Manchester: Manchester U.P., 1978), p. xi.

51   Keston Sutherland, 'The Trade in Bathos', *Jacket*, 15 (2001). Accessed: http://www.jacketmagazine.com/15/sutherland-bathos.html

plus ultra of true Modern Poesie!'[52] Cast in this light bathos is associated with a misjudging of poetic language and it is linked with extreme and posturing artifice; the treatise describes the bathetic as an 'anti natural way of thinking' (18). The linguistic representation of the world becomes the ability to cloud, deform and subvert the natural. The poet's eyes 'should be like unto the wrong end of a Perspective Glass, by which all the Objects of Nature are lessen'd'(18). Intractability, obscurity and hermeticism are key characteristics Pope advances: 'His Design ought to be like a Labyrinth, out of which no body can get you clear but himself' (51). Moreover 'A genuine Writer of the Profund will take Care never to magnify any Object without clouding it at the same time' and the technique Pope associates with bathos is 'The Hyperbole, or Impossible' (51).

I am not suggesting that Moxley's poetry is intentionally hyperbolic, but Pope's initial mock manifesto had at its core a self-reflexive awareness that is identified as a key element of contemporary poetics. In reading Moxley's poetry there is also a distinct sense of belatedness, that indicates more than the inclusions of archaisms and slipped aphorisms. More than any other poet in this study, Moxley's work is immersed, often nostalgically in the diction of an English lyric tradition. Yet Moxley is careful to distinguish between abstraction and obscurity. She associates an extreme obscurity with a 'wilful' hermeticism that 'risks passing, like a spectre, right through those "things" the Modernists wanted to put in their poems, and wandering off into a netherworld of misty and undefined idea.'[53] Linguistic abstraction contrastingly 'strives for a more reflexive representation of materiality.' In responding to Ezra Pound's famous admonition 'to go in fear abstractions',[54] Moxley recognises that 'abstract' words such as love and liberty are 'both abstract but neither is particularly obscure ... The burden of the poet who uses such words, then, is to write in such a way that our definition of them is enriched and enlivened, though

52   Alexander Pope, *The Art of Sinking in Poetry*, ed. Edna Leake Steeves (New York: King's Crown Press, 1952), p. 6.
53   Moxley, 'To Whom It May Concern "sphere of generality"/on content.'
54   Pound, 'A Retrospect', in *The Literary Essays of Ezra Pound* (London: Faber, 1968), pp. 3–14 (p. 5).

not simplified, by the poem's content, without destroying what is general and accessible.' In gesturing to what she calls the 'sphere of generality' (a shared space communication, empathy and action focused on contemporary living), she proposes that 'A good poet will often recontextualize this sphere, so that we feel both comforted by the familiar references and excited by the chance to distance ourselves from them, via a new or, perhaps, a clearer understanding gained through the poet's insight.'[55] Moxley treads carefully here, while she does not use terms such as defamiliarisation or estrangement, her easy reference to ideas of a recontextualising of the everyday is informed by the legacy of Language Writing. As has been noted by Evans, the reception of poetry after Language Writing as purely the 'perceived rehabilitation of lyric forms' performs a disservice to the new compositional forms.[56] In turn, he proposes that new writing in response to Language offers 'a commitment to what can be called the democracy of perception (with its origins in Whitman)' (655).

'Line of Descent' from *Imagination Verses*, addresses this issue of poetic inheritance and lineage. In considering a democratic poetics Moxley gives us the wry statement 'I was as hopeful as quoted Whitman' (81). The 'line' that the poem refers us to is a series of errancies and detours through literary history. Without a definitive programme or definable poetics 'This is a story lacking flight plans/ or verity' (81). The poem set with its 'evening appearance' (81) and 'wing tips' (81) is reminiscent of William Carlos Williams's 'Landscape with the Fall of Icarus', inspired by Pieter Brueghel's painting. Undoubtedly Moxley interrogates the erratic pattern of development, inclusion and exclusion of literary work within a tradition or canon. There are moreover intimations of literary theft at the close with the 'pocketed lineage' of 'Hemingway in the house, or Ibsen's pistol' (82). Against this stock of male authors our heroine is presented anachronistically as a figure from early romances and melodrama: 'I wept, derivatively'

---

55   Moxley, 'To Whom It May Concern "sphere of generality"/on content'
56   Evans, 'The American Avant-Garde After 1989: Notes Towards a History', in
      *The World in Time and Space: Towards a History of Innovative American
      Poetry, 1970–2000* (Issues 23–26), eds. Edward Foster and Joseph Donahue
      (Jersey City: Talisman Press, 2002), pp. 646–73 (p. 655).

(82) 'perchance to exit in various possible outcomes' (82). Perhaps most threatening overall is Moxley's analogy for the passage of memory; the protagonist becomes a vessel of 'storage' encumbered by the threat 'you will father undue memory' which becomes the terrifying solipsism of 'I will watch no daily gestures' (82).

It is clear that the poems from *Imagination Verses* are highly charged, emotive and dynamically lyric in a way that challenges the more immediate revelations of confessionalist verse. A key characteristic of this volume is Moxley's ability to suture intense personal perception and political observation with a nostalgia for mass social activism. Situating these poems in time can also be a difficult prospect. 'Ode on the Son' appears to place us in a quest for epic and romance with the questioning: 'Where is my field of wheat, / my flock my ocean / my arsenal, my knight errant' (17), while one of the longer poems from this volume, 'Ten Prolegomena to Heartbreak' makes reference to acts of duelling in conjunction with 'the Avant-Garde lover/ of hope' (85) and a protagonist who dreams of 'filmic meetings with big scores' (88). There are failures in the verses of this sequence, even a hesitant will to be an O'Hara poem 'like the poem I wish I'd written/ In Memory of My Feelings' (85). Moxley's language is moreover one of constant detour and transgression, she states 'I am such an inept navigator/ of woe betide, a miserable egomaniac' (85). Yet we should not be fooled that errancy means aimlessness or the lack of a critical programme. There is an intention at work in her poetry, and while it may not have a pedagogical poetics 'Ten Prolegomena to Heartbreak' alerts us to a development: 'pay off the press/ beforehand, but first we'll write/ a left a friendless lyric poem/ to warn you we're coming' (86).

In *Imagination Verses* lyricism can appear to be a doubtful strategy for political change and the nostalgia for a communal space for activism haunts the book. Feelings of hesitation and self-interrogation dominate the poems. At points there is a remnant of a collective, but one whose aesthetics can appear too esoteric as in 'The Right to Remain Silent': 'Singing together/ we know not who/ we serenade,/ if not ourselves/ who are no selves/ and broken/ we look to bedtime,/ elope with big/ distance in mind' (55). There is also a search for patterns of interconnection and responsibility, Oppen's 'Of Being

226

Numerous' haunts sections of Moxley's work. She urges in 'Ode on the Particle' 'so forget the time you dwelt in insolence pretending to be unique' (71), and seeks instead 'the unseen connection to any specific body' (72). In 'Wreath of a Similar Year' Moxley places into practice her propositions on the 'sphere of generality'. Taking that pivotal word 'Hope', the poem creates an atavistic scene. Moxley proposes that our anticipation of possibility often makes for an unmappable journey. If we recall Error is often figuratively portrayed as blind, walking a passage of unmediated detours. Hope too is represented as a blind figure 'of untold direction/ it sounds' (90). The poem is far from offering political solutions or possibilities when one considers that language is described as 'blind as the first letter on the first stone/ written down/ as if a wreath to circle/ the last sound spoken/ on some distant though similar/ Earth' (90). The momentum of this patterning necessitates an immediate devolving from one image to another, creating a detour within the propositions set up in the poem. These images shift from the birth of written language, to burial, apocalypse and space. In this contextualisation, Hope becomes a necessary element for action and agency. The effect is not unlike the contingencies and deviations that Adorno sees as integral to Paul Valéry's lyrics:

> Deviation was a constituent of his own anachronistic insistence on concepts like order, regularity, and permanence. For him, deviation is the guarantee of the truth. Valéry expresses sharp opposition to the commonsense view of knowledge: 'Unless it is new and strange, every visualization of the world of things is false. For if something is real it is bound to lose its reality in the process of becoming familiar. Philosophic contemplation means reverting from the familiar to the strange, and in the strange encountering the real.' [57]

'Lucky so and so' from *Imagination Verses* present a provocative reading of the lyric in contemporary American poetry, particularly 'after' Language Writing. Not unlike 'Line of Descent', the poem questions a lineage or seeks to find where continuities, ruptures and conflicts may lie within tradition. Counting herself as 'an orphan' (77) the speaker in this poem goes on to declare 'From this moment on there'll

---

57   Adorno, 'Valéry's Deviations', *Notes to Literature 1*, pp. 137–73 (p. 143).

be only/ whoop de do dear, no more signification' (77). While 'Lucky so and so' is not a direct attack on Language Writing, there is certainly playfulness in Moxley's reference to the constant analogies to reference and signification that dominated early Language debates. Moxley does not see experimentation as an aesthetic merely to be plundered, sampled or emulated since she comments: 'How poets write rather than what they are saying seems to take precedence in much contemporary poetic discourse, where the word "avant-garde" has come to be synonymous with a group of recognisable formal gestures rather than a position as regards both the poet's role in and engagement with society.'[58] In 'Lucky So and So' there is the formidable proposition that 'Immanence and transcendence will meet/ at the capital, everyone will be moved' (77). The curious conflation of both 19th Century lyric ambition for poetry as transcending the mundane and the role of imagination as a vehicle for political thought, jars against the word 'immanence.' It is between these two propositions of 'immanence' and 'transcendence', that one can close with a reading of *The Sense Record* and a recent critical proposition for a 'circumspective' lyric.

A question to be asked of Moxley's poetry is whether a 'post' Language lyric creates a texture of writing generative of lyrical transcendence, or the sensation of what Ihab Hassan refers to as postmodern 'Interdetermanaces.'[59] Hassan's general observations on the aesthetics of postmodernism focuses an attention upon the term 'immanences'. He gestures to a capability of an artwork to generate its own self-referential symbolic structure:

> I call the second major tendency of postmodernism *immanences*, a term which I employ without religious echo to designate the capacity of mind to generalize itself in symbols, intervene more and more into nature, act upon itself through its own abstractions and so become increasingly, immediately its own environment. This noetic tendency may be evoked further by such sundry concepts as diffusion, interdependence, which all derive from the emergence of human beings as language animals. Homo pictor or Homo significans, gnostic creatures constituting themselves, and determinedly their universe, by symbols of their own making. (153)

58   Moxley, 'Ancients and Contemporaries', *The Poker*, 2 (Spring 2003), 64–80 (p. 64).
59   Ihab Hassan, 'Towards a Concept of Postmodernism', *Postmodernism: A Reader*, ed. Thomas Docherty (New York: Columbia U.P., 1993), pp. 146–56 (p. 153).

This impetus to create a textual world, a labyrinth of linguistic trajectories comes to the fore in postmodern poetics. Clearly this passage points us to poetics as epistemology, a poetics enquiring after linkages generated by its own linguistic landscape. For Hassan this gestures towards an incessant self-referential circuitry. No doubt the extent of these ideas of self-reference enable Andreas Husseyn to declare that: 'The American postmodernist avant-garde therefore is not only the endgame of all avant-gardism. It also represents the fragmentation and the decline of the avant-garde as a genuinely critical and adversarial culture.'[60] In gesturing to a postmodern lyric one might well be tempted to consider this degree of self-reference as indicative of a political apathy or absence of agency. Peter Hühn indicates that the foregrounding of poetic strategies and devices is a protective strategy creating an opaque smokescreen. He poses that 'When self observation extended to the speaker's capacity as a writer and to his poetic creativity and its sources' the result is 'self doubt, self-paralysis and literary sterility.'[61] Hühn suggests that self-referentiality enables 'the poet speaker to continue writing ... shielding one's self, one's own consciousness from self-inspection, strategies of making oneself intransparent (220)

Turning to Moxley's *The Sense Record* the reader is struck by a poem that takes its title from Whitman's poem written on the outbreak of the American Civil War 'From the Cradle Endlessly Rocking'. Moxley's own 'Out of the Cradle Endlessly' interrogates creative production, social responsibility and political engagement. Her critique is evident in such lines as 'daughters of the new Obscurantism' 'swollen liberal guilt wing' and the slippage in 'dim lands of piecemeal ideology' (48). The latter of course being a reinscription of Pound's critique of abstraction in 'A Retrospect': 'Don't use such an expression as "dim land of peace." It dulls the image. It mixes an abstraction with the concrete' (5). The 'vanity of youth' that features in the poem attempts to

60   Andreas Huyssen, 'The Search for Tradition: Avant-Garde and Postmodernism in the 1970s', in *Postmodernism: A Reader*, pp. 220–36 (p. 228).
61   Peter Hühn, 'Watching the Speaker Speak: Self Observation and Watching and Self-Intransparency in Lyric Poetry', in *New Definitions of the Lyric: Theory Technology and Culture*, ed. Mark Jefferys (New York and London: Garland Publishing, 1998), pp. 215–44 (p. 220).

adjudicate the role of poetic production during time of war. Scathingly the poem links the language of economic scams and get-rich-quick strategies to literary production: 'The *soi-distant* Avant-Gardist builds/a pyramid scheme, a last ditch pitch /to the lure of Empire' (48). Even that most staple element of the mechanics of a poem, the stanza, becomes co-opted by the language of automobile production 'lost in a forest of Nissan stanzas' (48). The economic factors continue in the poem as we are told of 'target audience honesty' and 'stock piling weapons against the second coming' (48). The much lauded modernist belief of the revolution of the word becomes instead a 'world where Art/ is as late for this year's revolution/ as that cycle of judges drawing the Makers/ down on the sacred word of compromise' (48).

As scathing as this politicised lyric is, Moxley's lyricism cannot be neatly pinpointed as postmodernist satire or self-referential immanence. The sense of a lyric belatedness in her writing and an archaic syntactical texture evokes a tradition of lyrical writing. There is a dialectic at work in Moxley's lyric between what she proposes as 'the desire for the representation of a human totality and the impossibility of realizing that desire except through its mute particulars. It is a paradox that proposes the need to risk settled definitions at every point' (57). Hence in 'Grain of the Cutaway Insight' there is the berating of lyric form as a compulsion for order pitted against the desire to commit thought as momentum and investigation: 'My thoughts are too awkward, too erratic to rest/ at ease in the beautiful iamb' (6). The engagement of Moxley's lyric in the world seeks to counter what Charles Olson called the 'lyrical interference of the individual as ego.'[62] She states 'the lyric "I" is not a political universal, nor the guardian of the rights of men, but neither is it the flaccid marker of an outdated bourgeois egotism' (57). At the beginning of the 21st Century we are still striving to reconvene on ideas of the lyrical and how to address the conundrum raised by Hejinian in *My Life* 'Both subjectivity and objectivity are outdated filling stations.'[63]

62   Charles Olson, 'Projective Verse' in *Poetics of the New American Poetry*, eds. Donald Allen and Warren Tallman (New York: Grove Press, 1973), pp. 147–58 (p. 156).
63   Lyn Hejinian, *My Life* (Los Angeles: Sun & Moon Press, 1987), p. 99.

It is precisely the emphatic association of the lyric with intense introspection that is challenged by Daniel Barbiero. He proposes that the evolution of the lyric at the recent fin-de-siècle is invariably tied to an informed understanding of language theory and practice. Barbiero identifies 'a willingness to take a disillusioned look at oneself as part of a collective form of life, with special emphasis on the role language plays in constituting the conditions for such a collective life. The rejection of plain language, sincerity and the consequent emphasis on poetic artifice may be seen as one way of coming to this recognition.'[64] Arguing for an understanding of a socialised non-alienated lyric, he proposes that Language Writing's legacy to a generation of emerging poets is 'a particular understanding of the subjective as a factor dependent on social, linguistic and other structures ... For if inwardness is the pivot of the traditional lyric, the current lyric by contrast pivots on a sense of inwardness as outwardly constrained if not compromised' (363). Coining the term 'Circumspective Lyric', Barbiero suggests that recent poets' engagement with lyricism questions the more traditional concept of lyric inwardness and introspection by situating or inscribing the subject within a surrounding situation:

> Somewhat paradoxically though the circumspective view shows also that– by definition we are situated within the centre of circumstances surrounding us. But it is understood that such a center is not something we create, but rather it is a kind of point of insertion into the given. One takes one's place in a world already formed; already there one is pushed or pulled into place– into a given place. And that is the place from which the circumspective lyric speaks. (365)

This countering of the textual labyrinth of 'immanences', challenges to the sensations of inertia and textual cannibalism which threaten to immobilise postmodern poetics to a circuitry of language games. Moxley's disaffection with the '*soi-distant*' avant-garde indicates a desire to challenge as she puts it in a title 'To Those Who Would Equate the Public with Themselves' (70). Turning finally to the sixth section from the long title poem of *The Sense Record*, Moxley balances introspection with her desire to be situated among the

64   Daniel Barbiero, 'Reflections on Lyric, Before, During and After Language Poetry', in *The World in Time and Space*, pp. 355–66 (p. 362).

poplace: 'listening/ to the softly falling rain/ upon the rooftops of the city' (83). The poem acknowledges the difficulty of adequate expression that responsibly attends to the world: 'my heart has so much pain. / What I write in truth today/ tomorrow will be in error' (83). If as Barbiero states, the recent lyric attempts to navigate itself in the situation not as ego but as participant, responsive to the world, the situating of *The Sense Record* indicates the degree of difficulty this responsiveness incurs. The speaker at the beginning of this section seeks neutrality 'Eros tell me why, without love, / without hate' (83). Yet the words which situate this scene are accordingly 'mundane and repetitive' (83) and more threateningly untouched by an incentive for direct action 'With no job "to be done"/ nor doctrine to stand for' (83). In countering the uncertainties of the act of writing, Moxley does not seek to isolate the subject into paralysis. Instead the poem reads as responsive to the suffering the speaker identifies: 'And all small frightened things/ who spend existence seeking shelter/ become blank-slates on which I write/ this debt of ill-used care.' (83). Here the integration of economic language and empathy creates a form of social contract that dominates *The Sense Record*. Far from objectifying pain, Moxley in this section creates a passageway of nightmares to be encountered. Momentum, rewriting and errancy is suggested in the provocative lines: 'The evil spirits of the waking life/ spoil my clothes as I sleep/ the body a fragile vehicle/ its impotent words, its decomposition' (83).

Moxley's *The Sense Record* indicates that the recent lyric need not jettison tradition, but that its journeying and momentum can be responsive and empathetic to a world beyond self-reflexivity. Hélène Cixous comments upon the errancy that is involved in all writing and describes an errant passage that is pertinent to a reading of Moxley's lyric as an equivocatory dialogue with tradition, society and subjectivity:

> Writing is not arriving; most of the time it's not arriving. One must go on foot, with the body, one had to go away leave the self. How far must one not arrive in order to write, how far must one wander and wear out and have pleasure? One must walk as far as the night. One's own night. Walking through the self toward the dark.[65]

65   Hélène Cixous, *Three Steps on the Ladder of Writing* (New York: Columbia U.P., 1994), p. 65.

Conclusion

In considering the reconfiguration of the lyric in Charles Bernstein, Michael Palmer and Lyn Hejinian's poetry, I have strategically avoided proposing a new model of lyricism. It is tempting to coin new categories for the lyric for example, Bernstein's 'humorous lyric', Palmer's 'analytic lyric' or even a 'phenomenological lyric' for Hejinian's poetry. Alternatively, I have proposed that a conceptualisation of error provides a productive methodology for identifying the complex responses to the lyric in the work of the three poets, while also retaining the important conceptual differences between their poetics. Considering poetics itself as erring enables one to evaluate their poetry as establishing a dialogue with an earlier tradition of innovative writing and to begin reassessing the lyric impulse itself as a transitional locus. It is moreover, this sense of transition and tradition that comes to the fore in Jennifer Moxley's navigation of a lyric legacy following Language Writing.

Perhaps more problematically *Reading Error* indicates how a configuration of error allows us to consider the broader relationship between aesthetics, ethics and politics in poetry. In reflecting upon these claims overall one needs to consider what a conceptualisation of error as a method for reading recent innovative American poetry offers the reader, and whether this approach to the reconfiguration of the lyric can be extended to the work of other poets. Making this leap from aesthetics to ethics and politics is difficult and reconsidering the problems faced by the three poets in their engagement with the lyric marks out possibilities for the reader. All three share a commitment to rupturing the authority of the univocal lyric, and varying strategies (ideolects, malapropisms, the problematising of intertextuality and aphoristic slippage), open the lyric to provisionality and indeterminacy. The close scrutiny of the rhetorical impulse of the lyric can be linked not only to a suspicion of the ambitions of mastery, but can also be seen as a complex of aesthetic responses to a specific historical period. Hejinian indicates that the poetics of Language Writing were an initial response to the rhetorical 'fraud' of public discourse during the Vietnam War:

> My generation, shocked into awareness of atrocity by the Vietnam War, felt the urgency of seeing through the fraud endemic to the political culture of the times, and we believed– or perhaps at the time merely intuited– that poetry was the most available and best-prepared medium for undertaking the urgently required analysis and critique. Poetry provided the means for reopening the question of language; it was through poetry that a series of reinventions of language could be initiated ... The emphasis on language in our writing can be explained by our sense of the urgency of the need to address and, if possible, to redress social fraud.[1]

Viewed from this perspective, the small comforts of the expressive lyric with its impulse towards anecdotal recollection and epiphanic insight would seem a weak strategy to diminish the authority of reportage. Language Writing was premised on the belief that the disruption of established rules of grammar and syntax could be linked to the 'disclosure' of hierarchies of power. While these strategies are more readily identifiable in the work of Bernstein and Hejinian, even Palmer links his circumspectual rupture of the lyric to an opening of the text to epistemological uncertainty and an overarching political aim. He insists that poetry has a role 'as a critique of the discourse of power by undermining assumptions about meaning and univocality.'[2]

The configuration of these paradoxical strategies of 'disclosure' in the text read through error, also present some pertinent problems in making the leap from textual indeterminacy to political efficacy. While error may be aligned productively to a humorous critique of authority through misspellings and idiomatic slippage, there is also the danger that these strategies might veer towards the authoritarian distance of ironic commentary which all three poets are keen to avoid. Furthermore, in spite of Bernstein, Palmer and Hejinian's resistance to situating their work within a poststructuralist paradigm of play, a

1   Lyn Hejinian, 'Barbarism', in *The Language of Inquiry* (Berkeley: University of California Press, 2000), pp. 318–36 (pp. 324–5).
2   Michael Palmer, 'Interview: Conducted by Keith Tuma', *Contemporary Literature*, 30.1 (Spring 1989), 1–12 (p. 6).

reliance upon textual indeterminacy in itself may only serve to promote a vague political possibility as the only imminent vantage point
of their poetics.

These are criticisms which the three poets are evidently themselves acutely attuned to, registered perhaps most pertinently in Bernstein's essay 'The Revenge of the Poet Critic.' Here the poet observes
poignantly, but still apparently on fighting terms that 'words so often
fail us. They do so little and they are so disappointing, leading us
down blind alleys and up in smoke. But they are what we have, what
we are given, and we can make them do what we want.'[3] Another way
of reflecting on this problematic juncture between aesthetics, politics
and ethics in this difficult poetry is somewhat inevitably, to return to
the role of the reader. Rather than relying upon the reader as a
somewhat idealised point of reference, we might want to reconsider
what I originally gestured to as an erring poetics of readership; that is
a form of reading performed both in accordance with, and also
occasionally against the grain of the text.

Usefully in this context, Ann Vickery's study of the feminist
genealogy of Language Writing draws attention to the pedagogical
inflexion in the early poetics of male Language Writers.[4] Citing the
poetics of Ron Silliman and Barrett Watten in particular, she suggests
that their extensive use of theoretical citations could be read as an
anxious attempt to counter their manipulation 'by signs', through
reinforcing 'their role as the operators of signs' (110). While I have
some reservations regarding Vickery's Oedipal frame for reading the
theoretical density in the poetics of male language writers, she makes
a provocative claim asserting that citation 'has to do with paternal
anxiety and with control. It is a means to guide the reader away from
errancy and back into the fold' (110). Already we have examined the
transformative impulse in Hejinian's fusion of theory and poetics, and
how this marked tendency in her work demands an engagement which

---

3   Charles Bernstein, 'The Revenge of the Poet Critic, or the Parts are Greater
    than the Whole', in *My Way: Speeches and Poems* (Chicago: Chicago U.P.,
    1999), pp. 3–17 (p. 17).
4   Ann Vickery, *Leaving Lines of Gender: A Feminist Genealogy of Language
    Writing* (Hanover & London: Wesleyan U.P., 2000).

encourages the reader to test the assumptions and claims of the poetics within the performance of the poetry. Vickery's discussion continues by suggesting that the poetics of female poets such as Susan Howe, Carla Harryman, Joan Retallack and Leslie Scalapino provide an alternative approach to the explicitly theory driven discourse of early Language Writing through their mediation of theory within compositional strategies.[5] She suggests in surveying their work that, '[n]one of the typical signs are present. As such this theoretical double-take is often misread or viewed as revealing a lack of skill or mastery' (112).

While Vickery does not configure the approach of female poets within a conceptualisation of error, one can perhaps read this refutation of mastery as a productive strategy. Yet it seems somewhat perplexing, following Vickery's line of argument, that the pedagogical inflexion which Language Writers were so keen to avoid is merely replicated by the early poetics of male Language Writers.[6] Possibly her earlier comment on guiding the reader 'back to the fold', alerts us to the complex of responses that a retrospective consideration of this early period in the history of Language Writing now elicits. Without blurring the claims of Vickery's carefully articulated argument I would suggest that understanding the engagement demanded by the work of these writers as an erring performed by the reader, may be a way of alleviating the pedagogical anxieties induced by the early work. Certainly in considering Bernstein's poetics I have attempted to show how the reader can productively resist some of his rhetorical claims, to provide useful counter-readings of her own. Although an erring approach to reading the poetics does not give us an entirely interpretative free rein, the difficulty of this work does on occasion warrant readings outside the poet's own examinations.

5   See *Leaving Lines of Gender*, p. 111. Vickery cites the following works as examples: Howe's *My Emily Dickinson* (Berkeley: North Atlantic, 1985), Harryman's *There Never Was a Rose without a Thorn* (San Francisco: City Lights, 1995), Retallack's *The Poethical Wager* (Berkeley: University of California Press, 2003) and Scalapino's *How Phenomena Appear to Unfold* (Elmwood, Conn.: Potes & Poets Press, 1989).

6   For extended discussions surrounding pedagogy in modern and contemporary poetics see *Poetry and Pedagogy: The Challenge of the Contemporary*, eds. Joan Retallack and Juliana Spahr (New York: Palgrave, 2006).

The concept of the 'active' reader has now become perhaps too axiomatic for reading the poetry and poetics of these writers,[7] but these texts evidently do demand a considerably sophisticated engagement. Indeed, this testing out of assumptions in accordance with, and occasionally against the text aims to encourage the motivation to probe our own relationship to the social and political structures which are there to represent, what Bernstein calls 'the love of the public good.' Translating Bernstein's proposal of making words 'do what we want', or Hejinian's concept of poetry as a relationship of 'linkage' to the action of configuring the communities we may want, or alternatively refute, is admittedly an ambitious project. The most viable and important possibility that their poetry work offers the reader is the necessity of seeing those structures of power deemed to represent us, as necessarily provisional and ultimately answerable to our criticisms.

Finally it is worth reflecting upon whether a methodology of error as a way of approaching the lyric reconfiguration in Bernstein, Palmer and Hejinian's work has further relevance for reading the work of other poets. In Moxley's poetry I have suggested that error serves an important role in adjudicating the legacies of Language Writing for a younger generation, while mediating a connection to an earlier lyric tradition. Understandably, I am wary of 'promoting' an erring poetics as a paradigmatic model for a broad range of innovative poetry. It seems pertinent that an essay in Kathleen Fraser's *Translating the Unspeakable* focuses specifically on error as a productive strategy in her own poetics.[8] Fraser states in this work that 'error began to appear and then to figure consciously in my poems beginning around 1980'

7   See Charles Altieri's discussion of the reading of Language Writing in 'Some Problems about Agency in the Theories of Radical Poetics', *Contemporary Literature*, 37.2 (1996), 207–36. Altieri comments: 'Does the reader really need restoring? Are there any major traditional works that encourage readerly passivity ... There may be academics who confuse passivity and activity, but for the most part that particular opposition does not seem likely to generate the significant differences that radical writing claims to realize' (p. 211).

8   Kathleen Fraser, 'Faulty Copying', in *Translating the Unspeakable: Poetry and the Innovative Necessity* (Tuscaloosa and London: University of Alabama Press, 2000), pp. 77–88.

(77). Taking error as a means for countering the 'perfectibility' of poetic form, Fraser continues by staking her intention to illustrate where 'error has taken me– its unreliable path– and what error has given me, in the act of writing, that the goal of "perfection" cannot' (78). Initially Fraser focuses on error as unintentional typographical mistakes in early drafts of her work, and how these misspellings para-doxically generated a strategy of composition for her poetry. Her dis-cussion draws attention to the possibilities of error as a means for countering the ideal of the poem as a well-crafted, self-sufficient com-position, and as a method for opening the work to contingency. Equating error with provisionality, or what Fraser points to as the 'variables' of the poem (88), has become a familiar tenet of our dis-cussion. What is of particular importance is Fraser's gesture to error as a procedure of 'faulty copying.' Drawing her analogy from DNA research and the surprising contingency of scientific enquiry, error is not only related to isolate mistakes, but to an accumulative patterning of mutations and transitions. This 'erring' trajectory Fraser poses has both a pertinent metaphoric implication and practical application for the writing of poetry.

Taken at its most literal this gesture to 'faulty copying' could also be productively linked to the configuration of error in Howe's work. Howe's *My Emily Dickinson*, alerts one to protocols of reading and the erasures of the clarified edited text. Her focus upon the omissions of both literary history and the narratives of historical accounts, is frequently configured through the violent and graphic deformation of the poetic text. In approaching Howe's *Singularities* or her *A Bibliography of the King's Book or, Eikon Basilike*,[9] the reader frequently acts as palaeontologist, and the spatial co-ordinates of the poetry give definition to accounts that might have otherwise remained incoherent, lost or excluded. Cast in this light, Howe's poetry not only creates a typographical aesthetic of error but also a conceptual one mediated by the inclusion of 'stuttering', or 'stammering' voices in her poetry. The configuration of error in Howe's poetry points us to-

---

9   Susan Howe, *Singularities* (Hanover NH: Wesleyan University Press, 1990), *A Bibliography of the King's Book or, Eikon Basilike* in *The Nonconformist's Memorial* (New York: New Directions, 1993).

wards a process of lyric recovery and its collusion with a violent historical silence.

Possibly Jorie Graham's work might seem an unexpected inclusion to a consideration of the broader application of a methodology of error, to the formulation of the contemporary lyric. Graham's poetry is strongly identified with the predominance and proliferation of the workshop lyric of the eighties, and this would mark her poetry in direct opposition to the aesthetics of Bernstein, Palmer and Hejinian's poetry.[10] Yet the evolution of Graham's poetry presents a powerful claim for the urgent need to reconsider the configuration of the lyric in recent writing. One can situate her early volumes within the workshop aesthetic but the publication of *The End of Beauty* in the late eighties marks a notable rupture of the univocal lyric in her work.[11] The danger here is to equate the fracturing of the single speaking voice quite unproblematically with formal innovation, but it does seem pertinent that critical accounts of Graham's poetry register the shift in her work during this period as a movement from ecphrasis to iconoclasm.[12] The scrupulous painterly representations of her early work are forcefully broken down to focus on the scrutiny of perception, and its mediation through a certain linguistic textuality. Jed Rasula warns against making the assertion that Graham's recent work is indicative of a dispersal of Language Writing to the mainstream:

> Surely the initial investigations of Language Writing have been disseminated broadly if Jorie Graham ... can submit her work in *The End of Beauty* and *Region of Unlikeness* to strategies of forwarding the device; strategies that, a decade earlier, would hardly have endeared her to a critic like Helen Vendler.[13]

---

10 It is worth noting that Graham was a student at the Iowa Writers' workshop and has taught on their creative writing programme.

11 Jorie Graham, *Hybrids of Plants and Ghosts* (Princeton, NJ: Princeton U.P., 1980), *Erosion* (Princeton, NJ: Princeton U.P., 1983), *The End of Beauty* (New York Ecco Press, 1987).

12 For differing accounts of this 'benchmark' period in Graham's poetry see Bonnie Costello, 'Jorie Graham: Art and Erosion', *Contemporary Literature*, 33.2 (1992), 373–95, and Anne Shifrer, 'Iconoclasm in the Poetry of Jorie Graham', *Colby Quarterly*, 31.2 (1995), 142–63.

13 Jed Rasula, *The American Poetry Wax Museum: Reality Effects 1940–90* (Urbana, IL: National Council of Teachers of English, 1995), p. 392.

Rasula's forewarning indicates that Language Writing evidently cannot be viewed as a mere aesthetic to be plagiarised or imitated. But it does leave us with the problem of how to approach this transition in Graham's recent poetry.

Graham's volumes *The Errancy* and *Swarm*[14] make this dilemma even more acute and the poet demands to be read outside the reductive confines of a workshop aesthetic. The notes at the back of these volumes draw attention to Emmanuel Levinas's *Existence and Existents* and Gilles Deleuze's *The Fold*, as the basis for aspects of her work and in *Swarm* she dedicates specific poems to both Howe and Palmer. Evidently Graham's *The Errancy* makes the reading of her work through a configuration of error an alluring possibility. Understanding error initially as a rupturing of the lyric, what the poet gestures to in *The End of Beauty* as 'loving that error, loving that filial form, that break from perfection' (7), Graham's two volumes delineate an erring trajectory, frequently examining the phenomenological situating of the lyric impulse.

The 'errancy', or 'erring' momentum of Graham's latest work reads as an attempt to somehow 'suture' the flaws, gaps and holes which were the earlier preoccupation of *The End of Beauty*. What is most noticeable in *Swarm* is the equating of the ocular with a certain saturation in the text. The recurrent theme of blindness is also linked to the multiple references to a labyrinthine enfolding, which is evoked both thematically and linguistically throughout the volume. Bearing in mind that 'Error' is often allegorised as a blinded or blindfolded figure,[15] Graham appears to be setting up a complex correspondence between these two volumes. This complexity is made apparent when we are faced with lines such as 'the outwardoing of your blindness/ where the arcing seems to streak your gaze ... Sight never happens' (31). In an interview given around the same time as the publication of *The End of Beauty*, Graham comments:

14 Graham, *The Errancy* (New York: Ecco Press, 1997), *Swarm* (New York: Ecco Press, 2000).
15 See Jacques Derrida's discussion of the allegorical representation of error in Antoine Coypel's drawing *The Error, in Memoirs of the Blind: The Self-Portrait and Other Ruins*, trans. Pascale-Anne Brault and Michael Naas (Chicago and London: University of Chicago Press, 1990), p. 13.

I feel that if I can track in my own individual consciousness reasoning errors, slippages, misreadings, I might be able to find ways of altering them– at the very least in myself, by becoming aware, by understanding how we got here beached; and maybe not only in myself. Maybe in the *form* of the poem as well– which is, of course, the beginning of *others*.[16]

Reflecting upon these remarks, one might want to consider that error provides an attractive possibility for Graham's own poetic reinvention allowing her to stake a position away from the centre of mainstream poetry. Certainly Graham's latest work demands an engagement from the reader which one would not ordinarily associate with the more conventional registers of the eighties workshop lyric.

Reading Error has attempted to consider the role of the lyric in the work of recent innovative poets and its focus has been to illustrate the complex responses that a configuration of lyricism now elicits. Overall a configuration of error offers us a productive methodology for approaching these complexities, while also acknowledging an important lyric tradition which I argue continues to inform the work of these poets. In this final summation I am drawn to Maurice Blanchot's characterisation of error as an enquiry which navigates a way from the restrictions of a centralising nexus. Blanchot's words capture more eloquently the nature of the transitional locus I have attempted to map out in our consideration of the lyric in recent American poetry:

–Searching and error, then, would be akin. To err is to turn and to return, to give oneself up to the magic of detour. One who goes astray, who has left the protection of the center, turns about, himself adrift and subject to the center, and no longer guarded by it. More accurately, he turns about– a verb without complement; he does not turn around some thing or even around nothing; the center is no longer the immobile spur, the point of opening that secretly clears the space of advance.[17]

16   Graham, 'Interview', in Thomas Gardner, *Regions of Unlikeness: Explaining Contemporary Poetry* (Lincoln: University of Nebraska Press, 1999), pp. 214–37 (p. 237). Originally given in October 1987. Italics in original.

17   Maurice Blanchot, 'Plural Speech: Speaking Is Not Seeing', in *The Infinite Conversation*, trans. Susan Hanson (Minneapolis and London: University of Minnesota Press, 1993), pp. 25–32 (p. 26).

Bibliography

Abraham, Nicholas and Maria Torok. *The Wolf Man's Magic Word A Crypto-nymy*. Trans. Nicholas Rand. Minneapolis: University of Minnesota Press, 1986.

Abrahams M.H. *The Mirror and the Lamp*: *Romantic Theory and the Critical Tradition*. Oxford: Oxford University Press, 1977.

Adorno, Theodor. *Notes to Literature*: *Volume One*. Trans. Shierry Weber Nicholsen. New York: Columbia University Press, 1991.

Allen, Donald and George F. Butterick, eds. *The Postmoderns*: *The New American Poetry Revised*. New York: Grove Press, 1982.

Allen, Donald and Warren Tallman, eds. *The Poetics of the New American Poetry*. New York: Grove Press, 1973.

Altieri, Charles. *Enlarging the Temple*. Lewisburg PA: Bucknell University Press, 1979.

—— *Self and Sensibility in American Poetry*. Cambridge: Cambridge University Press, 1984.

—— *Painterly Abstraction in Modernist American Poetry*: *The Contemporaneity of Modernism*. Cambridge: Cambridge University Press, 1989.

—— *Subjective Agency*. Cambridge, Mass.: Blackwells, 1994.

—— 'Some Problems about Agency in the Theories of Radical Poetics.' *Contemporary Literature*. 37.2 (1996): 207–36.

Anders, Magnusson, Jonas and Olsson Jesper. Eds. 'After Language Poetry: 10 Statements.' *OEI*. 7–8 (2001). Accessed http://www.ubu.com/papers/oei/intro.html

Andrews, Bruce and Charles Bernstein, eds. *The L=A=N=G=U=A=G=E Book*. Carbondale: Southern Illinois University Press, 1984.

Armantrout, Rae. 'Mainstream Marginality.' *Poetics Journal* 6 (1986): 141–44.

Attali, Jacques. *Noise*: *The Political Economy of Music*. Trans. Brian Massumi. Manchester: Manchester University Press, 1985.

Baker, Peter. *Obdurate Brilliance*: *Exteriority and the Modern Long Poem*. Gainesville: University of Florida Press, 1991.

—— ed. *Onward Contemporary Poetry and Poetics*. New York: Peter Lang, 1996.

Bakhtin, Mikhail. *The Dialogic Imagination*. Ed. Michael Hoquist Trans. Caryl Emerson. Texas: University of Texas Press, 1981.

—— *Problems of Dostoevsky's Poetics*. Trans. Caryl Emerson. Manchester: Manchester University Press, 1984

Barthes, Roland. *The Pleasure of the Text*. Trans. New York: Hill and Wang, 1975.

—— *Music Image Text*. Trans. Stephen Heath. New York: The Noonday Press, 1977.

—— *Roland Barthes by Roland Barthes*. Trans. Richard Howard. London: Macmillan, 1977.

—— *Writing Degree Zero*. Trans. Annette Lavers and Colin Smith. New York: Hill and Wang, 1998.

—— *S/Z*. Trans. Richard Miller. Oxford: Blackwell, 2000.

Bartlett, Lee. 'What is Language Poetry?' *Critical Inquiry*. 12.4 (Summer 1986): 741–52.

—— *Conversations in the Workshop with Contemporary Poets*. Albuquerque: University of New Mexico Press, 1987.

Baudelaire, Charles. *Les Fleurs du Mal*. Trans. Richard Howard. Boston: David R. Godine, 1983.

Beach, Christopher. *ABC of Influence*. Berkeley: University of California Press, 1992.

—— *Poetic Culture*: *Contemporary Poetry Between Community and Institution*. Evanston, Illinois: Northwestern University Press, 1999.

—— ed. *Artifice and Indeterminacy*: *An Anthology of New Poetics*. Tuscaloosa and London: University of Alabama Press, 1998.

Belgrad, Daniel. *The Culture of Spontaneity*: *Improvisation and the Arts in Postwar America*. Chicago: Chicago University Press, 1998.

Bernstein, Charles. *Controlling Interests*. New York: Roof Books, 1980.

—— *Content's Dream Essays 1975–1984*. Los Angeles: Sun & Moon Press, 1986.

—— *The Sophist*. Los Angeles: Sun & Moon Press, 1987.

—— *Rough Trades*. Los Angeles: Sun & Moon Press, 1991.

—— *A Poetics*. Cambridge: Harvard University Press, 1992.

—— *Dark City*. Los Angeles: Sun & Moon Press, 1994.

—— 'Poetics of the Americas' in *Modernism/ Modernity*. 3.3 (1996): 1–23.

—— *My Way*: *Speeches and Poems*. Chicago: University of Chicago Press, 1999.

—— ed. *The Politics of Poetic Form*: *Poetry and Public Policy*. New York: Roof Books, 1990.

—— ed. *Close Listening: Poetry and the Performed Word* Oxford: Oxford University Press, 1998.

—— et al. 'Poetry, Community, Movement: A Conversation.' *Diacritics*. 26.3–4 (1996): 196–210.

Blanchot, Maurice. *The Infinite Conversation*. Trans. Susan Hanson. Minneapolis and London: University of Minnesota Press, 1993.

Breton, André. *Manifestos of Surrealism*. Trans. Richard Seaver and Helen R. Lane. Ann Arbor: University of Michigan Press, 1972.

Breuer, Rolf. 'Irony, Literature and Schizophrenia.' *New Literary History: A Journal of Theory and Interpretation*. 12 (1980): 107–18.

Bruns, Gerald L. 'Mallarmé: The Transcendence of Language and the Aesthetics of the Book.' *Journal of Typographical Research* 3 (1969): 219–34.

Byrd, Donald. *The Poetics of Common Knowledge*. Albany NY: SUNY Press, 1994.

Campbell, Bruce. '"A Body Disappears into Itself": Michael Palmer's *Sun.*' *Occident: Palmer/Davidson Issue*. 103.1 (1990): 67–80.

Caplan, David. *Questions of Possibility: Contemporary Poetry and Poetic Form*. New York: Oxford University Press, 2005.

Cavell, Stanley. *The Claim of Reason*. Oxford: Oxford University Press, 1979

—— *The Senses of Walden: An Expanded Edition*. San Francisco: North Point Press, 1981.

Celan, Paul. *Poems of Paul Celan*. Trans. Michael Hamburger. New York: Persea Books, 1995.

—— *Selected Poems and Prose of Paul Celan*. Trans. John Felstiner New York: Norton, 2001.

Cixous, Helen. *Three Steps on the Ladder of Writing*. New York: Columbia University Press, 1994.

Clark, Tom. 'Stalin as Linguist.' *Partisan Review*. 37.3 (1989): 299–304.

Clarke, Hilary. 'The Mnemonics of Autobiography: Lyn Hejinian's *My Life.*' *Biography*. 14.4 (1991): 315–35.

Collings, David. *Wordsworthian Errancies: The Poetics of Cultural Dismemberment*. Baltimore and London: Johns Hopkins University Press, 1994.

Cooley, Dennis. 'The Poetics of Robert Duncan.' *Boundary 2*. 8.2 (1980): 45–73.

Conte, Joseph M. *Unending Design: The Forms of Postmodern Poetry*. Ithaca: Cornell University Press, 1991.

Costello, Bonnie. 'Jorie Graham: Art and Erosion.' *Contemporary Literature*. 33.2 (1992): 373–95.

Culler, Jonathon. 'Changes in the Study of the Lyric.' *Lyric Poetry: Beyond the New Criticism.* Eds. Chaviva Hosek and Patricia Parker. New York, Ithaca: Cornell University Press. 1985. 38–54

—— ed. *On Puns: The Foundation of Letters.* Blackwell: London, 1988.

Critchley, Simon. *Ethics, Politics, Subjectivity– Essays on Derrida, Levinas and Contemporary French Thought.* London: Verso, 1999.

—— *The Ethics of Deconstruction: Derrida and Levinas.* Edinburgh: Edinburgh University Press, 1999.

Dana, Robert, ed. *A Community of Writers: Paul Engle and the Iowa Writer's Workshop.* Iowa: University of Iowa Press, 1999.

Dante. *The Divine Comedy: Hell.* Trans. Dorothy L. Sayers. Middlesex: Penguin, 1974.

Davidson, Donald. 'A Nice Derangement of Epitaphs.' *Truth and Interpretation: Perspectives on the Philosophy of Donald Davidson.* Ed. Ernest Le Pore. Oxford: Blackwell, 1986. 433–58.

Davidson, Michael. 'Hey Man, My Wave: The Authority of Private Language.' *Poetics Journal.* 6 (1986): 33–45.

—— *The San Francisco Renaissance.* Cambridge: Cambridge University Press, 1989.

—— *Ghostlier Demarcations: Modern Poetry and the Material Word.* Berkeley: University of California Press, 1997.

—— et al. *Leningrad: American Writers in the Soviet Union.* San Francisco: Mercury House, 1991.

Deleuze, Gilles. 'The Schizophrenic and Language: Surface and Depth in Lewis Carroll and Antonin Artaud.' *Textual Strategies: Perspectives in Post Structuralist Criticism.* Ed. Josue V. Harari. London: Methuen, 1980. 277–95.

—— *The Fold: Leibnitz and the Baroque.* Trans. Tom Conley. London: Athlone Press, 1993.

Deleuze, Gilles and Félix Guatteri. *Anti Oedipus: Capitalism and Schizophrenia.* Trans. Helen Lane, Mark Seem and Robert Hurley. New York: Viking, Penguin, 1977.

Delville, Michael. *The American Prose Poem: Poetic Form and the Boundaries of Genre.* Florida: Florida University Press, 1998.

Derrida, Jacques. *Positions.* Trans. Alan Bass. London: Athlone Press, 1981.

—— *Memoirs of the Blind: The Self-Portrait and Other Ruins.* Trans. Pascale-Anne Brault and Michael Naas. Chicago and London: University of Chicago Press, 1990.

—— *Politics of Friendship.* Trans. George Collins. London: Verso, 1997.

—— *Writing and Difference.* Trans. Alan Bass. London: Routledge, 1997

Dennis, Carl. 'Mid Course Corrections: Some Notes on Genre.' *Denver Quarterly*. 29.2 (1994): 120–146.

Dickinson, Emily. *The Complete Poems of Emily Dickinson*. Ed. Thomas H. Johnson. Boston: Little Brown, 1960.

Docherty, Thomas, ed. *Postmodernism: A Reader*. New York: Columbia University Press, 1993.

Dow, Philip, ed. *19 New American Poets of the Golden Gate*. San Diego: Harcourt Brace Jovanovich, 1984.

Duncan, Robert. *The Opening of the Field*. New York: New Directions 1973.

Eliot, T.S. *Collected Poems*. London: Faber & Faber, 1970.

—— *Selected Essays*. London: Faber & Faber, 1972.

Epstein, Joseph. 'Who Killed Poetry?' *Commentary*. 86.2 (August 1988): 13–20.

Evans, Steve. 'The Resistible Rise of Fence Enterprises'. Accessed http://www.third.factory.net/resistible.html

Finkelstein, Norman. 'The Case of Michael Palmer.' *Contemporary Literature*. 29.4 (1988): 518–37.

—— 'Michael Palmer's Songs for Sarah.' *Occident: Davidson/Palmer Issue* 103.1 (1990): 51–56.

—— 'The Problem of the Self in Recent American Poetry.' *Poetics Journal*. 9 (1991): 3–10.

—— *Lyrical Interference: Essays on Poetics*. New York: Sputyen Duyvil, 2003.

Forrest-Thomson, Veronica. *Poetic Artifice*. Manchester: Manchester University Press, 1978.

Foster, Edward, ed. *The World in Time and Space: Towards a History of Innovative American Poetry, 1970–2000 (Issues 23–26)*. Jersey City: Talisman Press, 2002.

Freud, Sigmund. 'The Uncanny.' *Art and Literature*. London: Penguin, 1985. 339–76.

Fraser, Katherine. *Translating the Unspeakable: Poetry and the Innovative Necessity*. Tuscaloosa and London: Alabama University Press, 2000.

Froula, Christine. *To Write Paradise: Style and Error in Pound's Cantos*. New Haven and London: Yale University Press, 1984.

Gardner, Thomas. 'Accurate Failures: The Work of Jorie Graham.' *The Hollins Critic*. 14.4 (1987): 1–9.

—— *Regions of Unlikeness: Explaining Contemporary Poetry*. Lincoln: University of Nebraska Press, 1999.

Gilbert, Roger. 'Textured Information: Politics, Pleasure and Poetry in the Eighties.' *Contemporary Literature*. 33.2 (1992): 242–72.

Gizzi, Peter, ed. *Exact Change Yearbook No. 1.* Boston: Exact Change, 1995.

Gizzi, Peter and Juliana Spahr, eds. *Writing from the New Coast: Technique* Providence: Oblek Editions,1993.

Golding, Alan. *From Outlaw to Classic: Canons in American Poetry.* Wisconsin: University of Wisconsin Press, 1995.

—— 'New, Newer and Newest American Poetries', *Chicago Review.* 43.4 (1997): 17–21.

Graham, Jorie. *Hybrids of Plants and Ghosts.* Princeton, NJ: Princeton Univeristy Press, 1980.

—— *Erosion.* Princeton, NJ: Princeton University Press, 1983.

—— *The End of Beauty.* New York: Ecco, 1987.

—— *The Dream of the Unified Field.* Manchester: Carcanet, 1996.

—— *The Errancy.* New York: Ecco, 1997.

—— *Swarm.* New York: Ecco, 2000.

—— ed. *The Best American Poetry 1990.* New York: Macmillan, 1990.

Greer, Michael. 'Ideology and Theory in Recent Experimental Writing or, The Naming of "Language Poetry."' *Boundary 2,* 16.2/3 (Spring 1989): 335–55.

Grimes, Tom, ed. *The Workshop: Seven Decades of the Iowa's Writers' Workshop.* New York: Hyperion Press, 1999.

Hacking, Ian. 'The Parody of Conversation.' *Truth and Interpretation: Perspectives on the Philosophy of Donald Davidson.* Ed. Ernest Le Pore. Oxford: Blackwell, 1986. 446–58.

Hamill, Sam. 'Lyric Miserable Lyric Or: Whose Dog are You?' *The American Poetry Review* 16.5 (1987): 31–35.

Hartley, George. *Textual Politics and the Language Poets.* Bloomington: Indiana University Press, 1989.

Hejinian, Lyn. *Writing is an Aid to Memory.* Berkeley CA: Figures, 1978.

—— 'Language and "Paradise."' *Line.* 6 (1985): 83–99.

—— 'The Rejection of Closure.' *Writing/Talks.* Ed. Bob Perelman. Carbondale: Southern Illinois University Press, 1985. 270–291

—— 'An Exchange.' *Jimmy and Lucy's House of 'K.'* 6 (1986): 1–17

—— 'Two Stein Talks: Language and Realism.' *Temblor* 3 (1986): 128–33.

—— *My Life.* Los Angeles: Sun and Moon Press, 1987.

—— *Oxota: A Short Russian Novel.* Great Barrington MA: Figures, 1991.

—— 'The Person and Description.' *Poetics Journal* 9 (1991): 166–70

—— *The Cold of Poetry.* Los Angeles: Sun & Moon Press, 1994.

—— *Happily.* Sausalito: Post Apollo Press, 2000.

—— *The Language of Inquiry.* Berkeley: University of California Press, 2000.

Holden, Jonathan. *Style and Authenticity in American Poetry*. Columbia: University of Missouri Press, 1986.

—— *The Fate of American Poetry*. Athens GA and London: University of Georgia, 1991.

Hölderlin, Friedrich. *Poems and Fragments*. Trans. Michael Hamburger. Cambridge: Cambridge University Press, 1980.

Hollander, John. *The Untuning of the Sky: Ideas of Music in English Poetry 1500–1700*. Princeton: Princeton University Press, 1961.

Hong, Cathy. 'Oppen Sesame: *The Sense Record* and Other poems' *Village Voice* (October 2–8 2002) http://www.villagevoice.com/books/0240, hong,38873,10.html

Hoover, Paul, ed. *Postmodern American Poetry: A Norton Anthology*. New York: Norton, 1994.

Hosek, Chaviva, and Patricia Parker, eds. *Lyric Poetry: Beyond the New Criticism*. New York, Ithaca: Cornell University Press, 1985.

Howe, Susan. *The Birth-mark: Unsettling the Wilderness in American Literary History*. Hanover, NH: Wesleyan University Press, 1993.

—— *The Nonconformist's Memorial*. New York: New Directions, 1993.

—— *Singularities*. Hanover, NH: Wesleyan University Press, 1990.

—— *My Emily Dickinson*. Berkeley: North Atlantic, 1985.

Hudgins, Andrew. *The Glass Anvil*. Ann Arbour: University of Michigan Press, 1997.

Huk, Romana, ed. *Assembling Alternatives: Reading Postmodern Poetries Transnationally*. Middletown, CT: Wesleyan University Press, 2003.

Irwin, Mark. 'Kite's Body and Beyond.' *Denver Quarterly* 31.1 (1996): 60–7.

Jackson, Richard, ed. *Acts of Mind: Conversations with Contemporary Poets*. Tuscaloosa: University of Alabama Press, 1983.

Jameson, Fredric. *Postmodernism, or The Cultural, Logic of Late Capitalism*. Durham NC: Duke University Press, 1991.

Jarman, Mark. 'The Grammar of Glamour: The Poetry of Jorie Graham.' *New England Review*, 14.4 (1992): 252–61.

—— 'The Pragmatic Imagination and the Secret of Poetry.' The Gettysburg Review, 1.4 (1988): 647–60.

Jarraway, David. 'My Life through the Eighties: The Exemplary Language of Lyn Hejinian.' *Contemporary Literature*. 33.2 (Summer 1992): 319–36.

Jay, Martin. *Downcast Eyes: The Denigration of Sight in Twentieth Century French Thought*. Berkeley: University of California Press, 1994.

Jefferys, Mark, ed. *New Definitions of Lyric: Theory, Technology and Culture*. New York: Garland, 1998.

Kalaidjian, Walter. *Languages of Liberation: The Social Text in Contemporary American Poetry.* New York: Columbia University Press, 1989.
—— *American Culture Between the Wars: Revisionary Modernism and Postmodern Critique.* New York: Columbia University Press, 1993.
Kalechovfsky, Robert. *Knowing and Erring: The Consolations of Error.* Marblehead MA: Micah Publications, 1997.
Kauffmann, David. 'Subjectivity and Disappointment in Contemporary American Poetry', *Ploughshares.* 17.4 (1991–2): 231–49.
Keats, John. *The Complete Poems.* ed. John Barnard. Middlesex: Penguin, 1973.
Keller, Lynn. *Re-Making it New: Contemporary American Poetry and the Modernist.* Cambridge. Cambridge University Press, 1987.
—— *Forms of Expansion: Recent Long Poems by Women.* Chicago: Chicago University Press, 1997.
Kristeva, Julia. *Revolution in Poetic Language.* Trans. Margaret Waller. New York: Columbia University Press, 1984.
Lacoue-Labarthe, Philippe. *Musica Ficta: Figures of Wagner.* Trans. Felicia McCarren. Stanford: Stanford University Press, 1994.
—— *Poetry as Experience.* Trans. Andrea Tarnowski. Stanford: Stanford University Press, 1999.
Lang, Candace. *Irony/ Humor: Critical Paradigms.* Baltimore & London: Johns Hopkins University Press, 1988.
Lazer, Frank. 'Opposing Poetry.' *Contemporary Literature.* 33.2 (1992) 123–38
—— *Opposing Poetries Vol. II: Readings.* Illinois: Northwestern University Press, 1996.
Lerner, Seth. *Error and the Academic Self: The Scholarly Imagination, Medieval to Modern.* New York: Columbia University Press, 2002.
Levinas, Emmanuel. *Emmanuel Levinas: Basic Philosophical Writings.* Eds. Adrian T. Peperzak, Simon Critchley and Robert Bernasconi. Bloomington and Indianapolis: Indiana University, 1996.
—— *Totality and Infinity: An Essay on Exteriority.* Trans. Alphonso Lingis. Pittsburgh: Duquesne University Press, 1969.
Lin, Tan. 'Language Poetry, Language Technology and the Fractal Dimension: Michael Palmer Prints Out a Kingdom.' *A Poetics of Criticism.* Eds. Juliana Spahr, Mark Wallace, Kristin Prevallet, Pam Rehn. Buffalo: Leave Books, 1994. 237–48.
Lodge, David. *The Modes of Modern Writing: Metaphor, Metonymy and the Typology of Modern Literature.* London: Edward Arnold, 1977.

Longenbach, James. 'Jorie Graham's Big Hunger.' *Denver Quarterly*. 131.3 (Winter 1997): 97–118.

Lyas, Colin. *Aesthetics.* London: University College London Press, 1997.

Mallarmé, Stephane. *Mallarmé: Selected Prose Poems, Essays and Letters.* Trans. Bradford Cook. Baltimore: Johns Hopkins University Press, 1956.

McCaffrey, Steve. 'Michael Palmer's LANGUAGE of language.' *North of Intention: Critical Writings 1973–86.* New York, Toronto: Roof & Nightwood, 1986. 44–53.

McGann, Jerome. 'Contemporary Poetry, Alternate Routes.' *Critical Inquiry.* 13.3 (Spring 1987): 624–47.

McHale Brian. *The Obligation Towards the Difficult Whole* Tuscaloosa; Alabama University Press, 2004.

Mead, George Herbert. *Mind Self and Society.* ed. Charles W. Morris Chicago: University of Chicago Press, 1962.

Mengham, Rod. 'Reading Jennifer Moxley: *Poems 1975–2000 Imagination Verses.' How 2.* 1.6 (2001). Accessed http://www.scc.rutgers.edu/however/v1_6_2001/current/alerts/mengham.html.

Merleau-Ponty, Maurice. *Phenomenology of Perception.* London: Routledge, 1999.

Messerli, Douglas, ed. *'Language' Poetries.* New York: New Directions, 1987.

—— ed. *From the Other Side of the Century: A New American Poetry 1960–90.* Los Angeles: Sun & Moon Classics, 1994.

Middleton, Peter. *Distant Reading: Performance, Readership, and Consumption in Contemporary Poetry.* Tuscaloosa: Alabama University Press, 2005

Middleton, Peter and Tim Woods. *Literatures of Memory: History, Time and Space in Postwar Literature.* Manchester: Manchester University Press, 2000.

Mileur, Jean Pierre. *The Critical Romance: The Critic as Reader, Writer, Hero.* Madison: University of Wisconsin, 1990.

Mitchell, W.J.T. *Iconology: Image, Text, Ideology.* Chicago: University of Chicago Press, 1987.

Molesworth, Charles. 'Jorie Graham: Living in the World.' *Salmagundi.* 120 (1998): 276–83.

Moxley, Jennifer. *Imagination Verses.* New York: Tender Buttons, 1996.

—— 'To Whom It May Concern "sphere of generality" /on content.' *The Open Letter.* (Fall 2001) Accessed http://slought.org/files/downloads/publications /openletter /04a.pdfshelley

—— 'Ancients and Contemporaries.' *The Poker* 2 (2003): 64–80.

—— *The Sense Record.* Cambridge: Salt, 2003.

—— *Often Capital.* Chicago: Flood Editions, 2005.

—— 'Lyric Poetry and the Inassimilable Life' *The Poker* 6 (2005): 49–58.

Mulhall, Stephen. *Stanley Cavell: Philosophy's Recounting of the Ordinary.* Oxford: Oxford University Press, 1996.

Muller-Zettelmann, Eva and Margarete Rubik, eds. *Theory into Poetry: New Approaches to the Lyric.* Amsterdam: Rodopi, 2004.

Nathanson, Tenney. 'Collage and Pulverization in Contemporary American Poetry: Charles Bernstein's Controlling Interests.' *Contemporary Literature.* 33.2 (1992): 302–18.

Naylor, Paul. 'MisCharacterizing Charlie': Language and the Self in the Poetry and Poetics of Charles Bernstein.' *Sagetrieb.* 14.3 (1995): 119–38.

—— *Poetic Investigations: Singing the Holes in History.* Illinois: Northwestern University Press, 1999.

Nealon, Jeffrey T. *Alterity and Politics: Ethics and Performative Subjectivity.* Durham and London: Duke University Press, 1998.

Nicholls, Peter. 'Difference Spreading: from Gertrude Stein to Language Poetry.' *Contemporary Poetry Meets Modern Theory.* Eds. Antony Easthope and John Thompson. Toronto: University of Toronto Press, 1991. 116–27.

—— *Modernisms: A Literary Guide.* Basingstoke & London: Macmillan, 1995.

—— 'Unsettling the Wilderness: Susan Howe and American History.' *Contemporary Literature* 37.4 (1996): 586–601.

—— 'Of Being Ethical: Reflections on George Oppen.' *Journal of American Studies.* 31.2 (1997): 153–70.

—— 'The Poetics of Opacity: Readability and Literary Form.' *Psychopolitics and Cultural Desires.* Eds. Janet Campbell and Janet Hardboard. London: UCL Press, 1998. 158–70.

—— 'Beyond *The Cantos*: Ezra Pound and recent American Poetry.' *The Cambridge Companion to Ezra Pound.* Cambridge: Cambridge University Press, 1999. 139–60.

—— 'Phenomenal Poetics: Reading Lyn Hejinian.' *The Mechanics of the Mirage: Postwar American Poetry.* Eds. Michel Delville and Christine Pagnouelle. Liège: Université de Liège, 2000. 241–52.

Nietzsche Friedrich. *Human all too Human.* Trans. Marion Faber and Stephen Lehmann. Lincoln: University of Nebraska Press, 1996.

Oppen, George. 'Interview with L.S. Dembo.' *Contemporary Literature*. 10.2 (1969): 159–77.

Palmer, Michael. *Notes for Echo Lake*. San Francisco: North Point Press, 1981.

—— 'Period: Senses of Duration.' *Code of Signals: Recent Writings in Poetics*. Ed. Michael Palmer. Berkeley: North Atlantic Books, 1983. 243–65.

—— *First Figure*. San Francisco: North Point Press, 1984.

—— 'Autobiography, Memory and Mechanisms of Concealment.' *Writing/Talks*. Ed. Bob Perelman. Carbondale: Southern Illinois University Press, 1985. 207–29.

—— 'A Conversation.' *American Poetry*. 3.1 (1986): 72–88.

—— 'Interview: Conducted by Lee Bartlett.' *Conversations in the Workshop with Contemporary Poets*. Ed. Lee Bartlett. Albuquerque: University of New Mexico Press, 1987. 125–48.

—— *Sun*. Berkeley: North Point Press, 1988.

—— 'Interview with Grant Jenkins with Teresa Aleman and Donald Prues.' *Sagetrieb*. 12.3 (1993): 53–64.

—— 'On Jess's Narkissos.' *Jess: A Grand Collage 1951–1993*. Ed. Michael Auping Buffalo: Albright-Knox Art Gallery/ The Buffalo Fine Arts Academy, 1993. 92–103.

—— *At Passages*. New York: New Directions Press. 1995.

—— 'Interview. Conducted by Peter Gizzi.' *Exact Change Yearbook No. 1*. Boston: Exact Change, 1995. 161–79.

—— 'Active Boundaries: Poetry at the Periphery.' *Onward Contemporary Poetry and Poetics*. Ed. Peter Baker. New York: Peter Lang, 1996. 265–86.

—— *The Lion Bridge: Selected Poems 1972–1995*. New York: New Directions, 1998

—— *The Danish Notebook*. Penngrove: Avec Books, 1999.

—— *The Promises of Glass*. New York: New Directions, 2000.

—— 'Poetry and Contingency: Within a Timeless Moment of Barbaric Thought.' *Chicago Review*. 49.2 (2003): 65–76

—— ed. *Code of Signals: Recent Writings in Poetics*. Berkeley: North Atlantic Books, 1983.

Parsons, Marnie. *Touchmonkeys: Nonsense Strategies in Contemporary Poetry*. Toronto: University of Toronto Press, 1994.

Perelman, Bob. *The Marginalization of Poetry: Language Writing and Literary History*. Princeton: Princeton University Press, 1996.

Perloff, Marjorie. *The Dance of the Intellect Studies in the Poetry of the Pound Tradition.* New York: Cambridge University Press, 1985.

—— *Poetic License: Essays on Modernist and Postmodernist Lyric.* Evanston, IL: Northwestern University Press, 1990.

—— *Radical Artifice: Writing Poetry in the Age of the Media.* Cambridge: Cambridge University Press, 1991.

—— 'Whose New American Poetry? Anthologizing in the Nineties.' *Diacritics.* 26.3 (1996): 104–23.

—— *Wittgenstein's Ladder: Poetic Language and the Strangeness of the Everyday.* Chicago and London: University of Chicago Press, 1996

—— *Poetry on and Off the Page: Essays for Emergent Occasions.* Evanston, Northwestern University Press, 1998.

—— 'Language Poetry and the Lyric Subject: Ron Silliman's Albany, Susan Howe's Buffalo.' Accessed http://wings.buffalo.edu/epc/authors/perloff/langpo.html

—— *Differentials: Poetry, Poetics, Pedagogy.* Tuscaloosa: Alabama University Press, 2005.

—— 'Yang Introduction to Younger American Poets.' Accessed http://wings.buffalo.edu/authors/perloff/yang.html

Pinsky, Robert. *The Situation of Poetry.* Princeton: Princeton University Press, 1976.

Pope, Alexander. *The Art of Sinking in Poetry.* Ed. Edna Leake Steeves. New York: King's Crown Press, 1952.

Pound, Ezra. *Literary Essays of Ezra Pound.* Ed. T.S. Eliot. London: Faber, 1960.

—— *ABC of Reading.* New York: New Directions, 1987.

—— *The Cantos.* London: Faber & Faber, 1990.

Quartermain, Peter. *Disjunctive Poetics: From Gertrude Stein and Louis Zukofsky to Susan Howe.* Cambridge, Cambridge University Press, 1992.

—— 'Syllable as Music in Lyn Hejinian's *Writing is an Aid to Memory.' Sagietreb.* 11 (1992): 17–31

Rankine, Claudia and Juliana Spahr, eds. *American Women poets in the 21st Century: Where Lyric Meets Language.* Middletown, Conn.: Wesleyan University Press, 2002.

Rasula, Jed. 'Literary Effects in the Wad: Handling the Fiction, Nursing the Wounds.' *Sulfur.* 24 (1989): 77–8.

—— *The American Poetry Wax Museum : Reality Effects 1940–90.* Urbana, IL: National Council of Teachers of English, 1995.

—— 'The Empire's New Clothes: Anthologizing American Poetry in the 1990s.' *American Literary History.* 7.2 (1996): 261–83.

——— *Syncopations: The Stress of Innovation in Contemporary American Poetry.* Tuscaloosa: Alabama University Press, 2004.

Reinfeld, Linda. *Language Poetry: Writing as Rescue.* Baton Rouge: Louisiana State University Press, 1992.

Reinsdorf, Walter. 'Schizophrenia, Poetic Imagery and Metaphor.' *Imagination, Cognition and Personality: Consciousness in Theory, Research, Clinical Practice.* 13.4 (1993–4): 335–45.

Retallack Joan. *The Poethical Wager.* Berkeley: University of California Press, 2003.

Riffaterre, Michael. *The Semiotics of Poetry.* Bloomington & London: Indiana University Press, 1978.

——— 'Interview.' *Diacritics.* 11.4. (1981): 2–11.

——— 'Compulsory Reader Response: The Intertextual Drive.' *Intertextuality: Theories and Practices.* Eds. Michael Worton and Judith Still. Manchester: Manchester University Press, 1990: 56–78.

Rilke, Rainer Maria. *The Selected Poetry of Rainer Maria Rilke.* Trans. Stephen Mitchell. New York: Vintage Press, 1989.

Rivkin, Julie and Michael Ryan, eds. *Literary Theory: An Anthology* (Oxford: Blackwell, 1998).

Rizzo, Carlo. 'Zanzotto, *"fabbro del parlar materno."'* *Selected Poetry of Andrea Zanzotto.* Trans. Ruth Feldman and Brian Swann. Princeton: Princeton University Press, 1975. 307–323.

Scharf, Michael. 'Imagination vs.' *Poets & Writers.* 27:2 (April 1999): 57–61.

Schultz, Susan. '"Called Null or Called Vocative": A Fate of the Contemporary Lyric.' *Talisman: A Journal of Contemporary Poetry.* 14 (1995): 70–80.

——— ed. The *Tribe of John: Ashbery and Contemporary Poetry.* Tuscaloosa and London: University of Alabama Press, 1995.

——— 'Visions of Silence in the Poems of Ann Lauterbach and Charles Bernstein.' *Talisman.* 13 (1994): 163–77.

Scroggins, Mark. *Louis Zukofsky and the Poetry of Knowledge.* Tuscaloosa: University of Alabama Press, 1998.

Selinger, Eric Murphy. 'Important Pleasures and Others: Michael Palmer, Ronald Johnson.' *Postmodern Culture.* 4.3 (1994). Accessed: http://jefferson.village.virginia.edu/pmc/text-only/issue.594/selinger594.html

Shelley, Percy Bysshe. *Shelley's Prose.* Ed. David Lee Clark. Albuquerque: University of New Mexico Press, 1954.

Shetley, Vernon. *After the Death of Poetry: Poet and Audience in Contemporary America.* Durham & London: Duke University Press, 1993.

Shifrer, Anne. 'Iconoclasm in the Poetry of Jorie Graham.' *Colby Quarterly* 31.2 (1995): 142–63.

Shklovsky, Victor. 'Art as Technique.' *Russian Formalist Criticism*: *Four Essays.* Trans. Lee T. Lemon and Marion J. Reis. Lincoln and London: University of Nebraska Press, 1965. 3–24.

Shoptaw, John. *From the Outside Looking In*: *John Ashbery's Poetry.* Cambridge, Mass.: Harvard University Press, 1994.

Silliman, Ron. *The New Sentence.* New York: Roof Books, 1987.

—— 'Canons and Institutions: New Hope for the Disappeared.' *The Politics of Poetic Form.* Ed. Charles Bernstein. New York: Roof, 1990. 149–74

—— ed. *In the American Tree*: *Language, Realism, Poetry.* Orno Maine: National Poetry Foundation, 1986

—— et al. 'Aesthetic Tendency and the Politics of Poetry: A Manifesto.' *Social Text.* 19/20 (Fall 1988): 261–75.

—— Silliman's Blog Monday, December 9, 2002. Accessed: http://ron silliman.blogspot.com/2002_12_01_ronsilliman_archive.html

Singer, Alan. 'Beautiful Errors: Aesthetic and the Art of Contextualization.' *Boundary 2.* 25.2 (1998): 7–34.

Smith, Lawrence, ed. *The New Italian Poetry*: *1945 to the Present.* Berkeley: University of California Press, 1981.

Soltan, Margaret. 'Hoax Poetry in America.' *Angelaki*: *Journal of the Theoretical Humanities* 5.1 (2000): 43–62.

Spahr, Julianna. 'Resignifying Autobiography: Lyn Hejinian's *My Life.'* *American Literature.* 68.1 (1996): 139–59.

—— *Everybody's Autonomy Connective Reading and Collective Identity.* Tuscaloosa University of Alabama, 2001.

Spicer, Jack. *The Collected Books of Jack Spicer.* Ed. Robin Blaser. Los Angeles: Black Sparrow Press, 1975.

Stefans, Brian Kim. 'Jennifer Moxley's *Wrong Life.'* *How 2.* 1.5 (2001). Accessed: http://www.scc.rutgers.edu/however/v1_5_2001/current/alerts/stefans.html

Stravinsky, Igor. *Poetics of Music.* Trans. Arthur Knodel and Ingolf Dahl. Cambridge Mass.: Harvard University Press, 1947.

Stein, Gertrude. *Look at Me Now and Here I am*: *Writings and Lectures.* Ed. Patricia Meyerowitz. Middlesex: Penguin, 1984.

Sturrock, John. *Structuralism and Since*: *From Levi Strauss to Derrida.* Oxford: Oxford University Press, 1979.

Sutherland, Keston. 'The Trade in Bathos.' *Jacket.* 15 (2001) Accessed: http://jacket magazine.com/15/sutherland-bathos.html

Taggart, John. *Songs of Degrees: Essays on Contemporary Poetry and Poetics*. Alabama: University of Alabama Press, 1994.

Taylor, Mark C. *Erring: A Postmodern A/Theology*. Chicago: University of Chicago Press, 1984.

Vanderborg Susan. *Paratextual Communities: American Avant-Garde Poetry Since 1950*. Carbondale: Southern Illinois University Press, 2001.

Vendler, Helen. *Soul Says: On Recent Poetry* (Cambridge, MA.: Belknap Press, 1995).

Vickery, Ann. *Leaving Lines of Gender: A Feminist Genealogy of Language Writing*. Hanover & London: Wesleyan University Press, 2000.

Wall, Thomas Carl. *Radical Passivity: Levinas, Blanchot and Agamben*. New York: SUNY Press, 1999.

Wallace, Mark. 'Definitions in Process, Definitions as Process/Uneasy Collaborations: Language and Postlanguage Poetries.' Accessed: http://www.flashpointmag.com/postlang.htm

Wittgenstein, Ludwig. *Philosophical Investigations*. Trans. G. E. M Anscombe. Oxford: Blackwell, 1963.

Woods, Tim. *The Poetics of the Limit: Ethics and Politics in Modern and Contemporary American Poetry*. New York: Palgrave, 2003.

Wordsworth, William. *The Poetical Works of William Wordsworth*. Ed. E. de Selincourt. Oxford: Oxford University Press, 1944.

Wordsworth, William and Samuel Taylor Coleridge,. *Wordsworth and Coleridge Lyrical Ballads*. Eds. R.L. Brett and A.R. Jones. London: Routledge, 2005.

Worton Michael and Judith Still, eds. *Intertextuality: Theories and Practices*. Manchester: Manchester University Press, 1990.

Zanzotto, Andrea. *Selected Poetry*. Trans. Ruth Feldman and Brian Swann. Princeton: Princeton University Press, 1975.

Zukofsky, Louis. *Prepositions: The Collected Critical Essays of Louis Zukofsky*. New York: Horizon Press, 1968.

—— *Complete Short Poetry*. London: Johns Hopkins University Press, 1991.

—— *'A'*. Baltimore & London: Johns Hopkins University Press, 1993.

Archive Material

Courtesy of *The Mandeville Special Collections Library* at the University of California San Diego.

Bernstein, Charles. Letter to Hejinian dated 21st March 1983 MSS 74/2/10
Hejinian, Lyn. Letter to Bernstein 4th March, 1983 MSS 74/2/10
—— Letter to Charles Bernstein 29th December 1984 MSS 74/2/10
Palmer, Michael. Letter to John Taggart 1st July 1985 MSS 11/17/13

Index

263

M o d e r n   P o e t r y

Series editors:
David Ayers, David Herd & Jan Montefiore, University of Kent

The Modern Poetry series brings together scholarly work on modern and contemporary poetry. As well as examining the sometimes neglected art of recent poetry, this series also sets modern poetry in the context of poetic history and in the context of other literary and artistic disciplines. Poetry has traditionally been considered the highest of the arts, but in our own time the scholarly tendency to treat literature as discourse or document sometimes threatens to obscure its specific vitalities. The Modern Poetry series aims to provide a platform for the full range of scholarly work on modern poetry, including work with an intercultural or interdisciplinary methodology. We invite submissions on all aspects of modern and contemporary poetry in English, and will also consider work on poetry in other language traditions. The series is non-dogmatic in its approach, and includes both mainstream and marginal topics. We are especially interested in work which brings new intellectual impetus to recognised areas (such as feminist poetry and linguistically innovative poetry) and also in work that makes a stimulating case for areas which are neglected.

For further details please contact Dr David Ayers (D.S.Ayers@kent.ac.uk).